Subjectivism and Objectivism in the History of Economic Thought

This book investigates the tensions between subjectivism and objectivism in the history of economics. The book looks at the works of Adam Smith, Carl Menger, Léon Walras, William Stanley Jevons, Oskar Morgenstern, Ludwig Mises, Piero Sraffa, and so on. The book highlights the diverse subjective and objective elements of their economic theories and suggests a reframing of methodology to better address the core problems of the theories.

Contributors of the volume are leading members of the Japan Society of History of Economic Thought who have provided a comprehensive overview on the economics methodology and the related problems. Hence, this book will be an invaluable asset to not only those who are interested in the history of economic thought, but also to scholars who are concerned with the methodological problems of economic science.

Yukihiro Ikeda is a historian of economic thought. He is currently with the faculty of economics of Keio University, Japan. He has been researching the Austrian School of Economics, with special attention to Carl Menger and Friedrich Hayek, for more than twenty-five years. He is also interested in research of the historical development of German economics and the introduction of the German Historical School of Japan.

Kiichiro Yagi, currently the Vice President of Setsunan University, Osaka, taught theory of political economy and history of economics over two decades in the Graduate School of Economics, Kyoto University. He served as Chairperson or President of several academic associations in his research fields, including the Japan Society for the History of Economics, the Japan Association for Evolutionary Economics, and the Japan Society of Political Economy.

Routledge studies in the history of economics

1. **Economics as Literature**
   Willie Henderson

2. **Socialism and Marginalism in Economics 1870–1930**
   Edited by Ian Steedman

3. **Hayek's Political Economy**
   The socio-economics of order
   Steve Fleetwood

4. **On the Origins of Classical Economics**
   Distribution and value from William Petty to Adam Smith
   Tony Aspromourgos

5. **The Economics of Joan Robinson**
   Edited by
   Maria Cristina Marcuzzo, Luigi Pasinetti and Alesandro Roncaglia

6. **The Evolutionist Economics of Léon Walras**
   Albert Jolink

7. **Keynes and the 'Classics'**
   A study in language, epistemology and mistaken identities
   Michel Verdon

8. **The History of Game Theory, Vol. 1**
   From the beginnings to 1945
   Robert W. Dimand and Mary Ann Dimand

9. **The Economics of W. S. Jevons**
   Sandra Peart

10. **Gandhi's Economic Thought**
    Ajit K. Dasgupta

11. **Equilibrium and Economic Theory**
    Edited by Giovanni Caravale

12. **Austrian Economics in Debate**
    Edited by Willem Keizer, Bert Tieben and Rudy van Zijp

13. **Ancient Economic Thought**
    Edited by B.B. Price

14. **The Political Economy of Social Credit and Guild Socialism**
    Frances Hutchinson and Brian Burkitt

15. **Economic Careers**
    Economics and economists in Britain 1930–1970
    Keith Tribe

16 **Understanding 'Classical' Economics**
Studies in the long-period theory
Heinz Kurz and Neri Salvadori

17 **History of Environmental Economic Thought**
E. Kula

18 **Economic Thought in Communist and Post-Communist Europe**
Edited by Hans-Jürgen Wagener

19 **Studies in the History of French Political Economy**
From Bodin to Walras
Edited by Gilbert Faccarello

20 **The Economics of John Rae**
Edited by O.F. Hamouda, C. Lee and D. Mair

21 **Keynes and the Neoclassical Synthesis**
Einsteinian versus Newtonian macroeconomics
Teodoro Dario Togati

22 **Historical Perspectives on Macroeconomics**
Sixty years after the 'General Theory'
Edited by Philippe Fontaine and Albert Jolink

23 **The Founding of Institutional Economics**
The leisure class and sovereignty
Edited by Warren J. Samuels

24 **Evolution of Austrian Economics**
From Menger to Lachmann
Sandye Gloria

25 **Marx's Concept of Money**
The god of commodities
Anitra Nelson

26 **The Economics of James Steuart**
Edited by Ramón Tortajada

27 **The Development of Economics in Europe since 1945**
Edited by A.W. Bob Coats

28 **The Canon in the History of Economics**
Critical essays
Edited by Michalis Psalidopoulos

29 **Money and Growth**
Selected papers of Allyn Abbott Young
Edited by Perry G. Mehrling and Roger J. Sandilands

30 **The Social Economics of Jean-Baptiste Say**
Markets and virtue
Evelyn L. Forget

31 **The Foundations of Laissez-Faire**
The economics of Pierre de Boisguilbert
Gilbert Faccarello

32 **John Ruskin's Political Economy**
Willie Henderson

33 **Contributions to the History of Economic Thought**
Essays in honour of R. D. C. Black
Edited by Antoin E. Murphy and Renee Prendergast

34 **Towards an Unknown Marx**
A commentary on the manuscripts of 1861–63
Enrique Dussel

35 **Economics and Interdisciplinary Exchange**
Edited by Guido Erreygers

36 **Economics as the Art of Thought**
Essays in memory of G. L. S. Shackle
Edited by Stephen F. Frowen and Peter Earl

37 **The Decline of Ricardian Economics**
Politics and economics in post-Ricardian theory
Susan Pashkoff

38 **Piero Sraffa**
His life, thought and cultural heritage
Alessandro Roncaglia

39 **Equilibrium and Disequilibrium in Economic Theory**
The Marshall–Walras divide
Michel de Vroey

40 **The German Historical School**
The historical and ethical approach to economics
Edited by Yuichi Shionoya

41 **Reflections on the Classical Canon in Economics**
Essays in honour of Samuel Hollander
Edited by Sandra Peart and Evelyn Forget

42 **Piero Sraffa's Political Economy**
A centenary estimate
Edited by Terenzio Cozzi and Roberto Marchionatti

43 **The Contribution of Joseph Schumpeter to Economics**
Economic development and institutional change
Richard Arena and Cecile Dangel

44 **On the Development of Long-run Neo-Classical Theory**
Tom Kompas

45 **F. A. Hayek as a Political Economist**
Economic analysis and values
Edited by Jack Birner, Pierre Garrouste and Thierry Aimar

46 **Pareto, Economics and Society**
The mechanical analogy
Michael McLure

47 **The Cambridge Controversies in Capital Theory**
A study in the logic of theory development
Jack Birner

48 **Economics Broadly Considered**
Essays in honour of Warren J. Samuels
Edited by Steven G. Medema, Jeff Biddle and John B. Davis

49 **Physicians and Political Economy**
Six studies of the work of doctor-economists
Edited by Peter Groenewegen

50 **The Spread of Political Economy and the Professionalisation of Economists**
Economic societies in Europe, America and Japan in the nineteenth century
Massimo Augello and Marco Guidi

51 **Historians of Economics and Economic Thought**
The construction of disciplinary memory
Steven G. Medema and Warren J. Samuels

52 **Competing Economic Theories**
Essays in memory of Giovanni Caravale
Sergio Nisticò and Domenico Tosato

53 **Economic Thought and Policy in Less Developed Europe**
The nineteenth century
Edited by
Michalis Psalidopoulos and Maria-Eugenia Almedia Mata

54 **Family Fictions and Family Facts**
Harriet Martineau, Adolphe Quetelet and the population question in England 1798–1859
Brian Cooper

55 **Eighteenth-Century Economics**
Peter Groenewegen

56 **The Rise of Political Economy in the Scottish Enlightenment**
Edited by *Tatsuya Sakamoto and Hideo Tanaka*

57 **Classics and Moderns in Economics, Volume I**
Essays on nineteenth and twentieth century economic thought
Peter Groenewegen

58 **Classics and Moderns in Economics, Volume II**
Essays on nineteenth and twentieth century economic thought
Peter Groenewegen

59 **Marshall's Evolutionary Economics**
Tiziano Raffaelli

60 **Money, Time and Rationality in Max Weber**
Austrian connections
Stephen D. Parsons

61 **Classical Macroeconomics**
Some modern variations and distortions
James C.W. Ahiakpor

62 **The Historical School of Economics in England and Japan**
Tamotsu Nishizawa

63 **Classical Economics and Modern Theory**
Studies in long-period analysis
Heinz D. Kurz and Neri Salvadori

64 **A Bibliography of Female Economic Thought to 1940**
Kirsten K. Madden, Janet A. Sietz and Michele Pujol

65 **Economics, Economists and Expectations**
From microfoundations to macroeconomics
Warren Young, Robert Leeson and William Darity Jnr.

66 **The Political Economy of Public Finance in Britain, 1767–1873**
Takuo Dome

67 **Essays in the History of Economics**
Warren J. Samuels, Willie Henderson, Kirk D. Johnson and Marianne Johnson

68 **History and Political Economy**
Essays in honour of P. D. Groenewegen
Edited by Tony Aspromourgos and John Lodewijks

69 **The Tradition of Free Trade**
Lars Magnusson

70 **Evolution of the Market Process**
Austrian and Swedish economics
Edited by Michel Bellet, Sandye Gloria-Palermo and Abdallah Zouache

71 **Consumption as an Investment**
The fear of goods from Hesiod to Adam Smith
Cosimo Perrotta

72 **Jean-Baptiste Say and the Classical Canon in Economics**
The British connection in French classicism
Samuel Hollander

73 **Knut Wicksell on Poverty**
No place is too exalted
Knut Wicksell

74 **Economists in Cambridge**
A study through their correspondence 1907–1946
Edited by M.C. Marcuzzo and A. Rosselli

75 **The Experiment in the History of Economics**
Edited by Philippe Fontaine and Robert Leonard

76 **At the Origins of Mathematical Economics**
The economics of A. N. Isnard (1748–1803)
Richard van den Berg

77 **Money and Exchange**
Folktales and reality
Sasan Fayazmanesh

78 **Economic Development and Social Change**
Historical roots and modern perspectives
George Stathakis and Gianni Vaggi

79 **Ethical Codes and Income Distribution**
A study of John Bates Clark and Thorstein Veblen
Guglielmo Forges Davanzati

80 **Evaluating Adam Smith**
Creating the wealth of nations
Willie Henderson

81 **Civil Happiness**
Economics and human flourishing in historical perspective
Luigino Bruni

82 **New Voices on Adam Smith**
Edited by Leonidas Montes and Eric Schliesser

83 **Making Chicago Price Theory**
Milton Friedman–George Stigler correspondence, 1945–1957
Edited by J. Daniel Hammond and Claire H. Hammond

84 **William Stanley Jevons and the Cutting Edge of Economics**
Bert Mosselmans

85 **A History of Econometrics in France**
From nature to models
Philippe Le Gall

86 **Money and Markets**
A doctrinal approach
Edited by Alberto Giacomin and Maria Cristina Marcuzzo

87 **Considerations on the Fundamental Principles of Pure Political Economy**
Vilfredo Pareto (edited by Roberto Marchionatti and Fiorenzo Mornati)

88 **The Years of High Econometrics**
A short history of the generation that reinvented economics
Francisco Louçã

89 **David Hume's Political Economy**
Edited by Carl Wennerlind and Margaret Schabas

90 **Interpreting Classical Economics**
Studies in long-period analysis
Heinz D. Kurz and Neri Salvadori

91 **Keynes's Vision**
Why the great depression did not return
John Philip Jones

92 **Monetary Theory in Retrospect**
The selected essays of Filippo Cesarano
Filippo Cesarano

93 **Keynes's Theoretical Development**
From the tract to the general theory
Toshiaki Hirai

94 **Leading Contemporary Economists**
Economics at the cutting edge
Edited by Steven Pressman

95 **The Science of Wealth**
Adam Smith and the framing of political economy
Tony Aspromourgos

96 **Capital, Time and Transitional Dynamics**
Edited by Harald Hagemann and Roberto Scazzieri

97 **New Essays on Pareto's Economic Theory**
Edited by Luigino Bruni and Aldo Montesano

98 **Frank Knight and the Chicago School in American Economics**
Ross B. Emmett

99 **A History of Economic Theory**
Essays in honour of Takashi Negishi
Edited by Aiko Ikeo and Heinz D. Kurz

100 **Open Economics**
Economics in relation to other disciplines
Edited by Richard Arena, Sheila Dow and Matthias Klaes

101 **Rosa Luxemburg and the Critique of Political Economy**
Edited by Riccardo Bellofiore

102 **Problems and Methods of Econometrics**
The Poincaré lectures of Ragnar Frisch 1933
Edited by Olav Bjerkholt and Ariane Dupont-Keiffer

103 **Criticisms of Classical Political Economy**
Menger, Austrian economics and the German historical school
Gilles Campagnolo

104 **A History of Entrepreneurship**
Robert F. Hébert and Albert N. Link

105 **Keynes on Monetary Policy, Finance and Uncertainty**
Liquidity preference theory and the global financial crisis
Jorg Bibow

106 **Kalecki's Principle of Increasing Risk and Keynesian Economics**
Tracy Mott

107 **Economic Theory and Economic Thought**
Essays in honour of Ian Steedman
John Vint, J. Stanley Metcalfe, Heinz D. Kurz, Neri Salvadori and Paul Samuelson

108 **Political Economy, Public Policy and Monetary Economics**
Ludwig von Mises and the Austrian tradition
Richard M. Ebeling

109 **Keynes and the British Humanist Tradition**
The moral purpose of the market
David R. Andrews

110 **Political Economy and Industrialism**
Banks in Saint-Simonian economic thought
Gilles Jacoud

111 **Studies in Social Economics**
By Leon Walras (translated by Jan van Daal and Donald Walker)

112 **The Making of the Classical Theory of Economic Growth**
By Anthony Brewer

113 **The Origins of David Hume's Economics**
By Willie Henderson

114 **Production, Distribution and Trade**
Edited by Adriano Birolo, Duncan Foley, Heinz D. Kurz, Bertram Schefold and Ian Steedman

115 **The Essential Writings of Thorstein Veblen**
Edited by Charles Camic and Geoffrey Hodgson

116 **Adam Smith and the Economy of the Passions**
By Jan Horst Keppler

117 **The Analysis of Linear Economic Systems**
Father Maurice Potron's pioneering works
Translated by Christian Bidard and Guido Erreygers

118 **A Dynamic Approach to Economic Theory: Frisch**
Edited by Olav Bjerkholt and Duo Qin

119 **Henry A. Abbati: Keynes' Forgotten Precursor**
Serena Di Gaspare

120 **Generations of Economists**
David Collard

121 **Hayek, Mill and the Liberal Tradition**
Edited by Andrew Farrant

122 **Marshall, Marshallians and Industrial Economics**
Edited by Tiziano Raffaelli

123 **Austrian and German Economic Thought**
Kiichiro Yagi

124 **The Evolution of Economic Theory**
Edited by Volker Caspari

125 **Thomas Tooke and the Monetary Thought of Classical Economics**
Matthew Smith

126 **Political Economy and Liberalism in France**
The contributions of Frédéric Bastiat
Robert Leroux

127 **Stalin's Economist**
The economic contributions of Jenö Varga
André Mommen

128 **E.E. Slutsky as Economist and Mathematician**
Crossing the limits of knowledge
Vincent Barnett

129 **Keynes, Sraffa, and the Criticism of Neoclassical Theory**
Essays in honour of Heinz Kurz
Neri Salvadori and Christian Gehrke

130 **Crises and Cycles in Economic Dictionaries and Encyclopaedias**
Edited by Daniele Bensomi

131 **General Equilibrium Analysis: A Century After Walras**
Edited by Pascal Bridel

132 **Sraffa and Modern Economics, Volume I**
Edited by Roberto Ciccone, Christian Gehrke and Gary Mongiovi

133 **Sraffa and Modern Economics, Volume II**
Edited by Roberto Ciccone, Christian Gehrke and Gary Mongiovi

134 **The Minor Marshallians and Alfred Marshall: An Evaluation**
Peter Groenewegen

135 **Fighting Market Failure**
Collected essays in the Cambridge tradition of economics
Maria Cristina Marcuzzo

136 **The Economic Reader**
Edited by Massimo M. Augello and Marco E.L. Guido

137 **Classical Political Economy and Modern Theory**
Essays in honour of Heinz Kurz
Neri Salvadori and Christian Gehrke

138 **The Ideas of Ronald H. Coase**
Lawrence W.C. Lai

139 **Anticipating the Wealth of Nations**
Edited by Maren Jonasson and Petri Hyttinen, with an Introduction by Lars Magnusson

140 **Innovation, Knowledge and Growth**
Edited by Heinz D. Kurz

141 **A History of Homo Economicus**
The nature of the moral in economic theory
William Dixon and David Wilson

142 **The Division of Labour in Economics**
A history
Guang-Zhen Sun

143 **Keynes and Modern Economics**
Edited by Ryuzo Kuroki

144 **Macroeconomics and the History of Economic Thought**
Festschrift in honour of Harald Hagemann
Edited by Hagen M. Krämer, Heinz D. Kurz and Hans-Michael Trautwein

145 **French Liberalism in the 19th Century**
An anthology
Edited by Robert Leroux

146 **Subjectivisim and Objectivism in the History of Economic Thought**
Edited by Yukihiro Ikeda and Kiichiro Yagi

Subjectivism and Objectivism in the History of Economic Thought

Edited by Yukihiro Ikeda
and Kiichiro Yagi

LONDON AND NEW YORK

First published 2012
by Routledge
2 Park Square, Milton Park, Abingdon, Oxfordshire OX14 4RN

Simultaneously published in the USA and Canada
by Routledge
711 Third Avenue, New York, NY 10017

First issued in paperback 2015

Routledge is an imprint of the Taylor & Francis Group, an informa business

© 2012 Yukihiro Ikeda and Kiichiro Yagi

The right of Yukihiro Ikeda and Kiichiro Yagi to be identified as the authors of the editorial material, and of the authors for their individual chapters, has been asserted in accordance with sections 77 and 78 of the Copyright, Designs and Patents Act 1988.

All rights reserved. No part of this book may be reprinted or reproduced or utilized in any form or by any electronic, mechanical, or other means, now known or hereafter invented, including photocopying and recording, or in any information storage or retrieval system, without permission in writing from the publishers.

Trademark notice: Product or corporate names may be trademarks or registered trademarks, and are used only for identification and explanation without intent to infringe.

British Library Cataloguing in Publication Data
A catalogue record for this book is available from the British Library

Library of Congress Cataloging in Publication Data
Subjectivism and objectivism in the history of economic thought/edited by Yukihiro Ikeda and Kiichiro Yagi.
  p. cm. – (Routledge studies in the history of economics; 146)
  Includes bibliographical references and index.
  1. Economics–History. 2. Subjectivity. 3. Objectivity. I. Ikeda, Yukihiro, 1959– II. Yagi, Kiichiro, 1947–
  HB75.S789 2012
  330.15–dc23
                                                        2012000000

ISBN 13: 978-0-415-70522-6 (pbk)
ISBN 13: 978-0-4156-0536-6 (hbk)

Typeset in Times New Roman
by Weraset Ltd, Boldon, Tyne and Wear

Contents

List of contributors   xv
Preface   xviii

Introduction: subjectivism and objectivism in the history of economic analysis   1
KIICHIRO YAGI

1 **Subjectivity, objectivity and biological interpretation in Smith's view on the real values of labour, money and corn**   11
TETSUO TAKA

2 **Individual rationality and mechanism in the history of microeconomic theory**   29
MASAHIRO KAWAMATA

3 **Quételet's influence on W. S. Jevons: from subjectivism to objectivism**   48
TAKUTOSHI INOUE

4 **Transforming of *rareté*? From Auguste to Léon Walras**   59
KAYOKO MISAKI

5 **Austrian subjectivism and hermeneutical economics**   73
YUICHI SHIONOYA

6 **Carl Menger's subjectivism: "types," economic subjects, and microfoundation**   91
YUKIHIRO IKEDA

7	**Böhm-Bawerk's objectivism: beyond Menger's subjectivism** SHIGEKI TOMO	108
8	**Ludwig von Mises as a pure subjectivist** HIROYUKI OKON	126
9	**Uncertainty and strategic interdependence in the interwar Viennese milieu** CHIKAKO NAKAYAMA	144
10	**Some evolutionary interpretations of the economic systems of Piero Sraffa and John von Neumann in the light of complexity** YUJI ARUKA	162
	Index	185

Contributors

Yuji Aruka is Professor of Economics at Chuo University, Japan. His publications include: *Evolutionary Controversies in Economics: A New Transdisciplinary Approach*, Tokyo/New York: Springer Verlag, 2001 (co-edited with Japan Association for Evolutionary Economics); *The Complex Networks of Economic Interactions: Essays in Agent-Based Economics and Econophysics*, Berlin: Springer Verlag, 2006 (co-edited with Akira Namatame and Taisei Kaizoji); *Complexities of Production and Interacting Human Behaviour*, Heidelberg: Physica, 2011.

Yukihiro Ikeda is Professor of History of Economic Thought at Keio University, Tokyo. His publications include: *Die Entstehungsgeschichte der Grundsätze Carl Mengers*. St. Katharinen: Scripta Mercaturae, 1997; "Carl Menger's Monetary Theory: A Revisionist View," *European Journal of History of Economic Thought*, 15 (13), 2008; *Austrian Economics in Transition: from Carl Menger to Friedrich Hayek*, London: Palgrave Macmillan, 2010 (co-edited with Harald Hagemann and Tamotsu Nishizawa).

Takutoshi Inoue is President of Kansei Gakuin University. His publications include: *The Thought and Economics of W. S. Jevons: From a Man of Science to an Economist* (in Japanese), Tokyo: Nihon Hyoronsha, 1987; "The Weeklong Blank in J. S. Mill's Sojourn in France: A Notebook Rediscovered," *Notes and Queries*, 250 (1), 2005; *Modern British Economics and Japan's Modernization: Japanese Students in Britain, Foreign Employees, and the Institutionalization of Economics* (in Japanese), Tokyo: Nihon Hyoronsha, 2006.

Masahiro Kawamata is Professor of History of Economic Thought at Keio University, Tokyo. His publications include: "Scientific Contributions to the International Journals," in A. Ikeo (ed.) *Japanese Economics and Economists since 1945*, London: Routledge, 2000; "The Negishi Method in the History of General Equilibrium Theory," in A. Ikeo and H. D. Kurz (eds.) *A History of Economic Theory: Essays in Honour of Takashi Negishi*, London: Routledge, 2009; "The Authorship of the Marginal Productivity Theory in 'the Old Quarrel,'" *Keio Economic Studies*, XLVI, 2010.

Kayoko Misaki is Professor of Economics at Shiga University, Japan. She was President of the International Walras Association (AIW) from 2008–2010. Her publications include: "La libre concurrence organisée chez Walras dans une perspective hayekienne," in Roberto Baranzini (ed.) *Léon Walras et l'équilibre général, Recherches récentes*, Paris: Economica, 2011; History, Philosophy, and Development of Walrasian Economics, 6.28.38 the Encyclopedia of Life Support System (EOLSS), the UNESCO, 2012.

Chikako Nakayama is Professor of Global Studies at Tokyo University of Foreign Studies, Tokyo. Her publications include: "An Investigation of Hayek's Criticism of Central Planning," in T. Aimar and J. Birner (eds.) *F.A. Hayek as a Political Economist: Economic Analysis and Values*, London/New York: Routledge, 2002; "A Lifelong Friendship: The Correspondence between Oskar Morgenstern and Luigi Einaudi," *Storia del Pensiero economico*, n.1, 2008 (co-authored with Giovanni Pavanelli); "Involvement of an Austrian Émigré Economist in America," in H. Hagemann, T. Nishizawa, and Y. Ikeda (eds.) *Austrian Economics in Transition: From Carl Menger to Friedrich Hayek*, London: Palgrave Macmillan, 2010.

Hiroyuki Okon is Professor of Economics at Kokugakuin University, Tokyo. His publications include: *Economics of the Austrian School of Economics* (in Japanese), Tokyo: Nihon Keizai Hyoron-sha, 2003 (co-edited with Tamotsu Hashimoto); "Evolutionary and Societal Rationalism of Ludwig von Mises" (in Japanese), in T. Hirai (ed.) *What is a Market Society?* Tokyo: Sophia University Press, 2007.

Yuichi Shionoya is Emeritus Professor of Economics at Hitotsubashi University, Tokyo. His publications include: *Schumpeter and the Idea of Social Science: A Metatheoretical Study*, New York: Cambridge University Press, 1997; *The Soul of the German Historical School: Methodological Essays on Schmoller, Weber and Schumpeter*, New York: Springer, 2005; *Economy and Morality: The Philosophy of the Welfare State*, Cheltenham: Edward Elgar, 2005.

Tetsuo Taka is Professor of History of Economic Thought at Kyushu Sangyo University, Fukuoka. His publications include: "The Place of Economic Man in Evolutionary Economics: Veblen and Commons Reconsidered," *Annals of the Society for the History of Economic Thought*, 44, 2003; "Veblen's Theory of Evolution and the Instinct of Workmanship: An Ethological and Biological Reinterpretation," *History of Economic Thought*, 47(2), 2005; "Instinct as a Foundational Concept in Adam Smith's Social Theory," *The History of Economic Thought*, 53(2), 2012.

Shigeki Tomo was teaching from April 1992 to October 2010 at Kyoto Sangyo Univesity, Kyoto. His publications include: *Eugen von Böhm-Bawerk: Ein grosser Österreichischer Nationalökonom zwischen Theorie und Praxis*, Marburg: Metropolis Verlag, 1994; *Eugen von Böhm-Bawerks Innsbrucker*

Vorlesungen über Nationalökonomie: Wiedergabe aufgrund zweier Mitschriften, Marburg: Metropolis Verlag, 1998; "Beyond Walras: On the Historicity of Walras's Market Equilibrium Concept," *History of Economic Thought*, 51, 2010.

Kiichiro Yagi is at present affiliated to Setsunan Universisty, Neyagawa City, Osaka. Previously, he taught theory of political economy and history of economics at Kyoto University for a quarter century. His publications include: *Competition, Trust, and Cooperation: A Compartative Study*, Berlin/New York: Springer, 2001 (co-edited with Yuichi Shionoya); *Melting Boundaries: Institutional Transformation in the Wider Europe*, Kyoto: Kyoto University Press, 2008 (co-edited with Satoshi Mizubata); *Austrian and German Economic Thought: From Subjectivism to Social Evolution*, London: Routledge, 2011.

Preface

This monograph, entitled *Subjectivism and Objectivism in the History of Economic Thought*, consists of papers by the members of the Japan Society for the History of Economic Thought. Although the Society has a long history, having approximately 700 members, it is still true that the research of the members is not necessarily well known in international academia due to the fact that the main results of the research continue to be published in Japanese.

Thus, the Society decided to publish a series of monographs to enhance the opportunity to have discussions with researchers with other cultural and linguistic backgrounds. A task force discussing a possibility of publication in English was set up formally in July 1993. In November the task force advised the council meeting of the Society to publish a series of monographs by the members of the Society. After positive reactions from the council members, a committee was organized to propose a concrete plan for the realization of the series and it came to the conclusion to publish a monograph on the history of economic thought of this country.[1] Thus, the first volume of the series was dedicated to the Japanese history of economic thought:

Economic Thought and Modernization in Japan, ed. by Shiro Sugihara and Toshihiro Tanaka, in association of the Society for the History of Economic Thought, Japan, Edward Elgar, 1998.

Fortunately the book contributed a great deal to the understanding of Japanese history of economic thought among English-speaking scholars in the broader sense of the term. Responding to the positive reactions from readers, the Society continues to publish a series every few years, the second of which was edited by Yuichi Shionoya, a well-known figure in the research of Joseph Schumpeter:

The German Historical School: The Historical and Ethical Approach to Economics (Routledge Studies in the History of Economics), edited by Yuichi Shionoya, Routledge, 2000.

The publication of the above volume can be partly reduced to the renaissance of the German Historical School in Europe, but also to the fact that Japan had introduced its doctrines in the Meiji Era.

And the third book in the series concerns itself with Scottish Enlightenment:

The Rise of Political Economy in the Scottish Enlightenment (Routledge Studies in the History of Economics), edited by Tatsuya Sakamoto and Hideo Tanaka, Routledge, 2003.

It is well-known among Western researchers that the study of Adam Smith has a very long outstanding tradition in Japanese academia. Influenced by the international upheaval of the study of the Scottish Enlightenment, the volume gives us new insights on the various figures of the movement.

Obviously another traditional field among the Japanese historians of economic thought is Karl Marx. The fourth publication appeared in a different series of Routledge:

Marx for the 21st Century (Routledge Frontiers of Political Economy), edited by Hiroshi Uchida, Routledge, 2005.

A short glance at the table of contents shows a variety of interests among the Japanese scholars in Marx.

All of these volumes are welcomed by Japanese and Western readers. This will be the fifth of the series published in association with the Japan Society for the History of Economic Thought. The editors of this volume have been concerned with the study of the Austrian School of Economics for a fairly long time, which necessitates our encounter with the methodological problems of economics, including subjectivism, allegedly one of the main methodological pillars of the School. We had planned to edit a volume concerning the tradition of subjectivism in the history of economic thought; but as it turns out, the volume has become a monograph dealing with the confrontations and differences between subjectivism and objectivism in economics. Therefore we have decided to change the original title slightly, which included only "subjectivism." In any case, this will be the first volume in the above-mentioned series which deals explicitly with the problem of methodology in the history of economic thought.

Publication of this volume was made possible by generous financial support from the Japan Society for the History of Economic Thought. Our special thanks go to Keiko Kurita, President of the Society, Toshiaki Hirai who is now responsible for this series, and council members of the Society.

Yukihiro Ikeda and Kiichiro Yagi

Note

1 The historical description of the planning of the series is based on: *Fifty Years of the Society for the History of Economic Thought*, edited by the Society for the History of Economic Thought, Japan, 2000.

Introduction

Subjectivism and objectivism in the history of economic analysis

Kiichiro Yagi

As a discipline, economic science investigates the processes in and the results of individuals' economic behavior. Thus, its study inevitably involves subjective elements that, in reality, affect the behavior of individuals. In this introduction, in using the terms "subjective" and "subjectivity," we refer to the states and content of comprehension as it takes place in the consciousness of individuals. Indeed, the coverage of "subjectivity" within economic science differs considerably, according to the focus of a given theorist. Nonetheless, we can refer to the attitude that stresses the significance of subjective elements as "subjectivism."

On the other hand, as a science that can provide definitive and meaningful information, economics requires objective elements that can determine or limit the range of economic behaviors of actors and their outcomes, independent of subjective comprehension. The quantities of available resources, the intensity and distribution of the needs of individuals, and knowledge of technology and consumption can all be considered "objective" elements. Further, in cases where the outcomes of the economic behavior of actors – as well as prices – are determined uniquely, they can in turn also be considered "objective" elements that influence the behavior of actors. Thus, economic theories involve both subjective and objective elements and aspects. If we consider the comprehension of economic actors as no more than a reflection of such objective elements, then "objectivism" is the antithesis of "subjectivism" in economics.

Here, we notice that "subjectivism" and "objectivism" – two topics with which this volume deals – are classifications of alternative positions in science, that is, elements of attentively controlled epistemology. No one can deny that economic behavior and its aggregation have elements of both subjectivity and objectivity. However, as a methodology or canon of a disciplined science, each position sets a priority among these elements in the course of their investigations.

Marxists – who consider the comprehension and motivation of economic actors, which are, in their view, ultimately determined by their position in a given set of social production relations – have a theory of labor value that is relevant to their "objectivism." Sraffian economists deduce a consistent value system from a set of technological coefficients and a distribution ratio between wage and profit; in this respect, they too are objectivists. Starting with bestowed labor or given technological coefficients is a process that reflects the objectivistic canon of sciences of which those economists conceive. However, as has been argued recently, under more realistic conditions involving joint production and plural technologies, even the concept of "class exploitation" cannot hold without introducing market prices; thus, the subjective element of demand is inserted into such species of objective economic analysis (Yoshihara and Veneziani 2009, Yoshihara 2010). The reinterpretation of the theorems of "objectivist" economics, by introducing into them "subjective" elements, is worth doing, as it may open a path to a new kind of integration.

It is common knowledge among historians of economics that a turn toward subjectivism occurred in the late nineteenth century, when the determination of prices by the maximization of utility of individuals was introduced to economic analysis. As the basic concept of "utility" can be traced back to the scholars of that age, the mainstream of present-day academic economics, that is, neoclassical economics, also belongs to the camp of "subjectivism"; however, it still represents a peculiar integration of subjectivism and objectivism. In the standard analysis of neoclassical economics, a set of possible alternatives (or the probability of their occurrence) is assumed to be known by all actors, and those actors are assumed to be able to attribute their utility estimates to every particular alternative. Regarding this assumption in addition to the assumption of non-existence of elements that cause market failures, it is argued that the rational behavior of individuals can produce a unique equilibrium solution. In other words, neoclassicism in economics represents the conviction that an objective outcome in economic analysis can be drawn by the subjective principle of utility maximization. Thanks to this synthesis of subjectivism and objectivism, economics in the twentieth century acquired the reputation of an advanced discipline within the family of social and human sciences.

Is this synthesis of subjectivism and objectivism tenable? Around the turn of the twentieth and twenty-first centuries, many theorists were no longer so optimistic as to assume that economic analysis could provide unique equilibrium solutions under any relevant condition. In fact, at present, many of them are skeptical of the assumption of perfect knowledge and even of the reality of utility maximization. Even if the concept of equilibrium were to be maintained, it can be indeterminate or intelligible, since there are plural equilibria, depending on the locality, path, or interpretation involved.

Criticism of the neoclassicist synthesis of subjectivism and objectivism can be traced back to a series of articles written by F.A. Hayek in the 1930s and 1940s (see Hayek 1948). As early as 1936 (Hyek 1937), Hayek criticized it in his famous article "Economics and Knowledge," wherein he argues that most knowledge that affects economic behavior is not that which is commonly shared, but rather *private* knowledge that is accessible only to an individual in action. In "Meaning of Competition," he further maintains that under the presupposition of attaining the unique and optimal equilibrium, the true meaning of the competitive process would disappear. Hayek thus abandoned the assumption of perfect knowledge and universal rational action, both of which are indispensable to the objective determination of a solution in equilibrium analysis. However, he retained the subjective element by which actors seek to attain their own aims and which reflects an individual's comprehension of his or her aims and environment. In other words, Hayek broke down the neoclassical synthesis of subjectivism and objectivism within equilibrium solutions and returned to the original sense of "subjectivism," as per the Austrian School in particular its founder, Carl Menger – wherein one gives priority to subjective elements in the comprehension of economic actors, rather than to the attainment of the optimal solution.

At present, theoretical economists endeavoring to advance economic analysis seem to have lost trust in the assumptions of perfect knowledge and universal rationality. Their interests have shifted to a world of imperfect knowledge, bounded rationality, and plural equilibria. Is all behavior of economic actors "rational?" Can the set of all possible selections be known? Even if economic actors were to behave rationally, do their interactions lead to a unique equilibrium? To all of these questions, contemporary theoretical economists are hesitant to answer "Yes."

Then, must they return to the position of empiricism, similar to that of natural scientists who collect empirical data in order to find regularities therein? This is the approach taken by some scientists trained in physics who work in the area of economic phenomena. However, as disputes in macroeconomics in recent decades have shown us, most economists have not been willing to take this direction. Most economic theorists have endeavored to ground their empirical findings by supplying a new scheme of economic behavior under the name of "micro-foundation." In our view, they have followed a conception consistent with the "subjectivist" canon of economic science.

The science canon we are using here is the mode of reasoning that exemplifies that specialized science, or otherwise distinguishes it from other sciences or nonsciences. In the first decade of the twentieth century, some economists held the view that a psychological law (i.e., Weber–Fechner's law on the psychological stimulus) might serve as the basis of the diminishing marginal utility, which economic theorists then assumed. It was Max Weber (1908) who opposed such a view and maintained that economic science need not borrow any foundation from another discipline. He argued that the very fact that the significance of rational economic action is confirmed in the daily lives of the people, including theorists, legitimizes the construction of an "ideal type" theory of economic science. Thus, in Weber's view, subjective economic rationality was not an objectively grounded principle, but a canon that researchers of economic science abstracted from their daily lives and of which conceived, for use in their discipline.

In his more popular article "Objectivity in the Recognition of Social Science" (1904), in which he proposes his theory concerning the "ideal type," Weber applies the term "objectivity" to the logically consistent outcome of the "ideal type" reconstruction of social life. "Objectivity" in the scientific sense does not consist in a correspondence to reality but in the logical consistency of reasoning within a given interest of recognition. What is necessary for a researcher is to be

Table I.1 "Objectivity" under the canon of subjectivism: the Weberian concept of the "ideal type" as a distinct canon of economic science

	Individual level	Plural individuals/social interaction
Epistemological dimension (legitimate dimension of subjective economics)	Rational economic action (aim and means)	Impartial and logical consequences from "ideal type" of construction
Ontological dimension (demarcated dimension)	Desire and its satisfaction as a psycho-physiological process	Existence of unique and determinate state

conscious of the given aim of the recognition and follow the ideal type of reasoning consistently, so that other researchers can obtain identical outcomes so long as they choose the same aim of recognition.[1]

Hayek, in his famous 1936 article (Hayek 1937), suggests that those economists who generally confine their agenda to a pure selection tend to reject the "ideal type" view of economic theory. In the "ideal type" reasoning, "objectivity" differs categorically from reality and signifies only an impartiality of recognition. In other words, it is an epistemological "objectivity" that has nothing to do with real or ontological "objectivity." However, for those economists who believed in the universality of rational action, no distinction existed between epistemological objectivity and ontological objectivity. If this belief is, at present, abandoned, then what functions as the bridge that combines the "objectivity" of the epistemological dimension and "objectivity" of the ontological dimension?

Further, we can apply the distinction of epistemology and ontology to the canon of subjectivism in economics.

At first, as far as comprehension and the behavior of an individual are concerned, epistemological "subjectivity" seems to coincide with ontological "subjectivity." However, if we agree with Weber's rejection of the psycho-physiological foundation of economic theory, the epistemological subjectivity that successfully passes the subjectivist canon consists of intellectual relationships among aims and means that are suited for logical and meaningful reconstruction by the researcher. The ontological "subjectivity" that includes the psycho-physiological process and which proceeds without consciousness or unintentional behavior is excluded. It is either neglected or considered a given presumption for economic science. However, today, with the growing interest in the apparently "irrational" behavior of economic affairs, many economists are joining in the investigation of the decision process and the behavior of individuals, under such rubrics as "behavioral economics" or "experimental economics." The author of this introduction, himself, feels some sympathy for such directions.

In the area of an individual actor, however, it is possible to confirm or modify the epistemological subjectivity through the use of the real ontological subjective process. However, what is the case with plural individuals, or society as a whole? The existence of other fellow human beings cannot be denied, and so we must think in terms of a society that consists of a number of actors who represent their own "subjectivity" of the same right as our own. Economic science establishes itself in the rank of social sciences only when it can address the interaction of plural actors and their outcomes. This signifies a real epistemological gap between plural subjectivities: how can we know of the comprehension of other individuals?

In the history of economic thought, several convenient devices have been known to fill this gap. One is the introduction of a collective entity (*society* or *nation*) that provides a collective subjective judgment/valuation of the relevant goods or services in question. There are many variations of such collective entities, from a mystical organic theory of national economy to a provisional statistical entity based on empirical data. Another is the assumption of the "representative consumer" or "representative firm," either of which can vindicate an extension of the analysis of the individual level to the social level, by way of simple aggregation. However, as seen from the ontological dimension, there are no legitimate grounds for such artificial assumptions.

In the real or ontological dimension, all human individuals as well as organizational entities such as firms compete and make transactions with each other, in order to live or survive. Thus, it is natural that some economists at the end of the nineteenth century anticipated the application of evolutionary theory to economic science (Veblen 1898, Marshall 1898). However, the emergence of advanced equilibrium economics (i.e., theory of general equilibrium) that does not need to deal with aggregate entities – at least not at the abstract, theoretical level – crowded out this premature direction of evolutionary economics. It was at the second generative stage of the evolutionary economics in the latter half of the twentieth century that the validity of the optimization postulate of firms/consumers and the selection process in the competitive market was first discussed seriously (see Nelson and Winter 1982). The result was the conclusion that the competitive pressure of the market economy does not necessarily generate the state in which all entities are the most efficient "representative" features of production/consumption and in which the existence and generation of heterogeneous entities are possible in various conditions. The subjective features

Table I.2 "Subjectivity" at the individual and social levels

	Individual level	*Social level/plural individuals*
Epistemological dimension	Intellectual comprehension	Collective organic entity/ representative entities/ heterogeneous comprehensions
Ontological dimension (developing dimension of advanced research)	Psycho-physiological subjectivity	Existence of heterogeneous entities/their interaction

of plural entities include various kinds of variation from which new compositions of economic entities (i.e., populations) emerge through their interactions. The epistemological constellation of comprehension vis-à-vis economic actors reflects the life situation of these actors in an ontological sense, and variations in the comprehension of actors affect both the direction and result of their economic behaviors. Thus, the viewpoint of evolutionary economics concedes an ontological constellation of plural entities with different subjective features and epistemological complexities.

One of the editors of this anthology holds an evolutionist view of the (future) development of economic science. To him, the Weberian distinction of this science from the intellectual subjective canon is too idealistic to deal with real economic phenomena.[2] In editing this anthology, he revisits the history of economics and explores the various types of relationships among the "subjective" elements and "objective" elements of the ideas of past scholars. He believes that such retrospection is useful not only for historians of economic thought, but also for all theoretical economists.

This volume consists of contributions by authors who belong to the Japan Society of the History of Economic Thought. Each of them has responded to the editors' proposal vis-à-vis the aim of this volume, in his or her own way.

First in this volume is Tetsuo Taka's biological interpretation of Adam Smith's theory of value. According to Taka, some of the alleged confusion surrounding Smithian value theory can be resolved by carefully reading the text – especially that pertaining to Smith's peculiarly organic and biological view of human beings and society. Indeed, Taka admits to the "subjective" nature of the Smithian judgment of value, but this "subjectivity" is a manifestation of the social instinct of man. Under the division of labor, a worker adjusts the quantity of labor he or she bestows on his or her product to the objective quantity of labor demanded by the market. The final outcome – namely, natural price – reflects the need to regenerate the lives of workers. Thus, the author of this chapter maintains that Smith's *Wealth of Nations*, as a text on economic value, aligns with essentially evolutionist views of the economic society of man.

The author of the second chapter, Masahiro Kawamata, understands the "subjectivist" canon as a general rubric of microeconomics in the modern sense, and that it presents a macroscopic view of its development. He maintains that microeconomic theory before the marginal revolution (i.e., utility theory) had essentially the same structure as that after the marginal revolution. What is missing from the former is the formulation of the rational behavior of individual economic agents and the mechanism by which their actions can be integrated. Kawamata does not consider this a decisive schism that splits what is otherwise the continuity of theoretical development, since the implication of the rationality formula and the understanding of market equilibrium go hand-in-hand with real economic development. He rather pinpoints the schism of the theoretical development of microeconomics in the twentieth century as having occurred when the theory of mechanism design emerged to cope with the problems of incentive compatibility. Microeconomic theory prior to this schism dealt with the mechanism of the competitive market and was based on the fundamental theorem of utilitarianism. However, recognition of the pervasive existence of market failures from the 1930s to the 1970s forced microeconomics to enter a new period of theoretical development.

In the third chapter, Takutoshi Inoue discusses the relationship of subjectivity and objectivity in an economic analysis of the work of William Stanley Jevons. Jevons began his investigation into economic theory by applying the utilitarian principle of maximization of happiness. However, there is a gap between individual "subjectivity" and "objective" economic phenomena. In Jevons's view, for economics to be a science, it must fulfill the criteria of rigidity and exactness. Here, Inoue reminds us of Jevons's background in mathematics and natural science and argues that the reception of Adolphe Quételet's statistical view of man is decisive in this respect. Thanks to Quételet's concept of "average law," Jevons believes, both the problem of "free will" and the difficulties inherent in measuring subjective utility can be evaded, and economics can fulfill the criterion of a science. Most present-day theoreticians in economics are not as optimistic as Jevons; however, how and what kind of statistic theory is useful in covering or uncovering the subjective elements of economics continues to be a question worth investigating.

Next, the fourth chapter deals with the concept of *rareté*, which Léon Walras inherited from his father Auguste Walras. Against the prevalent view of its origin in the French tradition of subjective utility theory of value, the chapter's author, Kayoko Misaki, argues that both Léon and Auguste meant to found an objective theory of value that could serve as a basis of the theory of property. Auguste defines *rareté* as the ratio of the number of persons wanting a good to the total available quantity of that good. Léon's interest in mathematical formulations of economic theory was aroused by the advice of his father. According to Misaki, the subjective content of marginal utility itself was not what Léon sought; rather, by naming it with the same word, *rareté*, Léon shares his father's conviction that objectivity is one of the necessary conditions for the theory of property, and thus a basis of social reform.

Now, we come to the Austrian School, which is often considered a representative school possessing the traits of subjectivism. In the fifth chapter, Yuichi Shionoya provides us with a hermeneutic reading of the tradition of subjectivism of and around the Austrian School. According to Shionoya, subjectivism has three aspects: desire, cognition, and interpretation, which are addressed by economics, psychology, and hermeneutics, respectively. As a School that grew while continuously interacting with contemporary philosophy and psychology on the continent, its theory – and particularly that of its founder, Carl Menger – contains hermeneutical elements that surpass those of mere economics, that is, the subjectivism of desire. Shionoya first summarizes Menger's view of the ontological structure of human economy and then follows with an outline of the development of hermeneutical thinking in economics, up to Joseph Schumpeter. He sees here a parallel development with the emergence of the hermeneutical ontology of Martin Heidegger.

In the sixth chapter, Yukihiro Ikeda examines Menger's subjectivism and its validity from a methodological viewpoint. He finds in Menger's *Principles* (Menger 1871) (*Grundsätze der Volkswirtschaftslehre*), particularly in its theory of goods, concepts that are not compatible with a strict subjectivist view of methodology. According to Ikeda, Menger in the polemical methodological investigation (Menger 1883) further misses the justification of reduction to the simplest element of economic phenomena and the formulation of "types." In Ikeda's view, Menger's position in terms of his real theory was not strict, but rather ambiguous. Thus, following a critical examination of Menger's text, Ikeda closes his contribution with a skeptical remark over the need for, and the possibility of, the microfoundation of economics.

In the seventh chapter, Shigeki Tomo deals with a confrontation between Menger and Böhm-Bawerk, from the viewpoints of "subjectivism" and "objectivism." Menger was definitely a "subjectivist" who saw in price no more than a contingent result of the behavior of actors in attempting to attain a fuller satisfaction of their wants. However, Böhm-Bawerk's tendency toward "objectivism" had been apparent since the early 1880s, when he started to consider price an "objective value." Böhm-Bawerk developed an objectivist interpretation of price, from an a-temporal version to an intertemporal version. Tomo further explores vacillations in "objective" and "subjective" interpretations of price within the Austrian tradition, and finally poses the question of whether or not the emergence of money is "objective," from the viewpoint of Mengerian subjectivism.

In the eighth chapter, Hiroyuki Okon presents Ludwig Mises as a "pure subjectivist." Mises rejected the inconsistent "subjectivism" of his senior generation, which admitted the possibility of value calculation. Friedrich Wieser, among others, went even further by speculating on a collective economy based on "natural value." However, for Mises, the subjective valuation of an individual is nothing but preference "a" over "b." The conclusion that individuals cannot make any calculations without money and monetary prices serves as the basis of his criticism of the socialist concept of a planned economy. Okon follows Mises's effort to develop his position, up to his *magnum opus*: the *Nationalökonomie* (Mises 1940) (*Human Action* in the later English edition).

In the ninth chapter, Chikako Nakayama focuses on the subjectivism Oskar Morgenstern held during his long career as an economic theoretician, since the interwar years. It was Morgenstern that integrated uncertainty, non-rationality, and strategic behavior into the subjectivist setting of the Austrian economists. Nakayama explains the influence of Karl Menger (the mathematician son of economist Carl Menger) on Morgenstern in Vienna, his friendly collaboration with Frank Knight in the United States, and the relationship between Morgenstern's work and the Keynesian concept of probability. Further, she reminds us of Morgenstern's initial interests in the forecast of business fluctuations, by situating her description within the context of the present-day uncertainty inherent in a finance-led global market.

Finally, in the tenth chapter, Yuji Aruka interprets Piero Sraffa and John von Neumann from the modern view of complexity. In the prevalent view, both

Sraffa's production system and von Neumann's growth model are considered "objective" models. However, in Aruka's view, the idea of heterogeneous interaction is common to both models. By receiving suggestions from John Holland that interprets von Neumann's growth model as a kind of complex adaptive system, Aruka seeks to formulate the Sraffian model with joint production, from the viewpoint of a complex, evolutionary system. Although Aruka does not use the term "subjectivism" in his description, the interaction of multiple heterogeneous agents supplies "subjectivism" of plural actors an appropriate setting for their functioning.

Thus, this volume provides the public with various considerations of the significance of and relationships between "subjectivism" and "objectivism," within the history of economics. At first sight, some of the chapters may seem to deviate from the editors' view of "subjectivism," as per the canon of economics. However, these chapters together suggest the possibility of an ontological constellation that involves the subjectivism of acting individuals. The postulate of "objectivism" is thus converted to the real ontological working of "subjectivism."

Notes

1 Another way to evade the substantial concept of "subjectivity" is to limit the perspective of the researcher to the empirical level that is manifest to anyone involved. It was once believed that Samuelson's concept of "revealed preference" (Samuelson 1938, 1949) successfully expelled the metaphysical concept of "subjective" utility. In reality, it was a device used to restate the "subjectivist" canon in a way palatable to positivists.
2 He published his research on the Austrian and German economists – including Carl Menger, Böhm-Bawerk, Friedrich Wieser, Karl Knies, Max Weber, and J.A. Schumpeter – as Yagi (2011). He summarizes the hidden shift in the academic interests of those scholars in the subtitle: "from subjectivism to social evolution."

References

Hayek, F.A. (1937) "Economics and knowledge," *Economica* (n.s.), 4: 33–54. Reprinted in F.A. Hayek (1948) *Individualism and Economic Order*. Chicago, IL: University of Chicago Press.
Hayek, F.A. (1948) "The meaning of competition," in F.A. Hayek, *Individualism and Economic Order*. Chicago, IL: University of Chicago Press, pp. 92–106.
Marshall, A. (1898) "Mechanical and biological analogies in economics," in A.C. Pigou (ed.) (1925) *Memorials of Alfred Marshall*. London: Macmillan, pp. 312–18.
Menger, C. (1871) *Grundsätze der Volkswirtschaftslehre*. Wien: Braumüller.
Menger, C. (1883) *Untersuchungen über die Methode der Sozialwissenschaften, und der Politischen Oekonomie insbesondere*. München und Leipzig: Duncker und Humblot.
Mises, L. (1940) *Nationalökonomie Theorie des Handelns und Wirtschaftens*. Geneva: Editions Unions Genf.
Nelson, R. and Winter, S. (1982) *An Evolutionary Theory of Economic Change*. Cambridge, MA: Belknap and Harvard University Press.
Samuelson, P.A. (1938) "A note on the pure theory of consumer's behavior," *Economica*, 5: 61–71.

Samuelson, P.A. (1949) *Foundations of Economic Analysis*. Cambridge, MA: Harvard University Press.

Veblen, T. (1898) "Why is economics not an evolutionary science?" *Quarterly Journal of Economics*, 12: 373–97.

Weber, M. (1904) "Die 'Objektivität' sozialwissenschaftlicher und sozialpolitischer Erkenntnis," *Archiv für Sozialwissenschaft und Sozialpolitik*, vol. 19. In M. Weber (1951) *Gesammelte Aufsätze zur Wissenschaftslehre*. Tübingen: J.C.B. Mohr (Paul Siebeck), pp. 146–214.

Weber, M. (1908) "Die Grenznutzlehre und das psychophysische Grundgesetz," *Archiv für Sozialwissenschaft und Sozialpolitik*, vol. 27. In M. Weber (1951) *Gesammelte Aufsätze zur Wissenschaftslehre*. Tübingen: J.C.B. Mohr (Paul Siebeck), 384–99.

Yagi, K. (2011) *Austrian and German Economic Thought: From Subjectivism to Social Evolution*. London and New York: Routledge.

Yoshihara, N. (2010) "Class and exploitation in general convex cone economies," *Journal of Economic Behavior and Organization*, 75: 281–96.

Yoshihara, N. and Veneziani, R. (2009) "Objectivist versus subjectivist approaches to the Marxian theory of exploitation," IER Discussion Papers, No. 514. The Institute of Economic Research, Hitotsubashi University.

1 Subjectivity, objectivity and biological interpretation in Smith's view on the real values of labour, money and corn

Tetsuo Taka

The purpose of this chapter is to reinterpret Adam Smith's labour theory of value which has long been criticized for mixing quantities of spent labour, labour commanded and sacrificed labour-disutility. Careful examination of his arguments reveals that the whole structure of his economic theory should be interpreted as an integral part of the organic and biological understanding of human being and society.

The reinterpretation resolves itself into the following three points. First, if we pay attention to Smith's distinction between the maintained quantity of labour and maintainable quantity of products, it is easy for us to understand why Smith declared that the unchangeable value of labour must be, in the short term, represented much better by money rather than by corn, however the latter represented it much better in the long term. Second, the labour theory of value elaborated in the first five chapters of the *Wealth of Nations* (hereafter abbreviated to *WN*) should be understood as an organically composite theory founded upon the physical and mechanical analysis of the increase of productive power through the division of labour: the whole product of labour became a "commons stock" of the society. The exchange value of each commodity was decided not only upon the subjective judgements of each owner but also upon the sympathy between buyers and sellers. Third and finally, Smith's theory of economic development was substantially the evolutionary theory about the quantitative increase of products and population resulting from the division of labour, the qualitative extension of the diversity of products (consumption) and human liberty. The distinctive means for escaping from Ricardian and Malthusian dismal sciences, therefore, seems to be found in the fact that Smith constructed his economics not only upon the instinctive working of sympathy explained in *The Theory of Moral Sentiment* (hereafter abbreviated to *TMS*), but also upon his own biological and evolutionary methods.

Division of labour and the propensity to exchange: physical reasoning and the role of sympathy

As Smith explicitly said that the greatest improvement in the productive powers of labour was the effects of the division of labour, he emphasized its decisive role for achieving physical and mechanical efficiency of production. The genius of Smith clearly appears in the short example of a small pin manufactory "where ten men only were employed, and where some of them consequently performed two or three distinct operations" (*WN*.I.i.3), A pin manufactory was very suggestive, since "changing fashions in dress were followed by people of all classes, pins were surely one of life's necessities" in the early seventeenth century (Thirsk 1977, 78). English pin making benefited by Dutch technological innovation started to employ children and gave opportunities for disabled soldiers and crippled paupers (ibid. 80–3), who earn "from 1s. to 2s. a week" in the description of Warrington (Young [1771]1967, vol. 3, 165).[1]

Smith cited three reasons for the increase of productivity. First, the division of labour increases the dexterity of workmen "by reducing every man's business to some one simple operation, and by making this operation the sole employment of his life" (*WN*.I.i.6). Second, "the advantage which is gained by saving the time commonly lost in passing from one sort of work to another is much greater than we should at first view be apt to imagine it". Smith asserted further that the habit of sauntering and of indolent careless application renders every country workman "almost always slothful and lazy, and incapable of any vigorous application even on the most pressing occasions" (*WN*.I.i.7). Third, the invention of machines which facilitated and abridged the labour. However, Smith attached great importance to "philosophers or men of speculation" rather than workers as sources of technological advance.

Smith's theory of division of labour is formalized fundamentally upon the physical and mechanical principle of the productivity enhancement in the social production of the necessaries of life, although it consists of two kinds of people, one engaged directly in production, like workers, and the other speculative work in order to accumulate scientific knowledge, like philosophers. It may, therefore, be an ideal case that "every workman has a great quantity of his own work to dispose of beyond what he himself has occasion for; and every other workman being exactly in the same situation" (*WN*.I.i.10). In short, the characterization of division of labour in the first chapter of *WN* is the explanation of physical and mechanical enhancement of productivity by individual workmen, and is a model of the barter system where all surplus products of labourers were to be exchanged with each other.

However, Smith presented different images in Chapter 2, since he declared that the different produce of geniuses and talents are brought, "as it were, into a common stock" by the general disposition to truck, barter and exchange (*WN*.I.ii.5).

> This division of labour, from which so many advantages are derived, is not originally the effect of any human wisdom, which foresees and intends that general opulence to which it gives occasion. It is the necessary, though very slow and gradual consequence of a certain propensity in human nature which has in view no such extensive utility; the propensity to truck, barter, and exchange one thing for another.
>
> (*WN*.I.ii.1)

Although this argument displays a distinctively anthropological and evolutionary conception of human nature, it seems worth noting that the guarded statement, "whether this propensity be one of those original principles in human nature" or "the necessary consequence of the faculties of reason and speech, it belongs not to our present subject to enquire" (*WN*.I.ii.2) in *WN* was finally extended to the confident belief in *TMS* in 1790. He said thusly.

> The desire of being believed, the desire of persuading, of leading and directing other people, seems to be one of the strongest of all our natural desires. It is, perhaps, the instinct upon which is founded the faculty of speech, the characteristical faculty of human nature. No other animal possesses this faculty, and we cannot discover in any other animal any desire to lead and direct the judgment and conduct of its fellows.
>
> (*TMS*.VII.iv.25)

This kind of distinctive reference to the instinct does not appear in *WN*, although Smith studied botany and enriched his conception of the instinct by reference to the twelfth edition of Linnés *Systema Naturae* (1766–8) in the latter part of "Of the External Senses" accomplished during his writing of *WN*.[2] While Smith used the term propensity in place of it, it was very close to the term instinct. He paraphrased the propensity to truck, barter and exchange thusly.

> Man has almost constant occasion for the help of his brethren, and it is in vain for him to expect it from their benevolence only. He will be more likely to prevail if he can interest their self-love in his favour, and shew them that it is for their own advantage to do for him what he requires of them. Whoever offers to another a bargain of any kind, proposes to do this. Give me that which I want, and you shall have this which you want, is the meaning of every such offer; and it is in this manner that we obtain from one another the far greater part of those good offices which we stand in need of.
>
> (*WN*.I.ii.2)

Today we know that Charles Darwin coined the same human nature into "the Social Instinct" of which "sympathy forms an essential part" (Darwin [1871]1874, 99), and what Frans de Wall called "reciprocal altruism" prevailed among animals who "seek and enjoy company" (de Wall 1996, 170). Although Smith's understandings attained less scientific maturity yet, it may safely be said that Smith's concept of propensity to exchange basically means sympathy, and this is almost the same concept as Darwin's social instinct and de Wall's reciprocal altruism.[3] This distinct biological feature of Smith's view of human nature enabled him to grasp a society with division of labour as an organism united through sympathy and reciprocal altruism, and therefore to insist that the whole product of labour becomes the common stock of society.

> Those different tribes of animals, however, though all of the same species, are of scarce any use to one another. The strength of the mastiff is not, in the least, supported either by the swiftness of the greyhound, or by the sagacity of the spaniel, or by the docility of the shepherd's dog. The effect of those different geniuses and talents, for want of the power or disposition to barter and exchange, cannot be brought into a common stock, and do not in the least contribute to the better accommodation and conveniency of the species.... Among men, on the contrary, the most dissimilar geniuses are of use to one another; the different produces of their respective talents, by the general disposition to truck, barter, and exchange, being brought, as it were, into a common stock, where every man may purchase whatever part of the produce of other men's talents he has occasion for.
>
> (*WN*. I.ii.5)

Then, Smith's argument that "it is by treaty, by barter, and by purchase, that we obtain from one another the greater part of those mutual good offices which we stand in need of", it will be safely said, depended on the role of sympathy and reciprocal altruism formulated in *TMS* on the one hand, and "the certainty of being able to exchange all that surplus part of the produce of his own labour, which is over and above his own consumption" (*WN*.I.ii.3) on the other hand. The certainty of exchange should be secured by making individual products into the common stock of society. The propensity to exchange, therefore, is the same kind of biological and anthropological understanding of human nature as Darwin's "sympathy as an instinct" or de Wall's "reciprocal altruism", so it became the foundation of the physical and mechanical understanding of the society with division of labour formulated in the first chapter of *WN*.

Therefore, Smith's argument will be summarized as follows. When people exchange their surplus produce with the necessaries of life produced by other people, the exchange rate – the price – should be determined in the marketplace according to their subjective judgements of the exchanging powers of their surplus produce, whether they exchange their own surplus with some part of the common stock or they exchange it directly with other people's surplus. While the market price (exchange rate) decided in the market is always objective for any participants and bystanders, there must be sympathy between them for the exchange to be approved as justifiable and agreeable whether the price was good or bad. The "objective" price (exchange rate) in *WN*, a kind of social decision, might be parallel to the decisions of the "impartial spectator" or "the arbiter" in *TMS*.

Then, it was appropriate and quite right for Smith to discuss further how individual producers subjectively meet with the objective price (exchange rate). Nevertheless, he turned his eye to the emergence of money, and emphasized its decisively contributive role for the extension of the division of labour and market economy.

Commercial society, money and the state: the institutionalist interpretation

The proper theme of Chapter 4 "Of the Origin and Use of Money" was the elucidation of "the manner that money has become in all civilized nations the universal instrument of commerce, by the intervention of which goods of all kinds are bought and sold, or exchanged for one another", and Smith achieved it from three perspectives: first, the transformation of human nature due to the transition from society with division of labour and barter to society with commercial exchange; second, the emergence of metal currency as a means of exchange; third, state assurance by stamping of the fineness and weight of the metal to promote commerce and industry.

First, the evolution to commercial society requires its members to adopt new spiritual attitudes of the merchant, making commercial society a distinctive institution. Smith says thusly.

> When the division of labour has been once thoroughly established, it is but a very small part of a man's wants which the produce of his own labour can supply. He supplies the far greater part of them by exchanging that surplus part of the produce of his own labour, which is over and above his own consumption, for such parts of the produce of other men's labour as he has occasion for. Every man thus lives by exchanging, or becomes in some measure a merchant, and the society itself grows to be what is properly a commercial society.
>
> (*WN*.I.iv.1)

That living by exchanging makes humans in some measure merchants means that nobody can live just relying on the instinctive human trait of reciprocal altruism which turns their produce into the common stock of the community. Smith was a distinguished institutionalist, in so far as he insisted that the evolution from the barter community to the commercial society could not occur until human beings establish new customs of thought proper to the merchant.

Second, Smith's interpretation of the evolution of money as a means of exchange seems, indeed, the typical conjectural history, despite not a few textual evidences after the period of the Roman Empire were cited. One example of conjecture is the statement that

> every prudent man in every period of society, after the first establishment of the division of labour, must naturally have endeavored to manage his affairs in such a manner, as to have at all times by him, besides the peculiar produce of his own industry, a certain quantity of some one commodity or other, such as he imagined few people would be likely to refuse in exchange for the produce of their industry.
>
> (*WN*.I.iv.2)

An example of evidence is the hearsay reports that "in the rude ages of society, cattle are said to have been the common instrument of commerce; a species of shells in some parts of the coast of India; tobacco in Virginia" (*WN*.I.iv.3). The comment that "there is at this day a village in Scotland where it is not uncommon, I am told, for a workman to carry nails instead of money to the baker's shop or the alehouse" seems but a gentle joke of opportunistic evidence.[4] However, notwithstanding his conjectural and opportunistic interpretations of the emergence of metal money – high corrosion resistance, easiness of division, fusion and carrying – his comment that the historical development from currency by weight to coin with stamp was the result of state activity to encourage its commerce and industry is worth noting.

Third, the coinage of money with stamp by the state occasionally enabled kings to devalue coins, damaging creditors but contributing to establish national confidence in money as a convenient means of exchange. The institution of coinage contributed to the making of a new custom of counting the value of money not by weight but by tale,[5] which was indispensable for the vital development of commercial society.

The commercial society imagined by Smith in *WN*, therefore, may be the society practising division of labour, where people produce all kinds of necessaries and conveniences of life as a common stock, exchange their surplus products according to the new way of thinking of their value on the basis of the tale of coin with stamp with the state assuring its weight and fineness. He, therefore, announced beforehand that "what are the rules which men naturally observe in exchanging them either for money or for one another, I shall now proceed to examine. These rules determine what may be called the relative or exchangeable value of goods" (*WN*.I.iv.12) at the end of Chapter 4.

Labour and value: the real measure of exchange value and the real value of commodities

At the beginning of Chapter 5, Smith said thus.

> Every man is rich or poor according to the degree in which he can afford to enjoy the necessaries, conveniencies, and amusements of human life. But after the division of labour has once thoroughly taken place, it is but a very small part of these with which a man's own labour can supply him. The far greater part of them he must derive from the labour of other people, and he must be rich or poor according to the quantity of that labour which he can command, or which he can afford to purchase. The value of any commodity, therefore, to the person who possesses it, and who means not to use or consume it himself, but to exchange it for other commodities, is equal to the quantity of labour which it enables him to purchase or command. Labour, therefore, is the real measure of the exchangeable value of all commodities.
> (*WN*.I.v.1)

While the essence of this paragraph, as E. Cannan presented, might be summarized as labour is the real measure of exchangeable value, the argument that labour is the real measure of the exchangeable value of all commodities should be interpreted as a completely new one, so long as we refer to Smith's previous arguments presented in *TMS* and *Lectures on Jurisprudence* (hereafter abbreviated to *LJ*(A)). At least two points may be cited.

It is obviously the fact that Smith abandoned utility as a determinant of values, although he distinctively acknowledged the difference between value in use and value in exchange in *WN*.[6] However, Douglas seems to be mistaken when he just criticized Smith's failure of comparing the total utilities yielded by varying types of objects rather than their marginal utilities (Douglas [1928]1966, 78). As Smith said in *TMS*, it is not the view of this utility or hurtfulness which is either the first or principal source of our approbation and disapprobation (*TMS*. IV.2.3), or the sentiment of approbation always involves in it a sense of propriety quite distinct from the perception of utility (*TMS*.IV.2.5), so the true reason of the abandonment should be figured out in the fact that Smith thought much of the concordance of sentiments between persons by sympathy rather than by the utilities of the objects themselves, whenever the proprieties of judgements or conduct of persons must be decided socially. The objects of the mutual sympathy of the parties concerned cannot be the satisfactions due to the consumption or attainment of the utility proper to each commodity, since Smith said explicitly that these sentiments are no doubt enhanced and enlivened by the perception of the beauty or deformity which results from this utility or hurtfulness. But still, I say, they are originally and essentially different from this perception (*TMS*. IV.2.3). That labour is the real measure of the exchangeable value of all commodities has strongly implied that the foundation of the sympathy between individual owners of commodities is not the utility of them but the labour to produce them.

Smith's analysis of the value and price mechanism made tremendous progress in *WN*. As he clearly said dearness and scarcity, abundance and cheapness, are we may say synonymous terms in *LJ*(A), so it is obvious that he connected directly scarcity and abundance with the price at that time, and firmly adhered to the quantitative theory of price determination.[7] In *WN*, however, the explanation becomes complicated but rigorous: whenever Labourers A and B exchange their surplus products with each other, their mutual sympathy for their partner's conduct (labour) becomes the prerequisite for their subjective decision to exchange at a certain exchange rate (price), the propriety of which must be approved not only by themselves but also by the community.

Although this is enough to ascertain the quality common to the exchange values of commodities in the society, it is not enough to fix their quantities. Therefore, Smith seemed to add complementary paraphrasing.

> The real price of every thing, what every thing really costs to the man who wants to acquire it, is the toil and trouble of acquiring it. What every thing is really worth to the man who has acquired it, and who wants to dispose of it or exchange it for something else, is the toil and trouble which it can save to himself, and which it can impose upon other people. What is bought with

> money or with goods is purchased by labour as much as what we acquire by the toil of our own body. That money or those goods indeed save us this toil. They contain the value of a certain quantity of labour which we exchange for what is supposed at the time to contain the value of an equal quantity. Labour was the first price, the original purchase-money that was paid for all things. It was not by gold or by silver, but by labour, that all the wealth of the world was originally purchased; and its value, to those who possess it and who want to exchange it for some new productions, is precisely equal to the quantity of labour which it can enable them to purchase or command.
>
> (*WN*.I.v.2)

While figurative expressions like purchased by labour or labour was the first price make clear understanding hard, the new points in Smith's argument are two: first, the real price of everything is reducible to the original quantity of labour; second, when we exchange goods, we exchange for what is supposed at the time to contain the value of an equal quantity.

The fact that the cost of acquiring goods is the toil and trouble, namely the sacrifice, seems to be the physical and mechanical fact requiring no further explanations here. It is the second point that is worth noting and interpreting as clearly as possible. When we express A as an owner of goods (a), and B as an owner of goods (b), the argument that they contain the value of a certain quantity of labour which we exchange for what is supposed at the time to contain the value of an equal quantity means strictly the following.

When both A and B exchange their good, A knows only the labour cost of (a) not of (b), which A can imagine or guess. This is the same to B, he can only imagine or guess about the labour cost of (a). Both A and B, therefore, compare subjectively the real production cost of their own goods with the supposed cost of others. However, if we look at it objectively, we will realize that what is really compared is the putative production cost of the other owner. The execution of exchange must come just after their putative production costs come in concord. Although A knows his product (a)'s cost directly with his own perceptions, his knowledge or estimation on the production cost of (b) can be established only by sympathy with B's own production cost (his toil and trouble). The only way to know another person's perception is by sympathy with the other person's perception by his own faculty of perceptions. As we have already seen above, Smith argued thus distinctly in *TMS*.

It is, however, certain that Smith's argument in the above paragraph extends beyond these two points. Although Smith carried the discussion assuming the barter exchange of the surplus produce of the necessaries of life, his argument that its value, to those who possess it and who want to exchange it for some new productions, is precisely equal to the quantity of labour which it can enable them to purchase or command indicates manifestly the following: first, there are exchanges not for the necessaries of life; second, the value of goods, in this case, will be determined only by the quantity of labour to be commanded or purchased, not by the labour as a cost.

The decisively important point in the above argument is the fact that the cost belongs to the past, but the quantity of labour to be commanded or purchased belongs to the future. A must assume and make judgements not only about the past costs (quantity of labour) but also the future quantity of labour which goods (a) and goods (b) severally can enable him to purchase or command. To put it slightly differently, both A and B try to tally and accord the past quantity of labour with the future quantity of purchasable labour, independently and subjectively at the time of exchanges. Although the cost of product, that is, the past quantity of spent labour and the future quantity of purchasable labour belong to different time dimensions, any accordance between them must be calculated on the basis of the present time, that is, on the quantities presented for exchange now. Therefore, Smith was obliged to add the following sentence in the third edition.

> Wealth, as Mr. Hobbes says, is power. But the person who either acquires, or succeeds to a great fortune, does not necessarily acquire or succeed to any political power, either civil or military. His fortune may, perhaps, afford him the means of acquiring both, but the mere possession of that fortune does not necessarily convey to him either. The Power which that possession immediately and directly conveys to him, is the power of purchasing; a certain command over all the labour, or over all the produce of labour which is then in the market. His fortune is greater or less, precisely in proportion to the extent of this power; or to the quantity either of other men's labour, or, what is the same thing, of the produce of other men's labour, which it enables him to purchase or command. The Exchangeable value of every thing must always be precisely equal to the extent of this power which it conveys to its owner.
>
> (*WN*.I.v.3)

Probably, Smith was afraid that the phrase the quantity of labour which it can enable them to purchase or command might include not only the political power but also the huge fortunes accumulated stock of past labour, so he wanted to show that his task was to discuss commodity exchanges on the bases of subjective and putative judgement of the quantity of labour contained in other men's products, that is, the cost of them. Adding the rigorous definition of the purchasing power or the exchanging power, he wanted to show explicitly that it is just the commanding power to the produce of labour then in the market, or to the common stock consisting of labour or produces of labour except accumulated capital stock and other estates of the community.

However, as Smith's statement that his fortune is greater or less, precisely in proportion to the extent of this power; or to the quantity either of other men's labour, or, what is the same thing, of the produce of other men's labour, which it enables him to purchase or command shows clearly, the exchange value of his fortune brought into the market should rise or fall precisely according to the quantity to be exchanged, so the exchange rate (price, or purchasing power) of commodities must be determined objectively at the meeting point of supply and demand. In the case of the quantity of labour purchased or commanded, the mutual sympathy between producers is not always the necessary condition for the exchange.

Then, it seems safe to say that labour has two dimensions in the real measure of exchange. First, it is the labour as a cost to acquire the necessaries of life, in other words, the toil and trouble which is always accompanied by sympathies of producer or labourer. Second, it is the quantity of labour capable of purchasing or commanding, which suits to those who possess it and who want to exchange it for some new productions beyond the limit of the barter system. This is a distinctive feature of the power to exchange or the purchasing power of commodities.

Smith, indeed, realized well that the theory and concept of labour value was too abstract to be used in daily life. The measure naturally fixed to money for two reasons: money is more convenient than labour for its accountability by numbers, and the frequency of commodity exchanges by money is strikingly high.

This institutionalist argument, in its turn, came to be criticized by Smith himself, because a commodity which is itself continually varying in its own value, can never be an accurate measure of the value of other commodities (*WN*.I.v.7). The discovery of abundant mines in America reduced the value of precious metal by about one-third in the sixteenth century, so Smith said this revolution in their value, though perhaps the greatest, is by no means the only one of which history gives some account (*WN*.I.v.7). Theorist Smith, therefore, was forced to find the unchangeable and ultimate standard of value.

> Equal quantities of labour, at all times and places, may be said to be of equal value to the labourer. *In his ordinary state of health, strength and spirits; in the ordinary degree of his skill and dexterity* [added in second edition], he must always lay down the same portion of his ease, his liberty, and his happiness. The price which he pays must always be the same, whatever may be the quantity of goods which he receives in return for it. Of these, indeed, it may sometimes purchase a greater and sometimes a smaller quantity; but it is their value which varies, not that of the labour which purchases them. At all times and places that is dear which it is difficult to come at, or which it cost much labour to acquire; and that cheap which is to be had easily, or with very little labour. Labour alone, therefore, never varying in its own value, is alone the ultimate and real standard by which the value of all commodities can at all times and places be estimated and compared. It is their real price: money is their nominal price only.
>
> (*WN*.I.v.7)

It is not easy to understand accurately the meaning of theory of labour sacrifice quoted above, because it is not easy to understand why Smith could believe that the labourer must always lay down the same portion of his ease, his liberty and his happiness.

The key to a solution of this problem seems to be the appropriate and balanced interpretation of the word value in Smith's argument that equal quantities of labour, at all times and places, may be said to be of equal value to the labourer. In this case, the value means not any objective goods or use value but something worth to reward for the sacrifice of labourer's ease, liberty and happiness.

In *TMS*, Smith admitted that the ideal of human life was the tranquility, that is, the life of pastoral tranquility and retirement which the elegant, the tender and the passionate Tibullus takes so much pleasure in describing, or a life of friendship, liberty and pose (*TMS*.I.ii.2.2). And he declared further. Except the frivolous pleasures of vanity and superiority, we may find, in the most humble station, where there is only personal liberty, every other which the most exalted can afford; and the pleasures of vanity and superiority are seldom consistent with perfect tranquility, the principle and foundation of all real and satisfactory enjoyment (*TMS*.III.3.31): in ease of body and peace of mind, all the different ranks of life are nearly upon a level, and the beggar, who suns himself by the side of the highway, possesses that security which kings are fighting for (*TMS*.IV.i.10).

If we look at the matter from such a world view, the value of the peace of mind, the tranquility as an ideal should be the same to everyone, so the quantity of it also should be equal to every labourer. So long as the assumption that every workman has fundamentally the same human nature, the ease of body and peace of mind, that is, the tranquility, ease, liberty and happiness must have an equal value to them. Presupposing Smith's argument on the basic view of human happiness in *TMS*, it seems to be a matter of course that the labourer must always lay down the same portion of his ease, his liberty and his happiness.

That such an argument on human happiness links itself deeply with the deception, stoic scepticism to the material opulence, probably demands no further elucidation here. However, if this argument is combined with the distinction between real and nominal prices, another interesting and important feature would come into sight. According to Smith, the value of labour seems different between the employer and employee (labourer).

Real and nominal price of labour

Smith scholars seem to have overlooked Smith's argument that the quantity of labour seemed to be different between the employer and employee, because the value of labour appeared to be changing to employers.

> But though equal quantities of labour are always of equal value to the labourer, yet to the person who employs him they appear sometimes to be of greater and sometimes of smaller value. He purchases them sometimes with a greater and sometimes with a smaller quantity of goods, and to him the price of labour seems to vary like that of all other things. It appears to him dear in the one case, and cheap in the other. In reality, however, it is the goods which are cheap in the one case, and dear in the other.
>
> (*WN*.I.v.8)

What the employer delivers to the employee (labourer) is substantially the necessaries of life as in the barter system. Therefore, employers believe the price of labour is high when they have to deliver more goods in exchange for a quantity of labour they employ, and conversely. However, since the value of labour is essentially invariable, the changes of value occurs only in goods not labour, so that the high price of labour means anything else than the low prices of good. Smith said so, but this kind of understanding is not limited only to the employer. Since labourers are usually paid their wages with money, this way of thinking gradually prevails throughout the community, and everybody begins to think in that manner.

> In this popular sense, therefore, labour, like commodities, may be said to have a real and a nominal price. Its real price may be said to consist in the quantity of the necessaries and conveniencies of life which are given for it; its nominal price, in the quantity of money. The labourer is rich or poor, is well or ill rewarded, in proportion to the real, not to the nominal price of his labour.
>
> (*WN*.I.v.9)

Therefore, it might be safely said that the real price of labour in Smith has two different meanings: first, it is the philosophical and purely theoretical meaning, such as the toil and trouble as a cost, and the sacrifice of tranquility. Second, it is the quantity of necessaries of life delivered as wages, and this is the popular sense of the real price of labour. As a result, the money price becomes the nominal price. The common notion about the real and the nominal price of labour does not prevail until the commercial society grows into the capitalist system constituted of employers and employees. It is worth noting that the distinction between the real and the nominal prices stemmed from the historical change of thinking, the institutional changes. Smith was indeed an Institutionalist here, meaning to think and theorize with specifying time and place.

> At the same time and place the real and the nominal price of all commodities are exactly in proportion to one another. The more or less money you get for any commodity, in the London market, for example, the more or less labour it will at that time and place enable you to purchase or command. At the same time and place, therefore, money is the exact measure of the real exchangeable value of all commodities. It is so, however, at the same time and place only.
>
> (*WN*.I.v.19)

Then, how about the cases of far distant ages?

> Equal quantities of labour will at distant times be purchased more nearly with equal quantities of corn, the subsistence of the labourer, than with equal quantities of gold and silver, or perhaps of any other commodity.

Equal quantities of corn, therefore, will, at distant times, be more nearly of the same real value, or enable the possessor to purchased or command more nearly the same quantity of the labour of other people. They will do this, I say, more nearly than equal quantities of almost any other commodity; for even equal quantities of corn will not do it exactly.

(*WN*.I.v.15)

Why can equal quantities of corn command or purchase nearly the same quantity of labour at distant times? Unfortunately, up to the present most of the Smith scholars who discussed his labour theory of value, not excluding S. Hollander,[8] have disregarded Smith's fundamentally biological and nutritional value conception that the same quantity of corn maintained nearly the same quantity of labour.

Nutritional value of corn: biological foundation of the labour theory of value

While he changed a word from value to price after the attack of James Anderson[9] in 1777, Smith had a deep belief that the nature of things has stamped upon corn a real value which cannot be altered by merely altering its money price (*WN*.IV.v.a.23).

The real value stamped upon corn, however, means what? Although Smith tried to show his own theory of composite price in order to demonstrate the rent is the result of price, not its cause in Chapter 11 of *WN*, now the question was the conception of the quantity of labour maintainable by corn. Smith said thusly.

> As men, like all other animals, naturally multiply in proportion to the means of their subsistence, food is always, more or less, in demand. It can always purchase or command a greater or smaller quantity of labour, and somebody can always be found who is willing to do something, in order to obtain it. The quantity of labour, indeed, which it can purchase, is not always equal to what it could maintain, if managed in the most economical manner, on account of the high wages which are sometimes given to labour. But it can always purchase such a quantity of labour as it can maintain, according to the rate at which that sort of labour is commonly maintained in the neighborhood.

(*WN*.I.xi.b.1)

There remain some ambiguities in the argument, but when we connect it with the insistence that land, in almost any situation, produces a greater quantity of food than is sufficient to maintain all the labour necessary for bringing it to market (*WN*.I.xi.b.2), we get abundantly clear understanding of Smith's meaning.

While the population of humans, like other animals, depends on the quantity of available food, it is quite possible for humans to acquire more food to maintain more labourers by cultivating the land. As there are men willing to provide their labour in exchange for food, so enough food will always be produced for maintaining the quantity of labour spent for cultivation. The price of labour, the quantity of food given to labourers, would be decided by comparing it with the rate at which that sort of labour is commonly maintained in the neighbourhood. In short, Smith was theorizing on a base of the quantity of labour maintainable per unit of food. And the most decisive feature, stamped by nature, was the fact that the most advantageous produce having the largest nutritive value was corn. Put it slightly differently, the quantity of labour maintainable per unit of corn always exceeds the quantity of labour spent in the production of one unit of corn. Smith said thusly.

> A corn field of moderate fertility produces a much greater quantity of food for man, than the best pasture of equal extent. Though its cultivation requires much more labour, yet the surplus which remains after replacing the seed and maintaining all that labour, is likewise much greater. If a pound of butcher's-meat, therefore, was never supposed to be worth more than a pound of bread, this greater surplus would everywhere be of greater value, and constitute a greater fund both for the profit of the farmer and the rent of the landlord. It seems to have done so universally in the rude beginnings of agriculture.
>
> (*WN*.I.xi.b.6)

What did Smith dignify by saying that the quantity of food produced in the moderate corn field is much greater than that in the best pasture? Although Smith's calculations seem too ambiguous for us to get a clear understanding, it may be safely said that two different but mutually connected things were put together. What Smith must say distinctively is that the total volume of nutrition of butcher's meat produced in a square mile of land was always less than that of the bread (corn) produced in the same square land, and nothing else. The nutrition of corn is so high that the surplus which remains after replacing the seed and maintaining all that labour, is likewise much greater.

Then, all arable land will be turned at once into corn fields? Absolutely not. Since the increase of population is much slower than that of food, the increase of one acre of corn fields would at first necessarily reduce one acre of pasture, that is, the increase of corn reduces the cattle (butcher's meat). However, the relative price of butcher's meat would go up at first, because the inferiority of the quantity must be compensated by the superiority of the price (*WN*.I.xi.b.9). Put slightly differently, while the nutritional value of butcher's meat remains the same, the increase of the quantity of corn which a pound of butcher's meat can purchase causes the enhancement of value of the latter. The absolute value, the nutritional value of corn never changes, so the value of labour also never changes from the biological point of view, because the degree of surplus produce of corn regulates the quantity of less nutritional foods such as hops, fruit, sugar, through the market's price mechanism; the nature of things had stamped a real value upon corn – the unchangeable nutritional and biological value of corn.

The above considerations should enable us to understand completely what Smith told us in his "Digression concerning the Variations in the Value of Silver" inserted in Chapter 11 of Book I of *WN*, and to realize that this argument corresponded precisely to the theoretical structure of the real standard of exchange value, that is, labour, money and corn extended in Chapter 5 of Book I. Smith said thusly.

> In every state of society, in every stage of improvement, corn is the production of human industry. But the average produce of every sort of industry is always suited, more or less exactly, to the average consumption; the average supply to the average demand. In every different stage of improvement, besides, the raising of equal quantities of corn in the same soil and climate, will, at an average, require nearly equal quantities of labour; or what comes to the same thing, the price of nearly equal quantities. Corn, it has already been observed, is, in all the different stages of wealth and improvement, a more accurate measure of value than any other commodity or set of commodities. In all those different stages, therefore, we can judge better of the real value of silver, by comparing it with corn, than by comparing it with any other commodity, or set of commodities.
>
> (*WN*.I.xi.e.28)

Concluding remarks

Smith's explanation of the real measure of exchange value was not only analytical but also historical and institutional, basing on nutritional and biological conceptions. Past critical interpretations of his labour theory of value, therefore, have failed to recognize core ideas of Smith's social and economic theory as an evolutionary theory of development. I would like to close this chapter with two quotations representing his keen comments on potatoes.

> The improvements of agriculture too introduce many sorts of vegetable food, which, requiring less land and not more labour than corn, come much cheaper to market. Such are potatoes and maize, or what is called Indian corn, the two most important improvements which the agriculture of Europe, perhaps, which Europe itself, has received from the great extension of its commerce and navigation. Many sorts of vegetable food, besides, which in the rude state of agriculture are confined to the kitchen-garden, and raised only by the spade, come in its improved state to be introduced into common fields, and to be raised by the plough; such as turnips, carrots, cabbages, &c.

"The circumstances of the poor through a great part of England cannot surely be so much distressed by any rise in the price of poultry, fish, wildfowl, or venison, as they must be relieved by the fall in that of potatoes" (*WN*.I.xi.n.10). In reality, the perishable nature of potatoes, noted by Smith himself, prevented them entering a staple diet and wide market transactions, however healthy and useful especially for the poor.[10]

Notes

1 Since pins were necessaries of life and their manufactories prevailed even in local and small towns by the early eighteenth century, Fitzgibbons' comment seems less appropriate: "It is not even certain that he visited the famous pin factory, since there was an article on the division of labour in pin manufacture in the French Encyclopedia" (1995, 92).
2 In detail, see Taka (2012).
3 Space limitation forced me simply to cite the highest appraisal of Smith's theory of sympathy by both Darwin and de Wall. See Darwin ([1871]1874, 106) and de Wall (2009, 1, 222).
4 According to E. Royston Pike, "although there were no naileries in Kirkcaldy itself, there were several in the immediate neighborhood", especially at Path-head (1974, 219–20).
5 Smith's explanation was excellent:

> The inconvenience and difficulty of weighing those metals with exactness gave occasion to the institution of coins, of which the stamp, covering entirely both sides of the piece and sometimes the edges too, was supposed to ascertain not only the fineness, but the weight of the metal. Such coins, therefore, were received by tail as at present, without the trouble of weighing.
>
> (*WN*.I.iv.9)

6 In the last paragraph of Chapter 4, Smith said thus.

> The word Value, it is to be observed, has two different meanings, and sometimes expresses the utility of some particular object, and sometimes the power of purchasing other goods which the possession of that object conveys. The one may be called "value in use;" the other, "value in exchange."
>
> (*WN*.I.iv.13)

7 I would like to quote from *LJ*(A).

> Whatever policy tends to raise the market price above the natural one diminishes publick opulence and natural wealth of the state. For dearness and scarcity, abundance and cheapness, are we may say synonymous terms. For whatever abounds much will be sold to the inferior people, whereas what is scarce will be sold to those only superior fortune, and the quantity will consequently be small. So far therefore as any thing is a convenience or necessary of life and tends to the happiness of mankind, so far is the dearness detrimental as it confines the necessary to a few and diminishes the happiness of the inferior sort. Whatever therefore raises or keeps up the price of them diminishes the opulence and happiness and ease of the country.
>
> (iv.84, 362)

8 Although S. Hollander noted that Smith's discussion on use value showed "the narrow sense of biological significance" and "cultural properties" (Hollander 1973, 136), these stimulating remarks remained yet "passing notes", because of his insufficient efforts to reconstruct Smith's thought as a constituent whole.
9 The special circumstances of this attack and the change of words were clearly shown in the letter from Smith to Andreas Holt (10 October 1780).

> In volume second page 101 of the first edition, I happened to say that the nature of things had stamped a real value upon Corn which no human institution can alter. The expression was certainly too strong, and had escaped me in the heat of Writing. I ought to have said that the surplus which remains after replacing the seed and maintaining all that labour, is likewise much greater a real value which could not be altered merely by altering its Money price. This was all that the

argument required, and all that I really meant. Mr Anderson takes advantage of this expression, and triumphs very much by showing that in several other parts of my Work I had acknowledged that whatever lowered the real price of manufactured produce, raised the price of rude produce, and consequently of corn. In the second edition I have corrected this careless expression, which I apprehend takes away the foundation of the whole argument of Mr Anderson.

(Smith 1977, 251)

10 Smith's characterization of potatoes seems very accurate. Both F.M. Eden and D. Davies showed that the chief merit of the potato was its low price, and it was taken into meals by the early eighteenth century mainly among the poor (Eden [1797]1966, 504–5; Davies [1795]1977, 35). According to J. Thirsk, cultivation of potatoes in England advanced rapidly after 1750 (traditionally peas and beans were more popular), mainly as a result of heavy food shortages in 1714–15 and in 1728–9. Its cultivation and use for meal, indeed, advanced slowly and showed geographical variation, although it had been popular in Lancashire and Cumberland in the 1670s and 1680s (Thirsk 2006, 179–81). Potatoes, along with other vegetables, represented "alternative agriculture" (Thirsk 1997, 59–60). C. Muldrew, studying the changing process of meals on the basis of calories, tells us that "both potatoes and turnips also became much more common features of the diet in stews and pottage during the late eighteenth century as a source of carbohydrates" (Muldrew 2011, 109). However, the cultivation of it seems to have remained for a long time mainly in the labourers' gardens.

References

Cannan, Edwin. ed. [1904] 1922. *An Inquiry into the Nature and Causes of the Wealth of Nations, with an Introduction, Notes, Marginal Summary an Enlarged Index*. London: Methuen & Co. Ltd.

Darwin, Charles. [1871] 1874. *The Descent of Man, and Selection in Relation to Sex*. 2nd edn, revised and augmented. 1874. London: John Murray.

Davies, David. [1795] 1977. *The Case of Labourers in Husbandry: Stated and Cconsidered with an Appendix*. Fairfield: Augustus M. Kelley.

de Wall, Frans. 1996. *Good Natured: The Origins of Right and Wrong in Humans and Other Animals*. Cambridge, MA: Harvard University Press.

de Wall, Frans. 2009. *The Age of Empathy: Nature's Lessons for a Kinder Society*. New York: Harmony Books.

Douglas, Paul H. [1928] 1966. "Smith's Theory of Value and Distribution". In J.M. Clark, Paul H. Douglas, Jacob H. Hollander, Glenn R. Morrow, Melchior Palyi and Jacob Viner, *Adam Smith 1776–1926*. New York: Augustus M. Kelley.

Eden, Frederic Morton. [1797] 1966. *The State of the Poor: Or, An History of the Labouring Classes in England*. 3 vols. London: Frank Cass & Co. Ltd.

Fitzgibbons, Athol. 1995. *Adam Smith's System of Liberty, Wealth, and Virtue: The Moral and Political foundations of the Wealth of Nations*. Oxford: Clarendon Press.

Hollander, Samuel. 1973. *The Economics of Adam Smith*. London: Heinemann Educational Books.

Muldrew, Craig. 2011. *Food, Energy and the Creation of Industriousness: Work and Material Culture in Agrarian England, 1550–1780*. Cambridge: Cambridge University Press.

Pike, E. Royston. 1974. *Human Documents of Adam Smith's Time*. London: George Allen & Unwin Ltd.

Smith, Adam. [1759] 1976. *The Theory of Moral Sentiments*. 6th edn, 1790. Clarendon Press: Oxford.

Smith, Adam. [1776] 1976. *An Inquiry into the Nature and Causes of the Wealth of Nations*. Oxford: Clarendon Press.

Smith, Adam. 1977. *The Correspondence of Adam Smith*. Edited by E.C. Mossner and I.S. Ross. Oxford: Clarendon Press.

Smith, Adam. 1978. *Lectures on Jurisprudence*. Edited by R.L. Meek, D.D. Raphael and P.G. Stein. Oxford: Clarendon Press.

Taka, Tetsuo. 2012. "Instinct as a Foundational Concept in Adam Smith's Social Theory", *The History of Economic Thought*, 53 2: 1–20.

Thirsk, Joan. [1997] 2006. *Alternative Agriculture: A History*. Oxford: Oxford University Press.

Thirsk, Joan. 2006. *Food in Early Modern England: Phases, Fads, Fashions 1500–1760*. London: Hambledon Continnuum.

Young, Arthur. [1771] 1967. *A Six Months Tour though the North of England*. 4 vols. New York: Augustus M. Kelley.

2 Individual rationality and mechanism in the history of microeconomic theory

Masahiro Kawamata

Introduction

The subjective theory of value characterizes the values of commodities based on the utilities of individual economic agents, and individual values are equalized to market prices through a market trade. We suppose that a certain stream of subjective theories of value consisted of the theory of UTILITY and scarcity before the marginal revolution,[1] the general equilibrium theory founded in the marginal revolution, and the theory of mechanism design described in terms of game theory. However, we prefer to group them together under the heading 'microeconomic theories' because all the fundamental topics they cover, to which we refer in this chapter, are included in *Microeconomic Theory* by Mas-Colell *et al.* (1995). Even though the theory of UTILITY and scarcity, the general equilibrium theory, and the theory of mechanism design are called by different names, they have distinct characteristics; however, they share the idea about value called utilitarianism in a wide sense of welfarism.

During the history of microeconomic theory, the marginal revolution has been considered one of the most historic events, but the structure of the theory of UTILITY and scarcity is very close to that of the general equilibrium theory, as Kawamata (2009) suggests.

Microeconomic Theory (Mas-Colell *et al.* 1995) covers the general equilibrium theory by using new welfare economics and game theoretical topics. In the general equilibrium theory, a competitive equilibrium (a resource allocation and a price system) is determined at the general equilibrium of a market economy. In a classical economic environment without factors of market failure, a competitive equilibrium is Pareto efficient, and any Pareto-efficient allocation is attainable as a competitive equilibrium through a certain reallocation of resources. This property of market mechanism is called the fundamental theorems of welfare economics, which is not held if the factors of market failure such as non-convexity, externalities, and public goods prevail in an economic environment. Regarding the problems of non-convexity, externalities are solvable within the framework of the general equilibrium theory by formulating public policy with recourse to the taxation system. However, the problem of public goods accompanies that of incentive compatibility, which needs the game theoretic framework of the theory of mechanism design. Game theory can overcome the difficulties suffered by the general equilibrium theory. Although the development of the theory of mechanism design is a more important historical event than was the marginal revolution, it has been rarely debated throughout the history of microeconomic theory. Thus, the purpose of this chapter is to characterize the properties of the theory of UTILITY and scarcity, the general equilibrium theory with new welfare economics, and the theory of mechanism design from the viewpoint of mechanism theory and to review the history of microeconomic theory.

As Carr (1961/64) points out, a history is a dialogue between the past and the present. A past theory may implicitly assume certain factors that are explicitly assumed in the present theory. It follows that we can better understand past theories by interpreting them in the present theory which has developed from past theories and vice versa. In order to logically understand a theory, it must be formulated as a consistent axiom system (Shoenfield 1967). According to an axiomatic approach, any theory can be characterized by a language and an axiom system described in terms of that language. In particular, microeconomic theory is described by an economy or a non-cooperative game and the equilibrium of the economy or of the game. By characterizing economic theories as axiom systems and comparing them with each other, we can more clearly see the characteristics of economic theories. For example, the economic theories used before and after a scientific revolution in economics such as the marginal revolution or Keynesian revolution, when characterized by their respective axiom systems, are distinct from one another. Since most original texts are incomplete as an axiom system, we cannot help interpreting the original theory based on a complete axiom system relative to a certain set of theorems, which is an extension of the original theory and thus is not equivalent to it.

This chapter is organized as follows. In the next section, we examine the theory of UTILITY and scarcity before the marginal revolution, finding that it had the same structure as has the marginal utility theory, while the subsequent section covers the general equilibrium theory after the marginal revolution, which is systematized on the basis of the rational behavior of economic agents and the market mechanism. The microeconomic theories in these periods can be characterized by the fundamental theorems of welfare economics. The chapter goes on to refer to the original development of the theory of mechanism design, which follows the general equilibrium theory to resolve market failures. In the last section, I summarize the results.

Theory of UTILITY and scarcity

The subjective theories of value before the marginal revolution are called the theory of UTILITY and scarcity, because this defines the values of commodities depending on the concepts of UTILITY and scarcity. Most historians of economics agree that the theory of UTILITY and scarcity are close to the marginal utility theory but that they lack the concept of marginal utility.[2] We examine the theory of UTILITY and scarcity and compare its structures with that of the general equilibrium theory in this section in order to demonstrate the following two points. First, as Kawamata (2009) shows, the theory of UTILITY and scarcity is certainly a marginal utility theory, but it does not characterize the value of a commodity as a necessary and sufficient condition of the rational behavior of an individual economic agent. Second, in the theory of UTILITY and scarcity, the theory of exchange value crucially depends on the specification of the economic environment, while the general equilibrium theory is based on the price mechanism of a market economy.

Structure of the theory of individual value

Things that were considered to be common knowledge when Galiani, Turgot, and Condillac were developing the theory of UTILITY and scarcity are not explicitly described in their original texts. Therefore, we cannot textually demonstrate what kinds of assumptions are lacking in the original theory. Logically, however, we can reconstruct a certain consistent theory in which the theorems in the original theory are provable, and then interpret the original theory in this reconstruction (Shoenfield 1967: ch. 4). This reconstructed theory has to be an extension of the original theory. If the reconstruction is consistent, then the interpretation of the original theory in the reconstruction is consistent. Thus, what kinds of assumptions are considered to be lacking in the original theory depends on how we derive the reconstruction. As Katzner (1970: 5–13) suggests, we assume that the theory of UTILITY and scarcity before the marginal revolution supposed that UTILITY was measurable, separable, and additive.

Now I put together the propositions of the theory of UTILITY and scarcity into an axiom system.[3] Turgot (1769/1977: 137) states 'this sense of the word value would be appropriate to a man in isolation, without any communication with other men.' Given the resources of commodities, the value of a commodity is a subjective evaluation by an individual. Turgot defines the value of a commodity as consisting of two components: wants and scarcity over a given period. Turgot states the following:

> The savage has killed a calf, which he takes to his hut; on his way he finds a roe; he kills it and takes it instead of the calf in the expectation of eating a more delicious meat. In the same way a child, who had first filled his pockets with chestnuts, empties them in order to make room for some sugared.
>
> This, then, is a comparison of value, an evaluation of the different objects in the judgements of this savage and this child; but these appraisals are not permanent, they change continually with the need of the person. When the savage is hungry, he values a piece of game more than the best bearskin; but let his appetite be satisfied and let him be cold, and it will be the bearskin that becomes valuable to him.
>
> (137–8)

In this passage, Turgot supposes that the UTILITY of a commodity h is a UTILITY $U_h(\cdot)$. This means that an individual obtains by consuming a unit quantity c_h of the commodity in question where the individual has already satisfied his or her needs with the quantity x_h of the commodity. That is, for every commodity h, the UTILITY means an additional utility of a unit c_h, when the quantity x_h has already been consumed. If total utility is denoted as occurring when the quantity x_h is consumed as $U_h(x_h)$ for every commodity h, then the UTILITY of c_h is defined by the formula $U_h(x_h+c_h)-U_h(x_h)$. As we saw in the passage, c_h is typically a unit of quantity, for example, 'a piece of game.' In order for the level of UTILITY to be independent of a scale of unit quantity, the UTILITY has to be expressed by the ratio

$$u_h(x_h) = \frac{U_h(x_h+c_h)-U_h(x_h)}{c_h}.$$

Taking a limit, namely $c_h \to 0$, then $U_h(x_h)$ comes to be equal to

$$\frac{\partial U_h}{\partial x_h}(x_h).$$

Then, Turgot states that the UTILITY $U_h(\cdot)$ decreases as the consumed quantity x_h increases. 'When the savage is hungry, he values a piece of game more than the best bearskin; but let his appetite be satisfied and let him be cold, and it will be the bearskin that becomes valuable to him.' This means $U_h(x_h)$ is a decreasing function of x_h. In the theory of UTILITY and scarcity by Galiani (1750/1803), Turgot (1769/1977), and Condillac (1776/1997), therefore, $U_h(x_h)$ cannot be total utility, because it is not an increasing function of x_h. This supports our interpretation of $U_h(x_h)$ as the marginal utility function.

Provided that the above-described results are valid, we proceed to reconstruct Turgot's theory as a consistent axiom system. Turgot definitely states that if the commodity h is scarce, that is to say, $v_h^* > 0$ and, therefore, the resource of the commodity h is exhausted $x_h^* = \omega_h > 0$, then a value v_h of the commodity h is equal to the marginal utility

$$\frac{\partial U_h}{\partial x_h}(x_h^*).$$

Turgot explains that the scarcity of a commodity is one of the factors that defines the value of the commodity:

> It is for this reason that water, in spite of its necessity and the multitude of pleasures which it provides for man, is not regarded as a precious thing in a well-watered country; that man does not seek to gain its possession, since the abundance of this element allows him to find it all around him.
> (1769/1977: 138)

This means that if a commodity is not scarce $x_h^* < \omega_h$, then $v_h^* = 0$. Having complemented the corner solution case such that if

$$\frac{\partial U_h}{\partial x_h}(x_h^*) < v_h^*$$

then $x_h^* = 0$ for every h, Turgot's conditions are coordinated with the following set of Kuhn–Tucker conditions:[4]

(Marginal Principle) If $x_h^* > 0$, then $\dfrac{\partial U_h}{\partial x_h}(x_h^*) = v_h^*$, for every h.

(Corner Solution) If $\dfrac{\partial U_h}{\partial x_h}(x_h^*) < v_h^*$, then $x_h^* = 0$, for every h.

(Scarce Goods) If $v_h^* > 0$, then $\omega_h = x_h^*$, for every h.

(Free Goods) If $\omega_h > x_h^*$, then $v_h^* = 0$, for every h.

It is clear that the theory of UTILITY and scarcity does not refer to the corner solution. This is understandable because this condition is not observable, whereas all the other conditions are. The corner solution means that the commodity is too costly to supply, and thus it is neither produced nor consumed, which is not observable. Thus, the theory of UTILITY and scarcity is considered to assume a set of conditions that are very close to the Kuhn–Tucker conditions.

If we define the function $U(x)$ appropriately, then the utility $u_h(x_h^*)$ is defined as a derivative of the total utility function

$$\frac{\partial U_h}{\partial x_h}(x_h^*).[5]$$

Using Kuhn–Tucker's equivalence theorem (Sundaram 1996), the Kuhn–Tucker conditions are equivalent to the problem of a consumer's choice such that

$$\max_{x_h} \sum_1^H U_h(x_h)$$

subject to $x \leq \omega$, that is to say,

$$\max_{x_h} \sum_1^H U_h(x_h) + \sum_1^H v_h(\omega_h - x_h)$$

where v_h is a Lagrangean multiplier that represents the value of the commodity h.[6] We can identify this principle of economic behavior and the economic implications of the Kuhn–Tucker conditions derived from it by using Menger's (1871/1950) theory of value. This means the theory of UTILITY and scarcity has almost the same structure as does the marginal utility theory of Menger.[7]

From the axiomatic point of view, the theory of UTILITY and scarcity is characterized by the axiom system consisting of the Kuhn–Tucker conditions. However, in modern microeconomic theory, the rational behavior of an individual economic agent is an axiom, and the Kuhn–Tucker conditions are theorems derived from the axiom. This means that in the theory of UTILITY and scarcity, UTILITY as a marginal utility is a basic concept that cannot be defined in terms of other concepts such as UTILITY or total utility. Moreover, the concept termed 'marginal utility' in the context of the marginal utility theory was named UTILITY in the specific context as shown above. For this reason, historians have considered the concept of marginal utility to be lacking in the theory of UTILITY and scarcity. However, it was typical to allow the concept of marginal utility to remain as given and to define total utility as an integral of marginal utility. Indeed, given the concept of the marginal utility function, Jevons (1871/1957: ch. 3) and Walras (1874–77/1954: ch. 8) define the concept of the total utility function in terms of the marginal utility function. Then, they explain the marginal conditions based on the rational behavior of an individual economic agent.

The theory of UTILITY and scarcity merely proposes characterizing the value of a commodity by the marginal conditions. This proposition is not based on any set of fundamental principles. One of the significances of the marginal revolution was to introduce the rational behavior of economic agents into the theory of marginal utility in order to demonstrate the group of propositions in the theory of UTILITY and scarcity on the basis of the rational behavior of economic agents.

Theory of exchange value

In the theory of UTILITY and scarcity, Turgot (1769/1977) and Condillac (1776/1997) clearly demonstrate that individuals exchange commodities because the allocation attained through an exchange is Pareto-improving relative to their status quo. Turgot describes the situation in which an exchange can occur:

> Suppose, for example, that on a desert island, in the middle of the northern seas, two savages land on different sides, one bringing fish with him in his boat, more than he can consume himself, the other carrying hides beyond what he can use to clothe himself and to make himself a tent. The one bringing fish is cold, the one bringing hides is hungry. It will eventuate that the latter will ask the owner of the fish for part of his provisions, and will offer to give him in return some of his hides: the other will accept. Here is exchange, here is commerce.
>
> (Turgot 1769/1977: 141)

Suppose we have an exchange economy consisting of two individuals and two commodities. Given an initial allocation of resources $((\omega_{A1}, \omega_{A2}), (\omega_{B1}, \omega_{B2}))$ where ω_{ih} denotes individual i's resource of the commodity h for every $i \in \{A, B\}$

and for every $h \in \{1, 2\}$, and an allocation $((x_{A1}, x_{A2}), (x_{B1}, x_{B2}))$ attained through exchange, the relative price

$$\frac{p_1}{p_2}$$

is equal to the exchange rate between the commodities

$$-\frac{\Delta x_{i1}}{\Delta x_{i2}},$$

and the individual value

$$\frac{v_1}{v_2},$$

namely Turgot's esteem value, at an allocation $((x_{A1}, x_{A2}), (x_{B1}, x_{B2}))$ is equal to the rate of marginal utility

$$\frac{\partial U_{i1}}{\partial x_{i1}}(x_{i1}) / \frac{\partial U_{i2}}{\partial x_{i2}}(x_{i2}).$$

What the concept of exchange rate between commodities means is ambiguous, because there are at least two interpretations of it: one is interpreting it as

$$-\frac{\Delta x_{i1}}{\Delta x_{i2}}$$

and the other as

$$-\frac{(\omega_2 - x_2)}{(\omega_1 - x_1)},$$

and Turgot does not keep them apart. The equality between them

$$-\frac{\Delta x_{i1}}{\Delta x_{i2}} = -\frac{(\omega_2 - x_2)}{(\omega_1 - x_1)}$$

is called the law of indifference by Jevons, and it must be proved as a result of market exchange.

Turgot continues as follows:

> This superiority of the esteem value attributed by the acquirer to the thing he acquires over the thing he gives up is essential to the exchange, for it is the sole motive for it. Each would remain as he was, if he did not find an

interest, a personal profit, in exchange; if, in his own mind, he did not consider what he receives worth more than what he gives.

(1769/1977: 142)

If, at an allocation $((x_{A1}, x_{A2}), (x_{B1}, x_{B2}))$,

$$\frac{\partial U_{i1}}{\partial x_{i1}}(x_{i1}) / \frac{\partial U_{i2}}{\partial x_{i2}}(x_{i2}) = \frac{dx_{i1}}{dx_{i2}} \neq \frac{p_1}{p_2},$$

then an exchange occurs. If the esteem value of commodity 1 is higher than is the price of commodity 1 for individual i, that is,

$$\frac{\frac{\partial U_{i1}}{\partial x_{i1}}(x^*_{i1})}{\frac{\partial U_{i2}}{\partial x_{i2}}(x^*_{i2})} \geq \frac{p_1}{p_2} \text{ for every } i \in \{A, B\},$$

then individual i demands commodity 1 and supplies commodity 2, and vice versa.

> Independently of this kind of mental evaluation by which each of them compares the interest he has of keeping to that of acquiring, both are also animated by a general interest independent of all comparisons, that is the interest of keeping as much of their own commodity as they can, and of acquiring as much as they can of that of the other. With this in mind, each will keep secret the mental comparison which he has made of his two interests, of the two values which he attached to the commodities for exchange, and he will sound out the owner of the commodity he desires by lower offers and higher demands. Since the other will follow the same procedure, they will discuss the conditions of the exchange, and as they both have a great interest in coming to an agreement, they will finally do so. Slowly each of them will increase his offers and reduce his demands, until they finally agree to give a certain quantity of corn for a certain quantity of wood.
>
> (Turgot 1769/1977: 142)

The exchange finishes at an exchange equilibrium,

$$\frac{\partial U_{i1}}{\partial x_{i1}}(x^*_{i1}) / \frac{\partial U_{i2}}{\partial x_{i2}}(x^*_{i2}) = \frac{p_1}{p_2} \text{ for every } i \in \{A, B\}.$$

This means that at the equilibrium, the marginal utility of one commodity is equal to the marginal utility of the other. However, in the theory of UTILITY and scarcity, the problem of how a price system is established through a market is not explicitly presented or solved. In this sense, the condition of equivalent exchange is not explicitly referred to.

Note that it is possible to distinguish between the concepts of value and price. The price of a commodity is its relative exchange rate (money or numeraire), which conveys the message by which all economic agents choose their optimal economic activity. The value of a commodity is an evaluation of its contribution to the UTILITY of an individual or to the social welfare of society. Throughout the history of the marginal utility theory, the concepts of value and price have been distinct from each other. In fact, in underlining these differences, Turgot (1769/1977: 144) notices that 'in commercial language, price is often confused with value without causing inconvenience, because in effect the stating of a price always involves the stating of a value. They are, however, different concepts which it is important to distinguish,' and clearly distinguishes the concept of exchange value from that of individual value (esteem value) as follows:

> This first value, to which we have given the name esteem value, is arrived at through the comparison which each separately makes between the two interests that contend with one another in his case; it exists only in the interest of each of the two taken separately. Exchange value on the contrary, is adopted by both the contracting parties, who recognise its equality and who make it the condition of the exchange.
>
> (Turgot 1769/1977: 143)

Turgot extends his reasoning to the two-agent, many-commodity exchange model and the two-commodity, many-agent exchange model in order to demonstrate that the law of indifference is generally valid. Those models house a unique price system common to the agents, which implies that equilibrium can be established without any institution organizing the exchange process. This means that Turgot's argument is just a conservative extension of and equivalent to the two-person, two-commodity model. Provided that the results mentioned above are valid, we can see that the theory of exchange value in the theory of UTILITY and scarcity is almost identical to Jevons's theory of exchange value (Kawamata 2009). Jevons's demonstration of exchange value depends on the specification of the exchange economy in terms of how every commodity is traded. In a two-consumer, two-commodity exchange model, it is clear which consumer supplies and demands which commodity. Each consumer supplies the commodity of smaller marginal utility and demands the commodity of larger marginal utility until they come to be equal to each other through exchange. However, in the more general case of a market economy consisting of many consumers and many producers with many commodities, it is practically impossible to specify and enumerate all the possible conditions of trades because of the numerous instances of indirect exchanges. Therefore, Jevons's framework in the theory of exchange value cannot be extended to the more general case of a market economy. In order to extend exchange theory to analyze more general economic environments, it is necessary to introduce a theory of market mechanism, which consists of the theories of consumer, producer, and market equilibrium. This was carried out by Walras (1874–77/1954).[8] The theory of competitive price was extended by Walras's general equilibrium theory to the more general case of a market economy. Thus, the introduction of a market mechanism by Walras was another achievement of the marginal revolution.

As long as we compare the structure of the theory of UTILITY and scarcity with that of the general equilibrium theory, the marginal revolution provides the following two original contributions: the formulation of the rational behavior of economic agents and the introduction of the theory of the price mechanism of a market economy.

Invisible hand and the fundamental theorems of welfare economics

Economics was established as a field of social sciences as the principle of the capitalist economy emerged. A capitalist economy assumes that resources are privately owned and that a certain market mechanism works. It is an autonomous mechanism, which has been the research object of economic analysis, including positive analysis and normative analysis. Adam Smith (1776/1976: part IV) suggests that every individual is 'led by an invisible hand to promote an end which was no part of his intension.' This implies that an index similar to GDP is maximized by the free market. Smith's idea of the invisible hand is considered to represent a normative analysis of the market economy, symbolizing the function of the market mechanism, which would go on to be studied by many economic scientists and formulated as the fundamental theorems of welfare economics.

In the 1710s, the French economy suffered a serious public financial problem caused by the enormous war costs. John Law built the so-called John Law's system from 1716 to 1720 to resolve France's financial problems, but the system instead subjected the French economy to economic crisis by creating economic bubbles. In the theory of UTILITY and scarcity, Galiani (1750) and Turgot (1769/1977) attribute the cause of the disorder to the system's failure to evaluate the values of commodities. They assume that a well-organized and freely competitive market would prevent an economy from the disorder caused by the misevaluation of commodities such as economic bubbles. Turgot states:

> The exchange value of the produce, the revenue, the wage rate, the population are things related to each other by a mutual dependence, which spontaneously reach their equilibrium according to a natural proportion; and this proportion is always maintained when commerce and competition are completely free.
>
> The single practical conclusion that can be drawn from this, is that wage labourers must be completely free to work for whom they desire, in order that the employers, by contending for them when they need them, may place a just price on their labour; and that, on the other hand, the employers must be completely free to use such men as they deem proper, in order that the local workers may not, by taking advantage of their small number, force them to increase wages above the natural proportion which depends on the

stock of wealth, the value of subsistence goods, the amount of work available and the number of workers, but which can never be settled by anything other than competition and freedom.

(1767/1977: 127)

Once the theory of the competitive market is established, the normative criterion is necessary for the invisible hand to be meaningful. In the theory of UTILITY and scarcity, it was recognized that a reallocation of resources through an exchange is Pareto-improving, but that the concept of optimality was not yet crystallized.

Gossen (1854/1983) was the first researcher to define the concept of optimal allocation on the basis of welfarism, and he tried to prove that the competitive market provided the optimal allocation. Gossen states 'the laws of enjoyment' as follows:

> To raise his life pleasure to the fullest, man must attempt the following:
>
> 1. To increase to the greatest possible extent both the number of available pleasures and also their absolute magnitudes.
> 2. To increase his strength and his skill in its application to the fullest possible extent.
> 3. To reduce as far as possible the labor required for achieving satiety of pleasures.
> 4. Depending on the individual's success in securing these conditions, to apply his strength to the satisfaction of the various pleasures as much as appears reasonable on the basis of the preceding calculations.
>
> [...]
>
> the Creator has assured by the laws of enjoyment that the human race constantly uses its intellectual and material powers so as to obtain at all times a maximum of life pleasures once the obstacles are removed preventing the individual from using his money in the best possible way and from entering the field of production that offers him the highest reward.
>
> (1854/1983: ch. 7, 95, 115–16)

Many economists before Pareto, such as Bentham, J.S. Mill, Jevons, and Menger, assumed that UTILITY was measurable, separable, and additive for every commodity. It follows that they implicitly assumed the interpersonal comparison of UTILITY. Thus, it would be natural for them to define the social welfare function as being utilitarian, namely the sum of all the individuals in an economy (Gossen 1854/1983: ch. 14). This implies that the optimal allocation maximizes the utilitarian social welfare function under the constraint of production technology and resources, and is independent of the initial allocation of resources. By contrast, a competitive equilibrium in a market economy crucially depends on the initial allocation of resources and, therefore, it is not always the same as the utilitarian solution. As the fundamental theorems of welfare economics imply, in order to characterize the competitive equilibrium of a market economy, it is necessary to introduce the ordinalist concepts of the ordinal utility function and the impossibility of the interpersonal comparison of utility to define Pareto's efficiency of allocation.

The general equilibrium theory was founded by Walras (1874–77/1954). Pareto (1909/1971) introduced ordinal utility into Walras's general equilibrium theory based on his methodology (Marchionatti and Gambino 1997) and tried to prove the existence and efficiency of equilibrium in a competitive market as well as the law of demand. As Debreu (1959) shows, we can assume that there exists an ordinalist economic environment in the case of no market failures, given proof of the existence and efficiency of the general competitive equilibrium in a private ownership economy.[9] Thus, we propose characterizing the theories in the period from the theory of UTILITY and scarcity to the general equilibrium theory as contributions to the theory of the competitive market and the fundamental theorems of welfare economics. In this period, economic scientists concentrated their studies on the performance of the competitive market mechanism in the absence of market failure.

At the end of the nineteenth century, the factors behind market failure were realized as economic problems. Externalities and non-convexity were put forward by Marshall (1890), and public goods by Wicksell (1896/1958). The problems of externalities and non-convexity were solved by Pigou (1920) on the basis of the utilitarian welfare criterion within the framework of partial equilibrium analysis. Pigou's analysis proposed constructive public policies and generated the field of welfare economics. Then, the general equilibrium theory and ordinalism were applied to welfare economics, which was called new welfare economics. However, in order to be fruitful within the framework of Pigovian cost–benefit analyses, public policies were not always so suggestive within the framework of the general equilibrium theory. It was necessary to devise a certain welfare criterion in new welfare economics. Thus, the conceptions of compensation principles and social welfare function were proposed. These proposals turned out to be unsuccessful according to Arrow's (1951/63) general impossibility theorem, because of the impossibility of deciding the optimal policy on the ordinalist basis of ordinal utility and the impossibility of the interpersonal comparison of utility (Suzumura 2002).

The constructive ideas of the welfare criterion are proposed in the cooperative game theory on the basis of the von Neumann–Morgenstern utility function, which is definable in the situation where the uncertainty equivalent is definite. We have cooperative solutions to the axiomatic bargaining game, such as the Nash solution and the Kalai–Smorodinsky solution, and to the games of characteristic functional forms, such as the Shapley value, the core, and the nucleolus.

Unlike externalities and non-convexity, public goods were a crucial problem in economic analysis, namely the problem of incentive compatibility. Wicksell (1896/1958) recognizes this as the free-rider problem:

> If the individual is to spend his money for private and public uses so that his satisfaction is maximized, he will obviously pay nothing whatsoever for

public purposes (at least if we disregard fees and similar charges). Whether he pays much or little will affect the scope of public service so slightly, that for all practical purposes, he himself will not notice it at all. Of course, if everyone were to do the same, the State would soon cease to function.

A solution to the problem of public goods was put forward by Lindahl (1919/58), but this proposal only came to reveal the serious economic problems caused by asymmetric information.

Incentives and mechanism design

In the history of microeconomic theory, the controversy about socialist economic planning is considered to be the turning point from the theory of the competitive market to the theory of mechanism design (Suzumura 2002; Hurwicz 1973). In this section, we trace how the theory of mechanism design developed from the theory of the competitive market.[10]

The controversy began with Mises's thesis (Hayek 1935). According to him, rational economic calculation is possible only when monetary prices exist, not only for consumption goods, but also for production goods of any order. Therefore, no production good will ever become the object of market exchange in a socialist state where, by definition, collective ownership prevails for all means of production. In light of this, Mises asserted that it is impossible to find necessary monetary prices for production goods of a higher order in a socialist state. Hayek (1935) put forward further difficulties of economic calculation in a socialist state. For example, in order for the central planning board to calculate efficiency prices by solving general equilibrium equations, it must gather information about technology, primary and intermediate resources, and consumers' preferences, which are widely dispersed and privately owned by a vast number of economic agents.[11] While this may be logically possible, it would be practically impossible to perform because it is a task beyond the human capacity.

Lange (1936–37/1938) asserts that these problems were solvable through the quasi-Walrasian *tâtonnement* process. He assumes a socialist state where consumers are free to choose their demand for consumption goods and the supply of labor services, and where their preferences are the guiding criteria in production and in the allocation of resources. In this system, there exist market prices for consumption goods and for labor services, but the prices of capital goods and productive resources other than labor only account for prices at the center. Some appropriate rules are applied to the distribution of social dividends to consumers. The accounting prices for capital goods and productive resources other than labor are formed and adjusted by the central planning board through the instrumental use of the Walrasian *tâtonnement* process, where the central planning board plays the role of the Walrasian auctioneer. This quasi-Walrasian *tâtonnement* process is now called the Lange–Lerner scheme of market socialism after Lange (1936–37/1938) and Lerner (1944). In this scheme, the central planning board can avoid the task of gathering widely dispersed private information for computing accounting prices at the center, because the necessary computation is in effect performed by every owner of private information. Moreover, the accounting prices found at the equilibrium of the quasi-Walrasian *tâtonnement* process in a socialist state have the same objective characters as do the competitive prices of a market economy.

The problem of mechanism design was first crystallized by Hayek (1945) as follows: since 'the data from which the economic calculus starts are never for the whole society given to a single mind,' the problem to be solved is 'how to secure the best use of resources known to any of the members of society, for ends whose relative importance only these individuals know.' In order to solve the problem of mechanism design, we must tackle the following three points. First, it is practically impossible to gather dispersed and privately owned information for the purpose of central computation. Second, the Lange–Lerner scheme of market socialism has no specific accounting rule that is compatible with the incentives of economic agents to strategically misrepresent their private preferences. That is to say, it lacks the property of incentive compatibility. Third, since the Lange–Lerner scheme of market socialism follows the Walrasian *tâtonnement* process, it only attains the efficiency of resource allocation. However, we must form a definite social goal, which prescribes the optimal allocation of resources, based on individual judgments.

Hurwicz (1960, 1972) put forward an analytical framework for mechanism design by introducing the concept of incentive compatibility.[12] A social goal is defined as a social choice rule that specifies, for each possible state of the world, which outcomes would be socially optimal in that state. It is considered to embody the welfare judgments of a social planner. The solutions of cooperative games mentioned in the previous section are alternatives to be chosen as a social choice rule. A mechanism, or game form, is considered to specify the rules of a game. The players are the members of society. The problem of implementation is that of designing a mechanism (game form) such that the equilibrium outcomes satisfy the criterion of social optimality embodied in the social choice rule. The social choice rule is implementable or incentive-compatible if a mechanism has the property such that, in each possible state of the world, the set of equilibrium outcomes equals the set of socially optimal outcomes identified by the social choice rule.

Whether or not a social choice rule is implementable may depend on which game theoretic solution is used. The most demanding requirement is that every agent should have a dominant strategy, which is optimal for that agent regardless of the actions of others. A mechanism with this property is called a dominant strategy mechanism. Since the planner does not know the true state of the world, he or she must rely on the agents' equilibrium actions to indirectly produce the socially optimal outcome. According to the revelation principle by Gibbard (1973), the search for dominant strategy mechanisms is restricted to 'revelation mechanisms' in which every agent reports their own personal characteristics such as preferences, endowments, productive capacity, and so on to the social planner. The planner uses this information to compute the state of the world and then chooses the outcome that the social choice rule prescribes in this state. A social choice rule is dominant strategy incentive-compatible, or strategy-proof, if the associated revelation mechanism has the property such that honestly reporting the truth is always the dominant strategy for every agent.

Unfortunately, there is no satisfactory strategy-proof social choice rule in many environments. Neither the Walrasian rule for the classical private goods economy nor the Lindahl rule for the classical public goods economy is strategy-proof. The Gibbard–Satterthwaite theorem (Gibbard 1973; Satterthwaite 1975) shows that for a general class of problems there is no hope of implementing satisfactory social choice rules in dominant strategies.

More positive results are obtained using less demanding solutions such as the Nash equilibrium. Maskin (1977/1999) shows that any Nash-implementable social choice rule must satisfy a condition of 'monotonicity.' Conversely, any social choice rule that satisfies monotonicity and 'no veto power' can be Nash-implemented. If the agents are incompletely informed about the state of the world, then the concept of the Nash equilibrium is replaced by the Bayesian Nash equilibrium (Dasgupta *et al.* 1979). Incentive compatibility is a necessary condition for Bayesian Nash implementation but, in other respects, the results closely follow those obtained using complete information.

Since the mechanism of the competitive market is one of alternative mechanisms, the theory of mechanism design is clearly an extension of the theory of the competitive market and, indeed, the former historically developed from the latter. Therefore, they together are considered to form a major stream of microeconomic theories.

Concluding remarks

The presented analysis demonstrates that the history of microeconomic theory can be divided into two periods: the first period when the competitive market mechanism was considered to be operational and the fundamental theorems of welfare economics were valid and the second period when market failures prevailed in the economic environment and the theory of mechanism design was developed to resolve the problems of incentive compatibility emerging from these market failures. The first period can furthermore be divided into two periods before and after the marginal revolution. Microeconomic theory before the marginal revolution had an almost identical structure to that after it, but the former lacked the formulation of the rational behavior of individual economic agents and the theory of the competitive mechanism to associate individual actions with one another. The implications of individual rationality and mechanisms have developed depending on the nature of the pervasive economic environment, which has varied as an economy has evolved. It follows from these results that in the history of microeconomic theory, the most remarkable turning point was not the marginal revolution in the 1870s, but rather the transition from the theory of the competitive market to the theory of mechanism design between the 1930s and 1970s.

It has been said that economics was founded by Adam Smith because he investigated the scientific laws of the capitalist economy that was emerging at that time. The pervasive capitalist economy became the research object of positive analysis for economic scientists. Scientific facts founded on the observation of the capitalist economy, which is defined as the competitive equilibrium of the market economy, guarantee the scientific validity of positive analysis in economic science. Once, however, the mechanism is considered not to be given but to be designed, scientific facts that guarantee the scientific validity of economic analysis must be reduced to observations on human nature, because the equilibrium concepts of market economy or games consist of axioms on the behavior of economic agents and those on mechanisms. The positive analysis of microeconomics is thus reduced to the investigation of human nature based on how to design a certain mechanism to implement a social choice rule. This would be a similar research program to the social thoughts of Hobbes, Locke, and Hume as far as economic institutions are concerned. The research fields of experimental economics, behavioral economics, and so on investigate human nature, and their results would lay the foundation on which the theory of mechanism design can be built. Such a situation in present day microeconomics would be a major reason why some game theorists have great interest in the social thoughts of Hobbes, Locke, and Hume.

Notes

1. We denote the concept of UTILITY in the theory of UTILITY and scarcity by the capital description of UTILITY, because in this chapter, UTILITY is interpreted not as total utility but as marginal utility.
2. See Schumpeter (1954: 297), Kauder (1965), Hutchison (1988), and Ekelund and Hébert (2002).
3. The fact that we understand a theory of the past implies translating the original theory into a consistent axiom system described in terms of the language by which the present theory is described.
4. The Kuhn–Tucker conditions of the utility maximization problem are as follows:

   (KT1) $\frac{\partial U_h}{\partial x_h}(x_h^*) \leq v_h^*, \left(\frac{\partial U_h}{\partial x_h}(x_h^*) - v_h^*\right) x_h^* = 0, x_h^* \geq 0,$

   (KT2) $\omega_h \geq x_h^*, v_h^*(\omega_h - x_h^*) = 0, v_h^* \geq 0.$

5. Define $U(x)$, where $x = (x_1, x_2, \ldots, x_H)$, by

   $$U(x) = \Sigma_i^H U_h(x_h) = \Sigma_i^H \int_0^{x_h} \frac{\partial U_h}{\partial x_h}(c_h) dc_h = \Sigma_i^H U_h \int_0^{x_h} u_h(c_h) dc_h(x_h).$$

6. The proposition such that a UTILITY is a decreasing function, with the suppositions of cardinality, separability, and additivity, implies the concavity of a total utility function, which is a sufficient condition for a solution of the Kuhn–Tucker problem to exist.
7. Jevons (1871/1957), Menger, and Walras (1874–77/1954) put forward the theory of marginal utility, but they are different from one another, as shown by Kawamata (2009). It was Menger who constructed the theory that implies the theorems in the theory of UTILITY and scarcity.

8 There is another approach to solving the problems emerging from more general economic environments. As Negishi (1989) shows, Jevons answers the problem of how a competitive situation becomes possible. Following Jevons, Edgeworth (1881) demonstrates his limit theorem in the replica economy consisting of the same types of economic agents. They are interpreted as primary contributions to the core, which is a solution concept of cooperative game theory.
9 See Arrow and Hahn (1971) for the detailed development of the general equilibrium theory.
10 See Suzumura (2002), Maskin and Sjöström (2002) and the references cited therein for the detailed development the theory of mechanism design. The author owes this section to them and Hurwicz (1973).
11 If information is symmetric across economic agents, the problem of resource allocation under conditions of uncertainty is solvable within the framework of the general equilibrium theory. Asymmetric information is crucial for the problems of mechanism design and incentive compatibility.
12 See Hurwicz (1973) for a detailed development of the theory of mechanism design before him.

References

Arrow, K.J. (1951/63) *Social Choice and Individual Values*, 2nd edn, New York: Wiley.
Arrow, K.J. and F.H. Hahn (1971) *General Competitive Analysis*, San Francisco: Holden-Day, Oliver and Boyd.
Carr, E.H. (1961/64) *What is History?* Middlesex: Penguin Books.
Condillac, É.B. de (1776/1997) *Le commerce et le gouvernement considerés relativement l'un a l'autre*, Paris: Jombert et Cellot. Trans. S. Eltis (1997) *Commerce and Government*, Cheltenham: Edward Elgar.
Dasgupta, P., P.J. Hammond, and E. Maskin (1979) 'Implementation of social choice rules: some general results on incentive compatibility,' *Review of Economic Studies*, 46: 181–216.
Debreu, G. (1959) *Theory of Value*, New York: Wiley.
Edgeworth, F.Y. (1881) *Mathematical Psychics*, London: Kegan Paul & Co.
Ekelund, R.B. Jr. and R.F. Hébert (2002) 'Retrospectives: the origins of neoclassical microeconomics,' *Journal of Economic Perspectives*, 16: 197–215.
Galiani, F. (1750/1803) *Della Moneta*, Napoli. Reprinted in P. Custodi (ed.) (1803) *Scrittori Classici Italiani di Economia Politica*, Parte Moderna, Tomo 3, Milano: Destefanis.
Gibbard, A.F. (1973) 'Manipulation of voting schemes: a general result,' *Econometrica*, 41: 587–601.
Gossen, H.H. (1854/1983) *Entwickelung der Gesetze des menschlichen Verkehrs, und der daraus fliessenden Regeln für menschliches Handeln*, Brunswick: Vieweg. Trans. R.C. Blitz (1983) with an introductory essay by N. Geogescu-Roegen, *The Laws of Human Relations and the Rules of Human Action Derived Therefrom*, Cambridge, MA: MIT Press.
Hayek, F.A. von ed. (1935) *Collectivist Economic Planning*, London: Routledge.
Hayek, F.A. von (1945) 'The use of knowledge in society,' *American Economic Review*, 35: 519–30.
Hurwicz, L. (1960) 'Optimality and informational efficiency in resource allocation processes,' in K.J. Arrow, S. Karlin, and P. Suppes (eds.), *Mathematical Methods in the Social Sciences*, Stanford, CA: Stanford University Press, pp. 27–46.

Hurwicz, L. (1972) 'On informationally decentralized systems,' in R. Radner and C.B. McGuire (eds.), *Decision and Organization*, Amsterdam: North-Holland, pp. 297–336.

Hurwicz, L. (1973) 'The design of resource allocation mechanisms,' *American Economic Review*, 58: 1–30.

Hutchison, T.W. (1988) *Before Adam Smith: The Emergence of Political Economy 1662–1776*, Oxford: Blackwell.

Jevons, W.S. (1871/1957) *The Theory of Political Economy*, 5th edn., London: Macmillan.

Katzner, D.W. (1970) *Static Demand Theory*, New York: Macmillan.

Kauder, E. (1965) *A History of Marginal Utility Theory*, Princeton, NJ: Princeton University Press.

Kawamata, M. (2009) 'The Negishi method in the history of general equilibrium theory,' in A. Ikeo and H.D. Kurz (eds.), *A History of Economic Theory: Essays in the Horner of Takashi Negishi*, London and New York: Routledge, pp. 120–36.

Lange, O. (1936–37/1938) 'On the economic theory of socialism,' *Review of Economic Studies*, 4: 53–71, 123–42. Revised and reprinted in B.E. Lippincott (ed.), with O. Lange and F.M. Taylor (1938) *On the Economic Theory of Socialism*, Minneapolis, MN: University of Minnesota Press, pp. 57–143.

Lerner, A.P. (1944) *The Economics of Control*, New York: Macmillan.

Lindahl, E. (1919/58) 'Positive Lösung,' *Die Gerechtigkeit der Besteuerung*, Jena. Trans. E. Henderson (1958) 'Just taxation: a positive solution,' in R.A. Musgrave and A.T. Peacock (eds.), *Classics in the Theory of Public Finance*, London: Macmillan, pp. 168–76.

Marshall, A. (1890) *Principles of Economics*. London: Macmillan.

Mas-Colell, A., M.D. Whinston, and J. Green (1995) *Microeconomic Theory*, New York: Oxford University Press.

Maskin, E. (1977/99) 'Nash equilibrium and welfare optimality,' *Review of Economic Studies*, 66: 23–38.

Maskin, E. and T. Sjöström (2002) 'Implementation theory,' in K.J. Arrow, A.K. Sen, and K. Suzumura (eds.), *Handbook of Social Choice and Welfare*, Vol. 1, Amsterdam: Elsevier, pp. 237–88.

Marchionatti, R. and E. Gambino (1997) 'Pareto and political economy as a science: methodological revolution and analytical advances in economic theory in the 1890s,' *Journal of Political Economy*, 105: 1322–47.

Menger, C. (1871/1950) *Grundsäze der Volkswirtschaftslehre*, Wien: Braumüller. Trans. J. Dingwall and B.F. Hoselitz, with an introduction by F.A. Hayek (1950) *Principles of Economics*, Glencoe: Free Press.

Negishi, T. (1989) *History of Economic Theory*, Amsterdam: North-Holland.

Pareto, V. (1909/71) *Manuel d'économie politique*, Geneve: Giard & Briere. Trans. A.S. Schwier (1971) *Manual of Political Economy*, New York: A.M. Kelley.

Pigou, A.C. (1920) *The Economics of Welfare*, London: Macmillan.

Satterthwaite, M.A. (1975) 'Strategy-proofness and Arrow's conditions: existence and correspondence theorems for voting procedures and social welfare functions,' *Journal of Economic Theory*, 10: 187–217.

Schumpeter, J.A. (1954) *History of Economic Analysis*, (ed.) E.B. Schumpeter, New York: Oxford University Press.

Shoenfield, J.R. (1967) *Mathematical Logic*, Reading, MA: Addison-Wesley.

Smith, A. (1776/1976) *An Inquiry into the Nature and Causes of the Wealth of Nations*, 2 vols, London: Strahan & Cadell. In A.S. Skinner and W.B. Todd (eds.) (1976) *The*

Glasgow Edition of the Works and Correspondence of Adam Smith, 6 vols, Oxford: Clarendon.

Sundaram, R.K. (1996) *A First Course in Optimization Theory*, Cambridge: Cambridge University Press.

Suzumura, K. (2002) 'Introduction,' in K.J. Arrow, A.K. Sen, and K. Suzumura (eds.), *Handbook of Social Choice and Welfare*, Vol. 1, Amsterdam: Elsevier, pp. 1–32.

Turgot, A.R.J. (1769/1977) 'Valeurs et monnaies,' in G. Schelle (ed.) (1919) *Œuvres de Turgot*, Vol. 3, Paris: Alcan. Trans. (1977) 'Value and money,' in P.D. Groenewegen (ed.), *The Economics of A.R.J. Turgot*, The Hague: Martinus Nijhoff, pp. 133–48.

Walras, L. (1874–77/1954) *Éléments d'économie politique pure*, Lausanne: Rouge. Trans. W. Jaffé (1954) *Elements of Pure Economics*, Homewood, IL: Irwin.

Wicksell, K. (1896/1958) 'Ein neues Prinzip der gerechten Besteuerung,' *Finanztheoretische Untersuchungen*, Jena. Trans. J.M. Buchanan (1958) 'A new principle of just taxation,' in R.A. Musgrave and A.T. Peacock (eds.), *Classics in the Theory of Public Finance*, London: Macmillan, pp. 72–118.

3 Quételet's influence on W. S. Jevons

From subjectivism to objectivism

Takutoshi Inoue

The evolution of Jevons's intellect and the formation of his view of science[1]

William Stanley Jevons was born on September 1, 1835 to a Unitarian family in Liverpool, England. Liverpool, having grown to the country's second largest city after London through the prosperous trade in tobacco, sugar, and slaves during the eighteenth century, was along with Manchester the new city that flourished most from England's industrial revolution and the policies of free trade.

From beginnings as humble nail manufacturers in Staffordshire, a center of small-scale metalworking firms, the Jevons family had steadily built up its fortunes, starting in William Stanley's grandfather's era, as members of the then-growing middle class of Liverpool. With financial support from a man named John Yeats, his grandfather had made himself into an independent iron merchant, and his first son, Thomas, through marriage to a daughter of reformist politician William Roscoe, solidified the family's social standing. The son of John Yeats, J. Y. Yeats was to play a major role in the founding of University College, which was where William Stanley was to pursue his higher education. From the beginning of the nineteenth century, Liverpool struggled with the social ills propagated in the shadow of prosperity by population increase and industrialization. In 1835 reforms were begun with the enactment of the Municipal Corporations Act, and one of the prominent figures in the instituting of the reforms was grandfather Roscoe. Thomas Jevons also had a profound interest in science and technology and counted among his friends railway engineers like George Stephenson (known as the Father of Railways) and his pupil Joseph Locke. A supporter of free trade, Roscoe also involved himself in the Corn Laws dispute. He was an astute businessman who advocated use of the decimal monetary system as a means of promoting trade.

Brought up in this lively environment, William Stanley Jevons first entered University College London, which was dedicated to education, not in specialized knowledge but in the general knowledge governing specialization – in other words, the liberal arts. He then went to the University College School. He studied under such famous scholars as mathematician Augustus De Morgan and chemist Alexander William Williamson. From De Morgan he learned about probability, trigonometry, and binomial theorems and realized the importance of mathematics and moral philosophy, expressing his desire "especially to become a good mathematician" (Jevons 1886, p. 119). Williamson impressed upon him the importance of experimentation and empirical verification.

Jevons not only pursued his studies of mathematics and natural science but, concerned about the dark side in the backdrop of the prosperity of the Victorian age, investigated the conditions of the poor in Liverpool and London. At the time of the national census (1851) based on the occupational categories developed by medical statistician William Farr (1807–1883), he developed an interest in the industrial structure and the workings of society (Jevons 1905, p. vi). While Jevons's intellectual interests were developing in this way, his father had great expectations for his son's future. Those expectations brought the young Jevons to confront the "liberty of the will" involved in the difficult question of "philosophical necessity". It was not until his encounter with a copy of the first English translation (1842) of Adolphe Quételet's *Treatise on Man and the Development of His Faculties*, which he purchased August 2, 1857, that he found the answer to this question of free will (Black 1981, vol. 7, p. 119).

Jevons left University College before completing his studies to take a position as assayer at the newly founded Australian Royal Mint in Sydney. While engaged in that work he gathered various meteorological data and published his findings in newspaper articles under the pseudonym "Honestas" (Black 1973, vol. 2, p. 237) and was called a "scientific gentleman" (La Nauze 1949, p. 29). It was through that work that Jevons realized that meteorology without gathering adequate data was only "half science" (Black 1972, vol. 1, p. 109), but he came to the belief that if one could

> present in an available form, such accurate numerical data as are attainable, and secondly, to group together general information ... so as to show what remarkable problems have to be solved, and what interesting connections of case and effect may ultimately be traced and proved.
> (Jevons 1859, p. 96)[2]

then meteorology could become a true science. In order to achieve that goal, Jevons worked to improve assaying methods and equipment and became interested in statistical methods for processing the data.

Jevons applied the statistics methodologies he picked up during his study of meteorology to his work on poverty issues in Sydney, and he began research in the social sciences, particularly economics, through his interest in railway expansion and nationalization. Compared to natural sciences, he saw that few had realized that human nature could also be the subject of scientific inquiry, and recognized in the social condition of man a perhaps difficult-to-grasp but fertile field for research.[3] Not long after he firmly embraced the potential for the "scientific investigation of *Man*,"[4] asserting his intention to pursue research in the social sciences. Human beings may possess free will, but they are "a phenomenon in which *effect* is always connected with *cause*"; and, he argued, "It follows that each individual man must be a creature of *cause & effect*.... To each individual the choice belongs, and so to yourself." He agreed with Adolphe Quételet's arguments on this subject but felt that the Belgian statistician and sociologist's ideas were "require[d] yet to be more completed proved."

This view of human nature that Jevons acquired from Quételet was easy for him to accept not only because of his recognition that "selfishness is the first and last principle of human nature,"[5] but because, for acquisition of wealth based on selfishness to be a path to morality, he thought that "for the happiness of one to be necessary for the peace of another, is nothing but *sympathy* between them."[6] It moreover offered a resolution to the question of the "liberty of the will" he had long confronted and was akin to Jeremy Bentham's utilitarian view that "Nature has placed mankind under the governance of two sovereign masters, *pain* and *pleasure*" (Bentham 1970, p. 11), and view of science as the study of cause–effect relationships (law of causality).

Having confirmed this view of human nature, Jevons arrived at the conviction that in an arena of fair competition, people who might very well be "really and entirely selfish" would "work together unconsciously or at least unintentionally each for the good of all." He became eager to demonstrate this idea, which he called "the principle of Individual Competition," and worked out the outlines of what he would later demonstrate as the perfect competitive market.[7]

Also noteworthy was that his study of the science of economics was getting underway at this time as he sought to "more fully develop and demonstrate the causes[,] mode of operation, and exact effects of Selfish Competition" (April 5, 1857), and that it was, rather than theoretical study, his attempt to verify the arguments that Quételet had presented. The key to proving them, he believed, was "exactness." He had, through his study of natural science, acquired a sense of the distinction between "exactness," which would show the relationship between fact and theory, and "rigorousness or strictness," which would be required for consistency of theory, as he explained in a letter announcing his arrival at "the true theory of economy," that is the marginal utility theory.[8] In "Notice of a General Mathematical Theory of Political Economy" he wrote:

> The main problem of economy may be reduced to a rigorous mathematical form, and it is only the absence of exact data for the inductive determination of the laws or functions which will always prevent it from becoming an exact science.
> (June 1862; Jevons 1863, pp. 158–9)

Distinguishing clearly between exactness and rigorousness, he argued that, as with the development of the natural sciences, statistically exact data was needed for a rigorous science to develop into an exact science.

Jevons already saw mathematics as the "solid foundation of all other scientific knowledge, thus recognizing that mathematics and the rigorousness required in mathematics," were vital for scientific research (January 5, 1855; Black 1972, vol. 1, p. 109). Saying, "I perfectly comprehended everything that may be deduced from Nature, as to design, order, unity of conception &c of the universe" (January 28, 1857; Black 1972, vol. 1, p. 155), he developed not only his world view but his conviction that economics should be developed into an exact science like natural science.

Through these explorations as a scientist, Jevons argued that science had to be rigorous, systematic, and exact, and he believed that this approach was the way Isaac Newton had viewed science.

Quételet's *Treatise on Man*

Jevons found that his own personal problem regarding the liberty of the will and the law of causality, which was basic to scientific analysis, were compatible. Moreover, while embracing Newton's idea that mathematics was basic to understanding and grasping the world, he distinguished the mathematical rigor of the natural sciences from empirical exactness and clearly separated mathematical science and statistical science. By balancing the two, he sought to make economics a science. What made this possible was the work of Quételet, whom Jevons called "the true founder of exact social science" (Jevons 1875, p. 492). Next, let us look at how Quételet viewed science and how he viewed statistics.

According to Quételet, the study of the "*Science of Man*" was completely uncharted territory, because as soon as the object of study was the "moral phenomena of mankind," he said, scholars gave up applying the rules of inquiry that they applied to the study of other laws of nature. The reason for this is that this study treats "the moral and intellectual faculties, over which our volition exercises an influence" (p. 5, right). Quételet declared that "the speculative sciences" and "*à priori* reasoning"[9] were invalid in the study of man, calling instead for the "sciences of observation" (p. 5 left).[10] Regarding the "sciences of observation," he emphasized the importance of regarding man as "a fraction of the species," not as "he exists in insulated, separate, or in an individual state." By putting aside "all which is accidental, and the individual peculiarities" that do not affect the mass, the observer could grasp the overall results. In other words, the more individuals are observed, the more effectively "individual peculiarities, whether physical or moral, [would be] effaced," bringing to the surface "*the general facts, by virtue of which society exists and is preserved.*" Quételet called this the "fundamental principle" (pp. 5–6).

The law of causality applies to moral phenomena just as to physical phenomena, he asserted, and the only reason that some are convinced "that moral phenomena did not obey this law, has been the too great influence ascribed at all time to man himself over his actions." He remarked on the remarkable fact that "the more extended human knowledge has become, the more limited human power, in that respect, has constantly appeared" (p. 6, right).

Human beings are constantly subject to various forces (causes) that impinge upon them as members of society and must bend to those forces, but Quételet acknowledged the "liberty of the will," observing how "as a man, employing all the energy of his intellectual faculties, he in some measure masters these causes, and modifies their effects, thus constantly endeavoring to improve his condition" (p. 7, left).

Through the work of Quételet, Jevons availed himself of the means to deal with the issues he faced when he shifted his research from the natural to the social sciences: (1) the applicability of the principle of causality in the natural sciences to the social sciences, (2) the compatibility of causality's inevitability with human free will, and (3) the generality and objectivity independent from individual human being's peculiarity or subjectivity.

Having explained his ideas as above, Quételet's *Treatise* proposes his specific methodology after expressing the purpose of this work: "to study in their effects the causes, whether natural or disturbing, which influence human development; to endeavour to measure the influence of these causes, and the mode according to which they mutually modify each other" (p. 8, left). What Quételet considered the prerequisite to laying the foundation of a social physics was the "*social man*," whom he likened to a center of gravity "around which oscillate the social elements." That social man was a "fictitious being, for whom every thing proceeds conformable to the medium results obtained for society in general" (p. 8, left). This fictitious being he called "the average man" (p. 96, right).

> may be of the most important service to the science of man and the social system. It ought necessarily to precede every other inquiry into the social physics, since it is, as it were, the base ... it is by having that central point in view that we arrive at the apprehension of all the phenomena of equilibrium and motion.
>
> (p. 96, right)

"Average" and "trading body"

Jevons had stated in his "Notice of a General Mathematical Theory of Political Economy" that the "main problem of economy may be reduced to a rigorous mathematical form," but without exact data, he knew it would not be possible to organize the laws or functions into an exact science. Then in his "Brief Account of a General Mathematical Theory of Political Economy" (1866; Jevons 1965, pp. 303–14), he introduced his concept of "average," saying:

> Of course such equations as are here spoken of are merely theoretical. Such complicated laws as those of economy cannot be accurately traced in individual cases. Their operation can only be detected in aggregates and by the method of averages. *We must think under the forms of these laws in their theoretic perfection and complication; in practice we must be content with approximate and empirical laws.*

Here Jevons clearly distinguished between the perfection and rigor that informs the mathematical laws of economics and the complexity and exactness that makes possible the empirical laws of economics. In the first edition of *The*

Theory of Political Economy (1871), the sections from 1 to 14 of the 17 sections of Chapter IV "The Theory of Exchange" discussed the mathematical aspects of economics and all but two of the 17 sections (these two being Section 15, "Mode of ascertaining the Variation of Utility" and Section 16, "Opinions of Economists on the Variation of Price") dealt with the empirical aspects of economics. In the second edition (1879), sections 1 to 21 of the 25 sections of Chapter IV discussed the mathematical aspects of economics and all but three of the 25 sections (Section 22, "Numerical Determination of the Laws of Utility," Section 23, "Opinions as to the Variation of Price," and Section 24, "Variation of the Price of Corn") dealt with empirical aspects of economics. Especially Section 24 was separated from the Section 16 of the first edition and given a new title; it treated the details of the price of corn. This was of course due to Jevons's research interests, but at the same time – actually perhaps more importantly – it was because of his interest in Quételet's proposition about the "sciences of observation." Previous interpretations of *The Theory of Political Economy* have rarely paid much attention to those sections that discuss the "sciences of observation," and yet judging from Jevons's intentions, we should accord importance to those sections.

A typical example is his attempt to arrive at an estimated regression equation in setting corn prices using past statistical data from J. Dalrymple, G. King, and C. Davenant (x is average volume of crop):

$$\text{price of corn} = \frac{0.824}{(x-0.12)^2} \doteqdot \frac{5}{6(x-1/8)^2}$$

Aside from the validity of this formula, his attempt to find an equation for setting prices from statistical data separate from the mathematical theory of exchange was outstanding, for this formula for calculating corn prices rested on an objective methodology without the interference of individual subjectivity. We can see how absorbed he became with statistics and then again econometrics, given the contributions he made throughout his life, first to meteorology, then social statistics, and also to statistical theory and the establishment of the British statistics bureau.[11]

Jevons's concept linking economics not only to mathematical theory but exchange theory and statistical data was that of the "trading body," which may have been inspired by Quételet's notion of the "social body." This concept does not appear in either "Notice of a General Mathematical Theory of Political Economy" or his "Brief Account of a General Mathematical Theory of Political Economy," but in the third Section of Chapter IV "The Theory of Exchange" of the first edition of *The Theory of Political Economy*. Based on those theses, this section was written during a brief period under the title "Definitions of Market and Trading Body." In the second edition, he divides this section into Section 6, "Definition of Market" and Section 7, "Definition of Trading Body." These new endeavors resulted from the publication of Jevons's *The Principles of Science* (1874, 1877, 1879), which corroborated the "trading body" in terms of scientific method – and in fact the second edition of *The Theory of Political Economy* refers to "fictitious mean."

For example, in the first edition of *The Theory of Political Economy*, he writes little more than the following:

> At the same time, it would be an obvious error to suppose that the particular character of an economical law holding true of a great aggregate will be exactly the same as that of any individual. Only when the individuals are of perfectly uniform character will their average supply or demand for any commodity represent that of an individual. But every community is usually composed of individuals differing widely in powers, wants, habits, and possessions. An average will therefore partly depend upon the comparative numbers belonging to each class.
> (Jevons 1995, p. 90)

In the second edition, under the definition of average, he writes:

> In such circumstances the average laws applying to them will come under what I have elsewhere called the "Fictitious Mean," that is to say, they are numerical results which do not pretend to represent the character of any existing things. But average laws would not on this account be less useful, if we could obtain them; for the movements of trade and industry depends upon averages and aggregates, not upon the whims of individuals.
> (Jevons 1970, p. 136)

Quételet's influence on Jevons can be seen in the latter borrowing from the idea of the "*social* man" in developing his concept of "averages" and in the way his "aggregates" or "trading body" corresponds to Quételet's "social body.[12]

Regarding "fictitious mean," Jevons wrote under "The Method of Means" in his book *Principles of Science* that he distinguished between (1) "fictitious mean" or "average result," (2) "precise mean result," and (3) "probable mean result." Under the influence of Quételet, thus, Jevons distinguished real averages from non-existing averages, calling the former "mean" and the latter "fictitious mean" or "average" (Jevons 1874, vol. 1, pp. 359–60). Reducing the former to the latter from a standpoint of non-realism, he emphasized the importance of the fictitious mean or average result.

As we have seen above, one of the ideas Jevons introduced on the premise of the exchange theory was the concept of "trading body." This concept not only secured the generalization and objectivity allowed by the use of fictitious mean, independent of the peculiarities and subjectivity of human individuals, but opened up the possibilities for verification in economics by mathematical principles. Black writes that Jevons's theory of the "trading body" was often criticized as ambiguous and ill defined. Black believes Jevons had sought to "generalize his equation of exchange, developed first for the case of two-party two-commodity barter trade, without clearly realizing that contract in such a case is indeterminate." This point was later cleared up by Francis Y. Edgeworth (1967, p. 31). Black goes on to say that a careful reading of the "Definition of Trading Body" section suggests that Jevons "developed the concept in an attempt to treat all cases as if they displayed that 'precise and continuous variation' which he realized to exist in the case of 'large aggregates'" (Jevons 1970, p. 267).

Elimination of subjectivity

The Marginal Utility School in economics, which includes Jevons's economics, was once known for its subjective economics, and the subjectivity involved in the concept of utility was debated and efforts were made in subsequent developments to eliminate subjectivity. This section looks at how Jevons viewed this problem.

Jevons's economics began with his June 1, 1860 letter in which he declared his formulation of "the true theory of economy," or marginal utility theory. In the "Notice of a General Mathematical Theory of Political Economy" (1862), he wrote, in line with Bentham: "A true theory of economy can only be attained by going back to the spring of human action – the feelings of pleasure and pain which accompany our common wants." His attention, thus, was focused not on individuals but on "our common wants," and by so doing, he presented his idea of "aggregates," which would lead to the "trading body." In addition, in the "Brief Account of a General Mathematical Theory of Political Economy" (1866) he wrote of the motives that inspire action: "economy does not treat of all human motives. There are motives nearly always present with us, arising from conscience, compassion, or from some moral or religious source, which economy cannot and does not pretend to treat." Economics is a science, he carefully asserted, that deals with the world of "what to be," not the world of "what ought to be."

This position was made even clearer when he included in *The Theory of Political Economy* the section entitled "Relation of Political Economy to Moral Philosophy" (in the second edition, the section "Relation of Economics to Ethics"), in which he stated, "My present purpose is accomplished in pointing out the hierarchy of feeling, and assigning a proper place to the pleasure and pains with which Economy deals. It is the lowest rank of feeling which we here treat" (Jevons 1970, p. 93).

With regard to measurement of feeling and motive, Jevons admitted it was hardly possible to "form the conception of a unit of pleasure or pain," and that expressing quantities of feeling numerically was impossible. But he believed, "if we can compare the quantities directly, we do not need the units."[13] He then argued that "the mind of an individual is the balance which makes its own comparisons, and is the final judge of quantities of feeling," and the reason for this was, he wrote, citing Alexander Bain, "it is this resulting action that alone determines which is the greater." Jevons expressed his approval of Alfred Marshall's "measurement of motive by money" (Marshall 1961, p. 15).[14]

Regarding the comparison of feeling and motivation among individuals, moreover, "I see no means by which such comparison can ever be accomplished" (Jevons 1995, p. 21; 1970, p. 85)[15] he argued. For Jevons, economics deals not with "individuals" but "an aggregate of individuals," and as far as there are "a sufficient number of independent cases," they are neutralized. "Regular laws," which are "capable of exact investigation," can thus be obtained. A note of explanation about "great masses and wide averages" (1995, p. 23; 1970, p. 86) was added to the second edition of *The Theory of Political Economy*. This note refers the reader to chapter XVI, "The Method of Means," in *The Principles of Science*.

In his mathematical theory in *The Theory of Political Economy* Jevons, fully aware of the difficulties of measuring feeling and motivation, pursued indirect measurement of feeling and motive in monetary terms. He still could not help admitting that such measurements would involve some sort of subjectivity. To verify his mathematical theory he engaged in statistical research as a "science of observation." In the study of theory and law, as for the estimated regression equation, he declared it was possible to obtain objectivity of theory and law. Hence, he had opened up his path to econometrics.

Notes

1 See Inoue 2007 and 1987.
2 I would note that Jevons distinguished between "verification which enabled a judgment whether something was true or false" and "proof," as a "policy-making methodology." See also Inoue 1987, pp. 20–1.
3 On August 4, 1858, he wrote:

> [c]omparatively few have perceived that Human Nature may also be the subject of a science.... But the social condition of man as influenced by the many internal and external circumstances is perhaps an indefinite but a wide and rich field for future research.
>
> (Black 1981, vol. 2, pp. 335–6)

4 On January 30, 1958, he wrote: "within the last years I have become convinced that more is really to be done in the scientific investigation of Man." Black 1981, vol. 2, p. 361 for this and quotations to the end of this paragraph.
5 July 9, 1853; Black 1981, vol. 2, p. 44.
6 February 15, 1856; Black 1981, vol. 2, p. 212.
7 April 14, 1857; Black 1981, vol. 1, p. 158.
8 June 1, 1860; Black 1981, vol. 1, p. 410.
9 The "speculative sciences" and "*à priori* reasoning" Quételet criticized probably refers to the ideas concerning man and society in the history of social thought in the UK and France such as the "social contract," "self-interest," "benevolence," and "sympathy" as proposed by John Locke, Jacques Rousseau, David Hume, and Adam Smith.
10 "[I]t has hitherto been deemed expedient by learned men to abandon the line of inquiry employed in the investigation of the other laws of nature, as soon as the moral phenomena of mankind became the object of research" (see Quételet 1968). Quotations from here to end of this section, identified by page numbers.
11 Inoue 1987; see chapter 8 on Jevons as a statistician.
12 Regarding Jevons's "trading body," as he wrote that "every trading body is either an

individual or an aggregate of individuals" (Jevons 1970, p. 135), it seems clear that he adapted this from Quételet's "social body."
13 The assertion that units are not needed to compare quantities was made because, if dimension of units is considered, units for the denominator and numerator are the same and therefore they eliminate each other, leaving only ratios and thus demonstrating magnitude correlation. As for important concepts of dimensions in natural sciences, sections on "Dimension of Value" and "Dimensions of Labour," for example, are introduced in the second edition of *The Theory of Political Economy*.
14 Marshall writes, "It is essential to note that the economist does not claim to measure any affection of the mind in itself, or directly; but only indirectly through its effects." Concerning "through its effects," he points out "the measurement of motive by money."
15 Jevons deleted the word "ever" in the second edition.

References

Bentham, Jeremy 1970, *An Introduction to the Principles of Morals and Legislation* [orig. pub. 1789], Athlone Press, London.

Black, R. D. Collison, ed. 1972–1981, *Papers and Correspondence of William Stanley Jevons*, Macmillan, London.

Edgeworth, Francis Ysidro 1967, *Mathematical Psychics* [orig. pub. 1881], A. M. Kelley, New York.

Inoue, T. 1987, *Jebonzu no shiso to keizaigaku: Kagakusha kara keizaigakusha e* [*The Thought and Economics of W. Stanley Jevons: From a Man of Science to an Economist*], Nihon Hyoronsha, Tokyo.

Inoue, Takutoshi 2007, "W. Stanley Jevons (1835–1882): From Man of Science to Economist," *Discussion Paper Series*, vol. 33, School of Economics, Kwansei Gakuin University, Nishinomiya, 23 pp.

Jevons, Harriet A., ed. 1886, *Letters and Journal of W. Stanley Jevons*, Macmillan, London.

Jevons, William Stanley 1859, "Some Data Concerning the Climate of Australia and New Zealand," *Waugh's Australian Almanac*, pp. 47–98.

Jevons, W. S. 1862 (1863), "Notice of a General Mathematical Theory of Political Economy," *Report of the British Association for the Advancement of Science*, British Association for the Advancement of Science, Cambridge.

Jevons, W. S. 1874, *Principles of Science*, 2 vols., Macmillan, London.

Jevons, W. S. 1875, "Comte's Philosophy: The Positive Philosophy of Auguste Comte," *Nature*, vol. 12, pp. 491–2.

Jevons, W. S. 1866, "Brief Account of a General Mathematical Theory of Political Economy," *Journal of the Statistical Society of London*, vol. 29, pp. 282–7 (reprinted in Jevons, W.S., 1965, pp. 303–14).

Jevons, W. S. 1965, *The Theory of Political Economy* [orig. pub. 1911], A. M. Kelley, New York.

Jevons, W. S. 1970, *The Theory of Political Economy*, R. D. Collison Black, ed. [orig. pub. 1879], Pelican Books, Harmondsworth, Middlesex.

Jevons, W. S. 1905, *The Principles of Economics: A fragment of a Treatise on the Industrial Mechanism of Society and other Papers*, with preface by Henry Higgs, Macmillan, London.

Jevons, W. S. 1995, *The Theory of Political Economy* [orig. pub. 1871], Diese Faksimile-Ausgabe, Düsseldorf.

La Nauze, John Andrew 1949, *Political Economy in Australia*, Cambridge University Press, Cambridge.

Marshall, Alfred 1961, *Principles of Economics*, Macmillan, Variorum Edition, London.

Quételet, Lambert Adolphe Jacques 1968, *A Treatise on Man and the Development of his Faculties* [orig. pub. 1842] (Trans. Robert Knox of *Sur l'homme et le développement de ses facultés*, 1835), Burt Franklin, New York.

4 Transforming of *rareté*?
From Auguste to Léon Walras[1]

Kayoko Misaki

Introduction

This chapter focuses on the continuities and discontinuities in theory and in policy that exist between Auguste and Léon Walras and introduces a new perspective on the textbook interpretation that considers the adoption of subjective theory of value by Léon Walras as the birth of modern economic theory.

Léon Walras established the general equilibrium theory and founded modern economic analysis. In order to achieve this, he introduced the marginal utility theory of value, which is a subjective approach based on consumers' behavior. It is generally considered to be one of the most important contributions made by Léon Walras as a progenitor of neoclassical economics.[2]

In his *History of Economic Analysis* (1954), Schumpeter claimed that France has a tradition of utility theory of value including those of Quesnay, Condillac, and J.B. Say, etc. ... and he claimed that Walras's marginal utility theory of value belongs to this tradition.[3] In contrast to Britain, where the classical school, based on the objective labor theory of value was replaced by the subjective marginal utility theory of value with the Jevons revolution, French economists, Schumpeter claims, were always under the influence of this utility tradition.

As a matter of fact, however, Léon Walras and his father Auguste criticized both approaches, the French utility tradition and the British labor theory of value, all their lives. Auguste has his own theory of value based on *rareté* (scarcity) and Léon inherited it when he started his career in economics. Later, Léon transformed it into the idea of marginal utility but continued to call it "rareté." For the two ideas always have a definitive common role. Auguste and Léon Walras believed that only their *rareté* theory of value could be true grounds for realizing the nationalization of land. Auguste Walras criticized the utility theory of value of J. B. Say from the viewpoint of justice. He claimed that Say's subjective approach could not offer a coherent theoretical basis for the property theory. Auguste believed that he could establish it with the objective theory of *rareté*, Léon Walras is believed to have finally adopted the subjective theory of marginal utility; however he maintained his father's critical attitude toward Say's political economy in terms of justice all his life. The two generations stuck to their purpose of realizing the nationalization of land until the end.

Auguste Walras on theory of value

In this section, we will see how Auguste's theory of value is intended to counter Say's political economy. According to Léon Walras, Auguste started his study of economics because he was disappointed with J. B. Say.[4] Auguste claimed that Say's political economy treats the right of property only from the viewpoint of advantageousness and disregards that of justice.

In his main work, *De la nature de la Richesse* (1831), Auguste argues that value comes from *rareté* not from utility, rejecting Say's view.

> I ask for Mr. Say's pardon: but it is not the utility of a thing that makes it desirable, strictly speaking, and that lead people to make a sacrifice in order to possess it. It is solely the limitation or the rareté of this useful thing; for, if the thing were unlimited, all of us could possess it, and we would not need to make the least sacrifice in order to ensure us the enjoyment of it.
> (Walras, A., 1990, p. 79)

Auguste explains as follows. The air and the light of the sun are very useful things but don't have value. As they are unlimited in quantity, no one possesses them, and therefore no one wants them in the economic sense, since no one is deprived of it. Say says that we don't give anything in order to have what is useless, which is true. We don't give anything either in order to get what we already have and what we are sure to always get.

Auguste concludes:

> Probably, only what is useful can be worth something, and all objects that would be useless, would have therefore no value. However, the utility alone is not sufficient to produce this quality; we need to add here the limitation or the rareté of the useful thing there. This is what I wanted to establish.
> (Walras, A., 1990, p. 79)

Here we must note that Auguste talks about value in terms of possession rather than of exchange. This approach is related to Auguste's intention to criticize Say's political economy on the grounds that it lacks a theory of property based on viewpoints of justice. We shall return to this point later.

Auguste's second objection to Say's utility theory is that value is not relative to utility. The most useful things have, in general, even the least price; and among the things that cost nothing, there is something so useful, so necessary that if we came to be deprived of them, we would die. Such are warmth and air, for example.[5]

Auguste tried to reveal the definitive difference between *rareté* and utility in terms of a ratio. *Rareté* is a ratio that exists between the sum of limited goods and the sum of the needs for their enjoyment. Utility is a ratio of *quality*, while *rareté* is a ratio of *quantity*.[6] With this objective idea of *rareté*, Auguste believed that he could overcome all the errors made by J. B. Say and establish a scientific foundation for property theory.[7]

Say always thought that the utility was the real foundation of the value in exchange and therefore of the social wealth. J.-B. Say never understood that the value in exchange originated from the *rareté* and that the social wealth was composed of rare utilities, of utilities limited in their quantity. In the economic system where he was situated, J.-B.Say could not explain this surplus value that the land acquired, from day to day, in a society that prospers; he could not explain the land owner's continual enrichment to the detriment of the society, which constitutes a real usurpation.

(Walras, A., 1997, p. 72)[8]

Thus Auguste's intention was to use his theory of value as the evidence to reveal the exclusive advantage of land owners in a progressive society. He aimed to present the injustice of the demesne of land and to realize nationalization of land. Auguste claims: "The community of the land is what I intend to establish; what I attack is the individual property" (Walras, A., 1997, p. 46).

Léon Walras on *rareté* at the early stage

According to his Autobiographical Note,[9] Léon started his career as an economist in 1859 by writing *L'Economie Politique et la justice* (1860) helped by his father Auguste's advice. Then he recognized two facts to be demonstrated in pure economics by using mathematics. One is the surplus value of rent in a progressive society and the other is the maximum of utility attained by adopting a free competition system.[10]

This work was intended to criticize Proudhon by showing how the theory of property and that of exchange are related, which suggests the future definition of his pure economics and social economics. In this book, Léon cited his father's conclusive remarks[11] in *De la nature de la Richesse* (1831) on the inequality caused by the increase of the rent and price of land in a progressive society.

> The conclusion that arises by itself is that, in a progressive society, the condition of the land owner becomes more and more convenient, more and more advantageous. Without giving himself the least pain, without having the least sacrifice to make, by the simple effect of the law that I have just indicated, the land owner has the rare advantage to see the exchangeable value of the capital that he possesses increase, and the amount of the income that this possession assures him.
>
> (Walras, L., 2001, p. 243)

Here Léon explains his reasoning in the same way as his father.

The extent of the land to which a society, prosperous or declining, has access, is determined: in any case, we can't increase the supply. The demand for land or its products, on the contrary, increases if the society prospers, and decreases if the society declines. He concludes that in a society that prospers the total value of land and the total amount of its income increase, and that the individual value of the land and their incomes also increase.

In a progressive society, saving gets easier so that the supply of capital increases, they suppose, faster than the increasing demand for it. The total value of capital and the total amount of interest may increase but the individual value of capital and interest will decrease. For the *rareté* of capital decrease and, according to their "Law I" the rate of income (value of interest/value of capital) decreases in a progressive society, which they did not demonstrate sufficiently.

On the other hand, wages are supposed to remain the same, for all people are both producers and consumers. In both cases, in a progressive and a declined society, the supply and demand of labor increases or decreases proportionally.

Thus, in the early stage, Léon followed his father's idea regarding progress. We will see later how Léon Walras applies these laws of value variations in a progressive society in his main work, *Elements of Pure Economics* (the first edition, 1874–77), where the definition of *rareté* is not the same as that of his father.

According to his Autobiographical Note, when Léon participated in the congress on taxation held in Lausanne in July 1860, he showed more clearly his idea of nationalization of land.[12] In "Souvenirs du Congrés de Lausanne" (1861), Léon Walras summarized his father's theory of value in order to explain how it relates to his plan.

> In *De la Nature de la Richesse et de l'Origine de la Valeur*, my father established, in 1831, that the fact of the value in exchange has its reason not in the fact of labor as A. Smith and Ricardo said, not in the fact of the utility as J.-B. Say said, but in the fact of the limitation in the quantity of the useful things. This theory is true, and it is the only theory from which we can conclude that the value in exchange has its measure in the *rareté* or in the ratio of the demand to the supply, which is the sum of the needs to the sum of the provisions.
>
> (Walras, L., 2001, p. 343)

More precisely, Auguste defined *rareté* as the ratio of the number of persons wanting the goods to the total quantity of the goods available. He presumed that each person wants only a single unit of the goods, which, he believed, would maintain the objectivity of that theory. At the same time, he puzzled over its irrelevancy as a price determination theory in mathematical form.

Auguste explains this difficulty to his son in his letter written on May 18, 1861.

> The real difficulty to appreciate the rareté and the market value from which it originates is to notice the needy unit. And here, pay much attention that it is not sufficient to count the number of the human heads or mouths. The population of a country can only provide a very imperfect data to appreciate the rareté and the value in exchange. The heads and the mouths differ under so many relations! The population of a country includes men, women, children, sick people, healthy people, the old and the young. People differ

essentially in their condition, in their fortune, in their character, in their habits, in their virtues and in their vices. A man who drinks a liter of wine per day is equivalent to two men who drink only a half-liter of it ... This is what prevents us from determining the unit of need for all the kinds of goods or commodities consumed in a society ... This is at least what will make it slower and more difficult to apply mathematics to the theory of social wealth.

(Walras, A., 2005, p. 492)

This advice impelled Léon to construct pure economics in mathematical form. It took more than ten years for him to succeed. In 1870, Léon obtained a position at the University of Lausanne (Lausanne Academy) and presented his price theory based on the idea of marginal utility in 1873.

Léon Walras's pure economics

According to his Autobiographical Notice, Léon Walras started to prepare to construct mathematical economics first by studying Cournot's work,[13] which was the only achievement in that field that he knew at that time.[14] However it was Paul Picard, professor of mechanics of the University of Lausanne that finally guided Walras to success by teaching him the principle of maximization.[15] He was a colleague at Lausanne University. The idea of this principle cannot be found in any writings of Walras before Picard's advice[16] and it guided Walras to solve his father's difficult problem by constructing a new price theory based on the idea of "the intensity of the last want satisfied by a quantity possessed." He presented this idea in 1873, which was behind Jevons in presenting the marginal utility theory of value but enabled Walras to found the general equilibrium theory for the first time in the world. He presented it in *Eléments d'Economie Politique Pure*, which was first published in 1874–77.

In the preface of his *Etudes d'Economie Sociale* (1896), Walras expresses his gratitude to Picard.

> I must particularly thank three of my colleagues and friends at the Academy of Lausanne. The first is Mr. Paul Picard, an engineer and former professor of industrial mechanics, whom I have, from the very beginning of my studies, often consulted fruitfully, and who, moreover, first drew my attention to the impact that the increase in the value of the rent,[17] once observed, must have on the price of land.
>
> (Walras, L., 1990, p. 5; Walras, L., 2010, p. liii)

Here we must note that Walras relates Picard's helpful advice directly to his argument on the increasing value of land and rent in a progressive society and therefore to his support of nationalization of land in his social economics. For Léon Walras, the marginal utility is nothing but the developed version of his father's concept of *rareté*. That's why he continued to call the marginal utility *rareté* in his *Eléments*. The intention to establish a just property theory based on this concept remains the same for Léon Walras.

Rareté *in Eléments*

William Jaffé, the English translator of *Eléments* decided to leave Walras's term "rareté" in French and italicize it whenever it is used to denote marginal utility (the intensity of the last want satisfied) for he thought that to translate it into "marginal utility" was "to rob the text of its characteristic Walrasian flavour."[18] Only when "rareté" is used in the ordinary literary sense, did he translate it into "scarcity."

Jaffé's translation gives us the clue to identify August's idea of *rareté* in Léon's pure economics, which is translated into "scarcity" and to see how it is related to the latter's "rareté" (marginal utility).

In the preface of the fourth edition of *Eléments*, we can find the definition of pure economics:

> Pure economics is, in essence, the theory of the determination of prices under a hypothetical régime of perfectly free competition. The sum total of all things, material or immaterial, on which a price can be set because they are scarce i.e. both useful and limited in quantity, constitutes social wealth. Hence pure economics is also the theory of social wealth.
> (Walras, L., 1988, p. 11; Walras, L., 1954, p. 40)

Walras claims that scarcity can have a scientific meaning by comparing it to the word "*velocity*" in mechanics and the word "heat" in physics.

> To the mathematician slowness means only less velocity: to the physicist cold means less heat.... In the same way, scarcity and abundance are not opposed for our purposes. In political economy, however abundant a thing maybe, it is scarce whenever it is useful and limited in quantity, just as in mechanics a body has velocity whenever it travels a given distance within a given time.
> (Walras, L., 1988, p. 46; Walras, L., 1954, pp. 65–66)

Here Walras derives from this scientific concept of scarcity three consequences.

1. Useful things limited in quantity are appropriable.
2. Useful things limited in quantity are valuable and exchangeable.
3. Useful things limited in quantity can be produced and multiplied by industry.

These three consequences are related to his three divisions of economics. Walras explains that value in exchange; industry and property are respectively the purposes of his pure, applied, and social economics.

It is important to note that Walras sticks to the idea of his father's *rareté* when he defines his economics even after establishing his general equilibrium theory. This drives us to the question of what Léon Walras thinks about the continuity between his and his father's *raretés*.

In "Principe d'une Théorie Mathèmatique de l'échange: Correspondance entre M. Jevons and M. Walras" (1874), Walras referred to this question when he showed that values in exchange are proportional to the *raretés*.

> It was the theory of my late father and my master that the rareté is the cause of the value in exchange. He had exposed it since 1831 in his work titled: *De la nature de la richesse et de l'origin de la value*.... My father defined the rareté by the double condition of the utility and the limitation in the quantity. However, I would like to note that the rareté defined as such is identical rigorously to the rareté that we have here, in other words, the intensity of the last want satisfied. There could not be indeed a last want satisfied if there were no want, if the commodity had neither extensive nor intensive utility, if it were useless. Moreover the intensity of the last want satisfied need would be zero if the commodity, which possessed a utility curve, existed in quantity superior to the extensive utility, if it was unlimited in quantity. My rareté is therefore the same as my father's rareté.
>
> (Walras, L., 1987, pp. 278–279)

Then Léon adds as the difference between the two concepts the fact that his idea of *rareté* is taken to be a measurable magnitude and proportionate to the value in exchange. Thus Léon Walras tries to show the identity of the two ideas of rareté. We can say that his intention was to improve his father's idea of *rareté* as a measuring concept by introducing the subjective approach based on marginal utility. His main purpose was not to deny his father's objective approach but to try to retain it by calling it "rareté" for he believed that objectivity was one of the necessary conditions that provides theoretical grounds for their property theory. We may say that it was rather accidental for him to introduce the idea of marginal utility thanks to his colleague's advice for this theoretical refinement.

Progressive society

In this section, we will see how Léon showed the laws of price variations in a progressive society, which he took over from his father, in Lesson 36 of *Eléments* (the fourth edition). Here Walras defines progress as "a diminution in the intensities of last want satisfied, i.e., in the *raretés* of final products, in a country with an increasing population."[19] Thus Walras uses *rareté* as the marginal utility in this discussion.

At the beginning of this part, Walras mentions the principle of the proportionality of the values of goods and services to their *raretés* in general equilibrium, which he has already demonstrated in the former parts of this book and proceeds to the law of the variation of equilibrium prices when *raretés* vary by reason of changes in the utilities or in the initial quantities possessed.

Walras continues:

> quantity of land cannot possibly increase though it is possible to increase the number of persons and the quantity of capital goods proper in an economy that saves and converts its savings into capital. We propose now, to reduce the consequences of this fact to a certain number of laws that are essential to the completion of the theory of the determination of prices in terms of numéraire. These are the laws of the variation of prices in a progressive society.
>
> (Walras, L. 1988, p. 584; Walras, L., 1954, p. 382)

Here we must pay attention to the title of this lesson "The Marginal Productivity Theorem. Increase of the quantity of products. The Law of General Price Movements in a Progressive Society."[20] It was from the fourth edition that Walras uses the marginal productivity theory for this discussion, which enabled him to introduce the idea of factor substitution. He presumes that the indefinite multiplication of products can only take place to the extent that capital services can be substituted more and more for land services though never wholly replacing them. We can say that this is one of the striking differences from his father's discussion about progress.

In this part, Walras mentions two sorts of progress; economic progress and technical progress and he concentrates on the former case. The former he defines as the case where only the magnitudes of the coefficients of production change as the coefficients representing the use of land-services decrease while those representing the use of capital-service increase. The latter he defines as the case where a change takes place in the very nature of the coefficients of production as additional technical coefficients are introduced while others are abandoned.

The diminution in the *raretés* of final products along with an increase in population is possible in spite of the failure of the quantity of land to increase, thanks to the increase in the quantity of capital goods proper, if this increase in the quantity of capital goods proper proceeds and is proportionately greater than the increase in population.[21]

Then Walras shows the price variations in a progressive society as follows.

I Prices of Products. The *rareté* necessarily fall in a progressive society. Prices, which are the ration of these *raretés* to the *raretés* of the commodity serving as the numeraire, can remain constant under the assumption that the *raretés* of the commodity serving as the numeraire also diminish in the same proportion.

II Prices of Services. In order to describe his idea of progress, he assumes that every member of the original economy will replaced, at the end of a certain period of time, by two members of the new economy. Each of them will possess (1) the same utility curves, (2) half the same land, (3) the same personal faculties unchanged in amount, and (4) such a proportionately greater quantity of the same capital goods proper as is necessary to enable entrepreneurs utilizing the original quantity of land and land-services and twice the amount of personal faculties and labor to produce at least twice as much of each of the products. Consequently, each of them will consume (1) half the same land-services, (2) an unchanged amount of the same personal services, (3) a quantity proportionately greater of the same services of capital goods proper, and (4) at least an equal quantity of the same products as before.

Consequently, the new equilibrium will be attained with variations of the prices of services as follows: "In a progressive society, the prices of labor [wages] remaining substantially unchanged, the prices of land-services [rent] will rise appreciably and the prices of capital-services [the interest charge] will fall appreciably" (Walras, L., 1988, p. 597; Walras, L., 1954, pp. 390–391).

III Rate of Net Income and Prices of Capital Proper and Land. If the prices of their services (the interest charge) fall appreciably as is shown above, while their own price, which is equal to their costs of production, remains constant, the rate of net income will fall appreciably.

As shown in the theory of Capital Formation and Credit of this book, the rate of net income is given by the ratio of the net interest charge to the price of capital proper. Once the rate of net income has been found, it is possible to calculate the prices of land by dividing this rate into rents. As rents increase, the price of land will rise.

Then Walras concludes: "In a progressive society, the price of capital goods proper remaining constant, the price of land will rise both by reason of the fall in the net income and by reason of the rise in rent" (Walras, L., 1988, p. 597; Walras, L., 1954, p. 391). At the end of this part, Léon summarizes:

> The truth is that progressive rise in the values of land and its services, which may take place without necessarily bringing about an increase in the value of its products, goes along with the expansion of capital and population, the essential characteristic of economic progress. By clearly demonstrating this truth, pure economics sheds as much light on social economics, as in other respects, it sheds on applied economics.
> (Walras, L., 1988, p. 598; Walras, L., 1954, p. 391–392)

Léon's evaluation of his pure economics in his later years[22] shows how he intended to reach the same conclusion as his father regarding the laws of price variations in a progressive society by using his new concept of *rareté* in pure economics. It gives him theoretical grounds for the support of nationalization of land.

> The pure economics provides us, at the same time, the means of a practical realization of the justice and the economic interest. The value is proportional

to the *rareté*. However, the *rareté* and the value of the land constantly increases with the social progress. Therefore, as Gossen saw it, it is possible for the State, in a progressive society to purchase little by little all the lands while paying off the purchase price thanks to the increase of the farm rent.

(Walras, L., 1987, p. 509)

"A consequence of the highest gravity that the economy pure mathematical formula is this: In a progressive society, the rent of the lands, whose quantity doesn't increase, rises appreciably" (Walras, L., 1987, p. 513). It enables his pure economics to give a basis for realizing not only effectiveness but also equity, which he longed for since his younger days.

Object of pure economics

As we have already seen, Auguste criticized J. B. Say mainly because his political economy lacks the viewpoint of social justice. In *Eléments*, we can also find Léon's critiques of the definition of Say's political economy. In the first part "Object and Division of Political and Social Economy," he points out that Say's political economy provides no room for discussing justice and social reform. Walras constructed pure economics, which is considered to be science that elucidates the natural laws of value in exchange, but he argues that all the domains of political economy should not be classified as pure natural science.

According to Walras, Say's definition of political economy[23] supposes that the production, distribution, and consumption of wealth take place in a manner somehow independent of the will of man and as though political economy consists entirely of a simple exposition of this manner of production, distribution, and consumption. He continues:

> What has proved so pleasing and at the same time, so misleading to economists in this definition is precisely its characterization of the whole political economy as a natural science pure and simple. Such a viewpoint was particularly useful to them in their controversy with the socialists. Every proposal to reorganize production, every proposal to redistribute property was rejected a priori and practically without discussion, not on the grounds that such plans were contrary to economic well-being or to social justice, but simply because they were artificial arrangement designed to replace what was natural.
> (Walras, L., 1988, p. 30; Walras, L., 1954, p. 55)

Walras claims that man is a creature endowed with reason and freedom, and possessed of a capacity for initiative and progress. Therefore, in the production and distribution of wealth, and in all matters pertaining to social organization, a man who has the choice between better and worse tends to choose the better part. That is why Walras divided his economics into three parts: pure economics, social economics, and applied economics. Among these three, social economics is considered to be a moral science that deals with distribution and property based on the viewpoint of justice.

> How could political economy be simultaneously a natural science and a moral science? How is such a science to be understood? On one hand, we have a moral science the aim of which is to determine how wealth ought to be distributed as equitably as possible; and on the other hand, we have a natural science the aim of which is to determine how wealth is produced as naturally as possible.... We shall undertake to look for it on our own account. If necessary we shall divide political economy into a natural science, a moral science and an art. To this end we shall first of all distinguish between science, art and ethics.
> (Walras, L., 1988, p. 33; Walras, L., 1954, pp. 56–57)

Conclusion

For Léon Walras, the most important purpose of pure economics was to demonstrate the laws of price variations in a progressive society, more precisely, the exclusive increase of the price of land and rent with economic progress, an idea which he took over from his father Auguste. He also sticks to his father's belief that Say's subjective utility theory of value cannot be a theoretical coherent basis for social justice and continued to call his idea of marginal utility "rareté." Contrary to the general interpretation, Walras's intention to introduce the idea of marginal utility was not to deny his father's objective approach to theory of value but to retain the objectivity of theory of value to present it as a theoretical basis for their support of the nationalization of land.

By reaching the subjective approach of marginal utility of value, Léon Walras succeeded in constructing the general equilibrium theory and demonstrating the efficiency of absolute free competition based on the principle of maximization of satisfaction. This gives him a theoretical basis for the argument of efficiency but his main purpose is to construct an economic system, where efficiency and justice are compatible. In order to attain this purpose, Walras had to demonstrate not only efficiency by using the static general equilibrium model but also complete the theoretical basis for justice by presenting the dynamic laws of price variations in a progressive society.

These two parts in *Eléments* were the subject of controversy of Jaffé and Morishima.[24] They focused on the question of which part in *Eléments* is more essential, the static general equilibrium part or the dynamic part arguing progress. Jaffé considered that the former part was essential by pointing out the normativeness existing in Walras's pure economics model while Morishima highly esteemed the latter part arguing that Walras's intention is to construct a positive model for scientific description of the reality. We may conclude that both researchers ignored Walras's real political and philosophical intention. Jaffé underestimates the significance of Walras's social economics and the incentives that it gave Walras to construct pure economics; on the contrary, Morishima evaluated the importance of the dynamic part of *Eléments* only from the theoretical viewpoints. He suggested the influence of Ricardo and its possible developments into Keynes.

We must note that if we concentrate on the formation process of Walras's general equilibrium model without paying attention to the scientific program of his pure, social, and applied economics, we will lose Walras's most important intention: the compatibility of efficiency and justice. Unfortunately, unlike his pure economics, his applied and social economics are unfinished. We must not forget that our modern neoclassical tradition is based on this limited heritage of Walras's contribution.

Notes

1. This research was supported by a grant from the Japan Society for the Promotions of Science (JSPS).
2. On the contrary, Jaffé (1972, 1976) points out the difference between Walras and the other two marginalists, Menger and Jevons. He shows that Walras's main purpose was to construct the general equilibrium theory and that the marginal utility theory of value was a collateral idea. Jaffé argues "Instead of climbing up from marginal utility to the level of his general equilibrium system, Walras actually climbed down from that level to marginal utility" (Jaffé, 1972, p. 313). We share the same view as Jaffé on this point. However, we believe that Jaffé overemphasizes the importance of general equilibrium as Walras's contribution, and pays little attention to the significance of Walras's social economics and his analysis of a progressive society related to the idea of *rareté*, which we will focus more on in this chapter.
3. Schumpeter, 1994, pp. 234, 828.
4. Walras, L., 1990, pp. 28–29.
5. Walras, A., 1990, p. 134.
6. Walras, A., 1990, p. 205.
7. Concerning this point, Jaffé explains that

    > being of a philosophical frame of mind, and no doubt influenced by the attacks of the socialists of his day on the legitimacy of private property, he sought a more logically coherent basis than the socialists had to offer for drawing the line between public property and private property.
    >
    > (1972, p. 298)

    Cirillo also points out that

    > it was Say who reasoned that utility was the motive force of economic activity and the strongest incentive for the accumulation of wealth. Auguste Walras could not accept this view; otherwise he would have had to justify the existence of private property (and wealth) on purely subjective grounds. The utility concept was based on self-interest, but the institution of private property had to be analyzed from the point of view of social justice.
    >
    > (1981, pp. 311–312)

8. This text is Auguste's manuscript titled "La verité sociale par un travailleur" (1848). Although he was preparing it for his property theory part of *Théorie de la richesse sociale* (1849), he never published this part.
9. Walras, L., 2001, p. 12.
10. The demonstration of these two facts composes the contrastive parts of *Elements of Pure Economics*, which gave rise to the argument of Jaffé and Morishima. On this subject, see Misaki (1999).

11 Walras, A., 1997, p. 155.
12 Walras, L., 2001, p. 12.
13 In the preface of *Eléments d'économie politique pure*, Walras refers to the influence of Cournot and his father but never to that of Paul Picard.
14 Walras, L., 2001, p. 16.
15 According to Jaffé, Léon Walras had to wait until Picard pointed the way because of Léon Walras's inadequate mathematical training (Jaffé, 1972, p. 305). We are not concerned here with the detail of the formation process of Walras's mathematical price theory before Picard. For this purpose, we must investigate the manuscripts entitled "Application des mathématiques à l'économie politique (1e tentative 1860)," "Application des mathématiques à l'économie politique (2e tentative 1869–1870)," "Application des mathématiques à l'économie politique (3e tentative-1871)." These texts are included in Walras, L. (1993). Concerning this subject, see Jolink (1991).
16 See the editor's notice in Walras, L., 1990, p. 426.
17 This word originally is the French word "la rente." It is translated into the English words "the produce of land" in Walras, L., 2010, p. liii. The translator points out that it means "the service of land not an amount of money" in Note x in p. liv.
18 Walras, L., 1954, p. 506.
19 Walras, L., 1988, p. 585; Walras, L., 1954, p. 383.
20 Jaffé translated the words "société progressive" in the original version into "progressive economy."
21 Walras, L., 1988, p. 592; Walras, L., 1954, p. 387.
22 "Ruchonnet et le socialism scientifique, Jublié" (1909).
23 Here Walras refers to the title of Say's main work (1803); *Traité d'économie politique, ou simple exposition de la maniére dont se forment, se distribuent ou se consomment les richesses*.
24 Jaffé (1980), Morishima (1977, 1980).

References

Cirillo, R. (1981) "The Influence of Auguste Walras on Léon Walras," *American Journal of Economics and Sociology*, 40(3): 309–316.
Jaffé, W. (1972) "Léon Walras's Role in the 'Marginal Revolution' of the 1870s," *History of Political Economy*, 4(2): 379–405, reprinted in D. A. Walker (ed.) (1983) *William Jaffé's Essays on Walras*, Cambridge, London, New York, Nes Rochelle, Melbourne and Sydney: Cambridge University Press.
Jaffé, W. (1976) "Menger, Jevons and Walras De-Homogenized," *Economic Inquiry*, 14(4): 511–524, reprinted in D. A. Walker (ed.) (1983) *William Jaffé's Essays on Walras*, Cambridge, London, New York, Nes Rochelle, Melbourne and Sydney: Cambridge University Press.
Jaffé, W. (1980) "Walras's Economics as Others See It," *Journal of Economic Literature*, 18(2): 528–549, reprinted in D. A. Walker (ed.) (1983) *William Jaffé's Essays on Walras*, Cambridge, London, New York, Nes Rochelle, Melbourne and Sydney: Cambridge University Press.
Jolink, A. (1991) *Liberté, Egalité, Rareté: The Evolutionary Economics of Léon Walras*, Thesis, Amsterdam: Tinbergen Instituut.
Misaki, K. (1999) "Walras on General Equilibrium in a Progressive Economy," *Revue européenne des sciences sociales*, 47(116): 73–81.
Morishima, M. (1977) *Walras's Economics: A Pure Theory of Capital and Money*, Cambridge: Cambridge University Press.

Morishima, M. (1980) "W. Jaffé on Léon Walras: A Comment," *Journal of Economic Literature*, 18(2): 550–558.

Say, J.-B. (2006) *Traité d'économie politique, ou simple exposition de la maniére dont se forment, se distribuent ou se consomment les richesses, Jean-Baptiste Say Œuvres Complètes*, Emmanuel Blanc, Pierre-Henri Goutte, Gilles Jacoud, Claude Mouchot, Jean-Pierre Potier, Michèle Saquin, Jean-Michel Servet, Philipe Steiner, and André Tiran (eds.), t.I, Paris, Economica.

Schumpeter, J. A. ([1954]1994) *History of Economic Analysis*, with a new introduction by Mark Perlman, New York: Oxford University Press.

Walras, Auguste (1990) *Richesse, Liberté et Société, Auguste et Léon Walras Œuvre Economique Complètes*, Pierre Dockès, Pierre-Henri Goutte, Claude Hébert, Claude Mouchot, Jean-Pierre Potier, and Jean-Michel Servet (eds.), t.I, Paris: Economica.

Walras, Auguste (1997) *La Vérité Sociale, Auguste et Léon Walras Œuvre Economique Complètes*, Pierre Dockès, Pierre-Henri Goutte, Claude Hébert, Claude Mouchot, Jean-Pierre Potier, and Jean-Michel Servet (eds.), t.II, Paris: Economica.

Walras, Auguste (2005) *Correspondence, Auguste et Léon Walras Œuvre Economique Complètes*, Pierre Dockès, Pierre-Henri Goutte, Claude Hébert, Claude Mouchot, Jean-Pierre Potier, and Jean-Michel Servet (eds.), t.IV, Paris: Economica.

Walras, Léon (1954) *Elements of Pure Economics or the Theory of Social Wealth*, trans. W. Jaffé, London: George Allen & Unwin Ltd.

Walras, Léon (1987) *Mélanges d'Economie Politique et Sociale, Auguste et Léon Walras Œuvre Economique Complètes*, Pierre Dockès, Pierre-Henri Goutte, Claude Hébert, Claude Mouchot, Jean-Pierre Potier, and Jean-Michel Servet (eds.), t.VII, Paris: Economica.

Walras, Léon (1988) *Eléments d'Economie Politique Pure, Auguste et Léon Walras Œuvre Economique Complètes*, Pierre Dockès, Pierre-Henri Goutte, Claude Hébert, Claude Mouchot, Jean-Pierre Potier, and Jean-Michel Servet (eds.), t.VIII, Paris: Economica.

Walras, Léon (1990) *Etudes d'Economie Sociale, Auguste et Léon Walras Œuvre Economique Complètes*, Pierre Dockès, Pierre-Henri Goutte, Claude Hébert, Claude Mouchot, Jean-Pierre Potier, and Jean-Michel Servet (eds.), t.IX, Paris: Economica.

Walras, Léon (1993) *Théorie Mathématique de la Richesse Sociale et Autres Ecrits d'Economie Pure, Auguste et Léon Walras Œuvre Economique Complètes*, Pierre Dockès, Pierre-Henri Goutte, Claude Hébert, Claude Mouchot, Jean-Pierre Potier, and Jean-Michel Servet (eds.), t.XI, Paris: Economica.

Walras, Léon ([1860]2001) *L'Economie Politique et La Justice, Auguste et Léon Walras Œuvre Economique Complètes*, Pierre Dockès, Pierre-Henri Goutte, Claude Hébert, Claude Mouchot, Jean-Pierre Potier, and Jean-Michel Servet (eds.), t.V, Paris: Economica.

Walras, Léon (2010) *Studies in Social Economics*, trans. J. Daal and D. A. Walker, London and New York: Routledge.

5 Austrian subjectivism and hermeneutical economics

Yuichi Shionoya

Introduction

This chapter intends to show that hermeneutical thinking could provide the philosophical foundation for a formulation of economics that serves as an alternative to current mainstream economics. The key figures in hermeneutics – also known as the philosophy of interpretation – are Dilthey (1883), Heidegger (1927), and Gadamer (1960); depending on the continental traditions of philosophy, these key figures have claimed that hermeneutics is the ontological basis of historical, social, and human sciences, each of which is distinct from the natural sciences. In hermeneutical thinking, ontology explores the meaning, significance, and value of entities as objects of knowledge; it also determines the orientation and perspective of that knowledge. This chapter argues that the best source for hermeneutical economics could be found in the development of Austrian subjectivism, in which the interaction of Austrian philosophy and Austrian economics builds a genuine foundation for the social sciences.

To clarify, subjectivism is viewed here from the three perspectives of economics, psychology, and philosophy, and these perspectives deal with the subjectivism of desire, cognition, and interpretation, respectively. The subjectivism of interpretation is the proper standpoint of hermeneutics, vis-à-vis philosophy; the subjectivism of desire and of cognition, meanwhile, belong to particular sciences, that is, economics and psychology, respectively. In view of the recently proliferating field of behavioral economics, the issue of the relevance of psychology to economics must be examined from the hermeneutical perspective, in order to complete the subjectivist trinity of economics, psychology, and philosophy – although, admittedly, it is not fully discussed here, owing to space limitations.

This chapter begins with an ontological analysis of Menger's (1923) economics in terms of alternative sets of basic concepts, forms of economy, and directions of economics. Menger unintentionally paved the way to a hermeneutical grasp of economy, which was later demonstrated by Polanyi (1971). In fact, some contemporary Austrian economists, including Ebeling (1986), Lachmann (1990), and Lavoie (1990), among others, advocate the possibility of hermeneutical economics.

The fundamental contention of Austrian subjectivism is that social-science explanations must begin with the subjective mental states of the actors under investigation (Horwitz 1994). The thrust of contemporary Austrian subjectivism is driven by its major concerns regarding time, expectation, and uncertainty; as such, it provides a unique meeting place for economics and philosophy in discussing the possibility of hermeneutical economics. Hermeneutics in Austrian economics involve a series of notions such as meaning, expectation, conjecture, knowledge, interpretation, and time, where external social phenomena are interpreted in terms of subjective perceptions and individual plans.

It is argued, however, that for hermeneutical economics to work, it requires more than the mere subjective aspects of individuals; it also needs an institutional framework and social values, neither of which is reducible to subjectivity. Moreover, the subjectivism of desires should be distinguished from the subjectivism of interpretation: the former has been customarily developed as a subjective economic theory following the Marginal Revolution, while the latter involves yet-to-be developed meta-economic theory. Hermeneutical economics is not economic theory but meta-economic theory or economic philosophy. It is further argued that hermeneutical economics will invoke the time horizon, which is the crucial viewpoint of the subjectivism of interpretation. The received view of time in economics (i.e., the superiority of the present) contrasts with Heidegger's future-oriented conception of time, as developed in his *Sein und Zeit* (1927). The time horizon for the decision making of an ontological self in hermeneutics covers the past, present, and future, with the utmost emphasis placed on the future.

To trace the hermeneutical moments of the Austrian School of economics, we examined the relevance of Franz Brentano, the Austrian philosopher whose phenomenology of intentionality gave rise not only to insights into Husserl and Heidegger, but also cohesion among a group of Austrian economists.

Following a short introduction to hermeneutics, our discussion touches upon the idea that Heidegger's thought is compatible with that of Schumpeter, the unique economist of Austrian origin, if both are compared from a hermeneutical perspective. To develop hermeneutical economics, we sought to integrate Heidegger's philosophical propositions with Schumpeter's economic and sociological ones, to obtain what might be called the "Heidegger=Schumpeter theses." These theses are concerned with various aspects of the "projection" (*Entwurf*) and "thrownness" (*Geworfenheit*) of the self, and of innovation and tradition in society. The latter half of this chapter draws upon my previous paper (Shionoya 2010).

Menger's ontology and its interpretation

According to Menger's *Grundsätze der Volkswirtschaftslehre* (second revised edition 1923), the basic nature of economy is explained from the following aspects: the "ultimate ground" of economy is human desire, the "ultimate measure" of economy is the significance of desire satisfaction for us, and the "ultimate goal" of economy is the provision of desire satisfaction (1923: 1).

The core of Menger's economic theory consists of three basic concepts: goods, desires, and values. He defines the relationships among them by using a single, concise phrase: "Values are the significance that concrete goods or its quantity acquired for us through our recognition that the satisfaction of our desires depends on the disposal of concrete goods or its quantity" (1923: 103, my translation). For Menger, an inquiry into the nature of economy amounts to conceiving of the values, significance, and meaning of economy. To use the terminology of Heidegger, this is no less than an "ontological" inquiry into the objects of economic research, whereas a study of their *modus operandi* (economics proper) is an "ontical" inquiry. To use Brentano's terminology, the values, significance, and meaning of an object exist only within the "intentionality," which is exclusively a mental phenomenon addressed to the object or entity in question; no physical phenomenon exhibits anything like it. Those factors that carry the intentionality in the economic world are human desires. Even if physical goods exist as the objects of external perception, they do not raise any economic problems unless they are the objects of human intentionality. Menger's ontology of economy was to fix the objects and themes of economic inquiry through the act of intentionality.

It is our interpretation that Menger's ontology consists of three dimensions: (A) the theory of desires, (B) two forms of economy, and (C) two directions of economic theory.

With regard to (A) – the concept of desires as the ground of economy – there are two notable points. First, Menger emphasizes that the actual pattern of human desires, including emotion, impulse, and appetite, should not be taken for granted, because human nature relates to the maintenance and development of "life and welfare," and desires must be correspondingly harmonious. For him, the concept of desires is an ideal and a type of normativity. Thus, he writes:

> In accordance with the complicated psychological-physical organization and the higher spiritual disposition of human beings, the economy of human being can find an appropriate ground only in the knowledge of human desires, i.e. the requirements for the maintenance and harmonious development of human nature as a whole.
>
> (Menger 1923: 3, my translation)

> Human desires are not a product of arbitrariness but given by the situation where we are located.... Human desires are not a product of invention; they must be discovered and therefore become an object of our cognitive effort. Thus, fallacy, ignorance, and passion affect and cloud the correct knowledge of desires, hinder and delay its progress.
>
> (Menger 1923: 4, my translation)

Menger, however, does not discuss in detail what the "true desires" (*wahre Bedürfnisse*) are, beyond the cursory remarks that knowledge and judgments of desires will become reasonable as human cognition progresses. Nonetheless, his normative idea of "true desires" is a touchstone in interpreting Austrian subjectivism as hermeneutics.

Second, while in the first edition of *Grundsätze* (1871) Menger considers the relation between goods and desires a "causal relationship," he revised the explanation in the second edition by identifying it as a "teleological relationship" (1923: 20–3). Although it is certain that there is a relation between goods and the satisfaction of desire, this relation implies that appropriate goods are chosen as a means to achieve the end, when the assumed end-and-means relations are subjectively given. In my view, the relation between goods and the satisfaction of desire in economy is better described as a "teleological causality," to distinguish it from both philosophical teleology and mechanical causality in physical phenomenon.

Thus, for Menger, economic theory is not an arbitrary construct of the human mind; rather, it helps discover and describe the essential structure of desires and the end-and-means relations in the economic world. Nonetheless, the ground of economic phenomena is not psychology and feelings as they actually exist. The object of economic theory, that is, economy based on true desires, is of an ideal type. Since the causes of economic phenomena comprise the teleological consciousness of human beings, economy cannot be presented in a mathematical form that describes the interrelationships among observable factors. Concerning the nature of Menger's economic theory, several interpretations have been proposed: Nakayama (1926) calls it "causal theory," in contrast with the "interdependent theory" of Walras's general equilibrium theory; Kauder (1957) calls it "philosophical realism," referencing Aristotle; and Hutchison (1981) calls it "methodological essentialism," referencing Popper. These plural labels point to the uniqueness of Menger's subjectivism, which is still in dispute. My interpretation is inclined toward yet another direction: hermeneutical thinking on the lines of Austrian philosophy. Before moving to the main theme, it is necessary to consider parts (B) and (C) of Menger's ontology.

That Menger's subjectivism is based on true desires as an ideal type is clarified by his argument regarding (B), the two forms of economy. He distinguishes between the "technical direction" (*technische Richtung*) and the "efficient or economizing direction" (*sparende oder ökonomisierende Richtung*) of resource allocation, as the two alternative forms of economy. The "efficient direction" of economy is a type of resource allocation that aims to realize true desires and is governed by economic rationality and efficiency. On the other hand, the "technical direction" of economy similarly utilizes resources and technology, but is characterized by "fallacy, ignorance, and lack of will, especially non-economic purposes that human beings pursue in combination with economic activity" (1923: 78–9, my translation). "Fallacy, ignorance, and lack of will" are the disturbing factors governed by emotion, impulse, and appetite, and they must be eliminated to discover the true desires. Although Menger treated the "technical direction" negatively, we find here possibilities of other forms of economy, including precapitalist and welfare-state economies, that transcend efficiency-oriented resource allocation.

These matters also relate to his discussion of (C), the two directions of economic theory. In his methodological work *Untersuchungen* (1883), Menger classifies theoretical economics into exact and empirical-realistic economics, warning against confusing the two.

> Exact economics by nature has to make us aware of the *laws of economic efficiency* [*die Gesetze der Wirtschaftlichkeit*], whereas empirical-realistic economics has to make us aware of the regularities in the succession and coexistence of the *real* phenomena of human economy (which, indeed, in their "full empirical reality" also contain numerous elements of *non-economic-efficiency* [*Unwirtschaftlichkeit*]!).
> (Menger 1883: 59; 1985: 72–3)

Since empirical-realistic economics records multiple realities without using theoretical abstractions or deductive formulations, it can address those phenomena that are outside the paradigm of economic efficiency.

It follows that Menger's entire perspective consists of two alternative series for the three dimensions of (A), (B), and (C): first is the main series (i.e., true desires: efficient resource allocation: laws of efficiency in exact economics), and second is the subsidiary series (real desires: non-efficient resource allocation: regularity of phenomena in empirical-realistic economics). Menger's concern in *Grundsätze* was with the exact economics of efficient resource allocation, based on the ideal type of true desires. In contrast, the interests of non-mainstream economics based on romanticism, historicism, and hermeneutics have been devoted to the life-world (*Lebenswelt*) with a full range of the human mind, rather than to the theoretical world created by reason and rationality. This corresponds exactly to the subject matter of Menger's subsidiary series.

Mainstream economic theory, in retaining Menger's main series, has not deeply considered the meaning of "true desires"; rather, it has simply accepted the given desires and developed a link between efficiency postulates and formal models. Moreover, mainstream economics definitely discarded concerns with multifarious psychological aspects of human behavior, reflecting the growth of behaviorism in the early twentieth century. However, Menger's alternative, albeit subsidiary, perspective of economics provided the Austrian School with room for various distinct attempts at non-mainstream economic theorizing.

Menger's alternative perspectives seemed to remain sterile for some time. It was Polanyi (1971), the economic anthropologist, who revived Menger's idea of the two directions of economy. According to Polanyi, Menger in his revision of *Grundsätze* had tried to include the non-market economy – usually the subject matter of history, anthropology, and sociology – by using the term "technical direction" of economy. Polanyi stepped forward to define the non-market economy in terms of "reciprocity" and "redistribution."

The conditions of economic efficiency, based on a scarcity of resources on one hand and the conditions of technical necessity for the maintenance of life on the other, are not necessarily equal. The term "economic" has two meanings:

formal and substantive (Polanyi 1977: ch. 2). For human beings to live, it is substantively necessary to acquire and produce goods. Managing the efficiency of production and consumption is a secondary formal issue. Under the assumption that a market economy is a social and cultural pattern, the formal meaning of economy (rational choice under scarcity) becomes the organizing principle of economy in its substantive meaning (maintenance of life); in this way, the two meanings become equal. However, in the non-market economy, the postulates of scarcity and life can diverge. "Reciprocity" and "redistribution" represent the patterns of social integration in a non-market system, in contrast to "market transaction" in the market system. Menger's ontology cast a light on the gap between economy and economization; it also disclosed the possibility of alternative non-market social systems and alternative non-exact economic theories.

Austrian economics and Austrian philosophy

A strategy to ascertain the hermeneutical moments in Austrian subjectivism is to examine the relationship between the Austrian School of economics and the Austrian School of philosophy, in their formative period at the end of the nineteenth century; the former includes Menger, Böhm-Bawerk, and Wieser, while the latter includes Brentano, Meinong, and Ehrenfels. The linkage between the two schools was the theory of values; indeed, they are called "two Austrian schools of values" (Rescher 1969: 30).

In contrast with German philosophy, Austrian philosophy in general was empirical, realistic, and objective; it also kept a close relation with the empirical sciences, including the social sciences, through contact with the growing science of psychology (Smith 1994: 1–5). Austrian empirical philosophy took two discrete directions. One is the quantitative and natural scientific direction, which was to come to fruition in the shape of the logical positivism represented by Mach. Another direction, led by Brentano, made much of the distinction between mental and physical phenomena according to whether or not intentionality exists; it also assumed universal and qualitative regularities for structured mental phenomena as a whole. It is this latter direction of Austrian philosophy with which we are concerned here.

Brentano was born in Germany and taught at the University of Vienna, mentoring a number of able scientists, including Husserl. He attempted a new type of empirical psychology as a basis of scientific philosophy and forged the concept of "intentionality": all mental phenomena have the property of the intentional reference to an object, while no physical phenomena have this property (Brentano 1874). In place of the traditional pattern of mental phenomena, that is, "presentations, feeling, and will," he proposed an alternative one – "presentations, judgments, and emotions of love and hate" – by uniting feeling and will into one category of "love and hate" or affirmation and negation in value judgments. In the field of psychology, Brentano's "descriptive psychology" was opposed to Wundt's "experimental psychology." Because the concept of intentionality is meant to emphasize the intentional reference of individuals to an external world, Brentano's psychology is called "act psychology," in comparison with Wundt's "content psychology," which explains mental phenomena as physiological phenomena related to sense factors. Brentano's thinking influenced the phenomenology and hermeneutics of Husserl and Heidegger, beyond the field of psychology. Dilthey, one of the modern proponents of hermeneutics, laid Brentano's psychology as the foundation of the human sciences.

Austrian subjectivism originated in Franz Brentano's psychologism, and his idea of intentionality was developed as the core concept of the subjectivism of both Austrian philosophy and economics. Concurrent with the rise of the Brentano school of Austrian subjective philosophy, the earliest achievement of subjectivism in economics was the subjective theory of value by Menger. Brentano's and Menger's schools were linked by the theory of values, which was supported by psychology as a science that deals with valuating an act of intentionality. The theory of values in philosophy involves an ethics of "good" (*Gut*), whereas the theory of values in economics involves a theory of "goods" (*Gütter*). The former concerns intrinsic good as an end, whereas the latter concerns extrinsic good as a means; both are combined by an end-and-means relationship and are engaged in the intentionality of valuation.

The philosophical background of the Austrian school of economics has been most often attributed to Aristotle's essentialism (Smith 1994). Although we take no issue with this interpretation, it seems more natural to regard Austrian economics as having been influenced directly by Brentano's psychology. Aristotelian influence, if any, might have been exerted on Austrian economists through contemporary Austrian philosophers, especially their leader Brentano, the Aristotelian. Among the trio of the early Austrian School of economics, Böhm-Bawerk most explicitly stated a dependence on Austrian psychology. In the second volume of his *Positive Theorie des Kapitales* (1921), entitled *Exkurse* (addendum) to the first volume, Böhm-Bawerk gave further explanations and detailed references on the major propositions presented in the first volume. There are frequent references to Austrian philosophers such as Brentano, Ehrenfels, Kraus, and Meinong.

Although Austrian subjective economics in its formative period was developed under the influence of Brentano's philosophy, it has not assimilated the subsequent achievements of Austrian subjective philosophy. This chapter urges a reconsideration of the possibility of Austrian economics in light of hermeneutics, which has been ultimately established in the development of Austrian subjectivism. The key to this reconsideration will be found in a fanciful dialogue between Heidegger and Schumpeter.

Husserl (1913), a pupil of Brentano, criticized his teacher's psychologism and developed phenomenology as an approach to philosophy to extract the essence from the intuitive experience of phenomena. However, he accepted Brentano's notion of intentionality: the notion that the characteristic of consciousness is always intentional and subjective. Heidegger developed Husserl's phenomenology, which was no more than the study of consciousness, into ontology, the study of beings or their Being. He was concerned about the Being behind all beings or entities, which could be grasped by the self-understanding of *Dasein* (human being).

Schumpeter (1912), from the Austrian School of economics, criticized the static nature of mainstream economics and took a unique approach to dynamic economics on the basis of the concept of innovation and development. However, his economic theory is part of his concept of a universal social science; he had a much broader vision of society that was based on a typology of *Dasein*, though he did not use this ontological term (Shionoya 1997). He distinguished between the hedonistic, adaptive, and static person on the one hand and the energetic, creative, and dynamic person on the other, and plotted out a research program to analyze the interaction between these two types of human agents in various social areas. It is possible, I argue, to interpret and develop Schumpeter's thought on a broad and holistic perspective of society in light of Heidegger's ontological hermeneutics.

The potentiality of Austrian subjectivism in economics can be exploited in different ways, and from different perspectives. As mentioned, some economists have advocated a sort of hermeneutical economics as the real contribution of the Austrian School in replacing mainstream neoclassical theory; however, they do not refer to Heidegger and Brentano as the intellectual resource of Austrian subjectivism. The combination of Heidegger and Schumpeter would suggest a new perspective, not only for economic philosophy but also for Austrian economics.

A very brief introduction to hermeneutics

Hermeneutics can be described as comprising theories of the interpretation and understanding of texts. Although hermeneutics has a long history dating to ancient Greece, it has attained a contemporary relevance in philosophy ever since Dilthey (1883, 1910) broadened the scope of hermeneutics by relating interpretation to all historical objectifications and by locating it as the methodological foundation of human and social sciences (*Geisteswissenschaften*, in his words).

Dilthey insists on building human and social sciences on a methodological basis different from that of natural science, comparing his project of a critique of historical reason to Kant's critique of pure reason, as applied to natural science. He distinguishes "understanding" as the task of the former from "explanation" in the latter, and tries to derive an interpretation of the historical world in terms of "experience, expression, and understanding" (*Erlebnis, Ausdruck, und Verstehen*) from the structure of life's "reason, feeling, and will" (*Vorstellung, Gefühl, und Wille*). The process of interpretation is characterized, above all, by what is called the "hermeneutical circle" between parts and the whole, between the mind and society, between agents and institutions, or between the psychological categories and historical ones.

Subsequently, Heidegger (1927) attempted the total reconstruction of the discipline of hermeneutics as a new approach to ontology, distinguishing between entities (*Seiende*) and Being (*Sein*), or between the ontical and ontological analysis of entities. While the ontical analysis (an empirical analysis in particular sciences) deals with the nature of entities as such, the ontological analysis (an a priori analysis in philosophy) asks for the meaning of their Being, focusing on the self-understanding of *Dasein* as the source of the meaning of existence. *Dasein* refers to an entity – the human being; since to exist means to be in a world already, a vague average understanding of Being is attributed to *Dasein* in advance. Ontology is what this vague self-understanding of *Dasein* is elaborated into, through a consciously clear formulation.

Heidegger's method of elaboration is to regard the essence of *Dasein* as temporality in terms of the past, present, and future. If *Dasein* has a different time horizon in understanding, the image of Being behind each entity will differ from that of the others. In other words, the meaning of Being depends on *Dasein*'s temporality, and it is to this that the title of his book *Being and Time* (*Sein und Zeit*) refers.

While *Dasein* is constrained by a number of factors occurring in the past and obliged to stay under restrictions characterized as "thrownness" (*Geworfenheit*), one can still open up a new vista of the future and create an active relationship to the world through the "projection" (*Entwurf*) of his or her own possibility. *Dasein*'s understanding, based on "thrownness" without "projection," would lead us to a "degradation" or "falling" (*Verfallen*) in life. Thus, human beings cope well with the present only by properly combining the past and future. Heidegger's ontological conceptions of "projection" and "thrownness" play a crucial role in synthesizing the temporality inherent in the understanding of Being. This understanding, consisting of the "projection" and "thrownness" of *Dasein*, contributes to a "thematizing" of historical knowledge as well as to a "prestructuring" of the framework of knowledge. Prescientific vision refers to a projection of the meaning of Being, which involves the stipulation of the objects, viewpoint, and concepts for scientific research.

A dialogue on innovation and routine

In Heidegger's ontological hermeneutics, the constitution of the understanding of Being depends on *Dasein*'s basic attitude toward the time horizon (i.e., the past, present, and future). We now raise hermeneutical questions about the empirical world, particularly, the economic world, from the viewpoint of temporality, focusing on a decision-making problem under circumstances of uncertainty. The questions may be answered through a type of dialogue between Heidegger and Schumpeter, in which Schumpeter is primarily Heidegger's interpreter, though sometimes the roles interchange.

For the sake of convenience, the dialogue will be divided into two parts: a dialogue on the modus operandi of *Dasein* (innovation and routine), to be discussed in the present section, and a dialogue on the consequences of *Dasein*'s operation (prestructure of science), to be discussed in the next section.

Heidegger's *Dasein* is characterized in several ways. First, it can be explained in the context of decision making under uncertainty. One cannot predict the future objectively. We are almost ignorant of the future because it does not exist in terms of perception. It is meaningless for any of us to try to predict the future without doing anything now. Hence, rather than asking how a decision will be made by each individual under uncertainty, it is more relevant to presume that the interaction of individual decisions will create the future. The decision making and present action will disclose and develop the possible future as the reality. For Heidegger, this is the role of "projection" of the authentic *Dasein* as "Being towards death," in anticipation of a possibility in the future. Heidegger argues on the leading role of "projection" in opening the future possibilities of the self and the world.

> Projecting has nothing to do with comporting oneself towards a plan that has been thought out, and in accordance with which *Dasein* arranges its Being. On the contrary, any *Dasein* has, as *Dasein*, already projected itself; and as long as it is, it is projecting. As long as it is, *Dasein* always has understood itself and always will understand itself in terms of possibilities.... Projection, in throwing, throws before itself the possibility as possibility, and lets it be as such. As projecting, understanding is the kind of Being of *Dasein* in which it is its possibilities as possibilities.
>
> (Heidegger 1962: 185)

Second, what is the motive of "projection" of *Dasein*? As Heidegger put it:

> We are still far from pondering the essence of action decisively enough. We view action only as causing an effect. The actuality of the effect is valued according to its utility. But the essence of action is accomplishment. To accomplish means to unfold something into the fullness of its essence, to lead it forth into this fullness. Therefore only what already is can really be accomplished. But what "is" above all is Being. Thinking accomplishes the relation of Being to the essence of man.
>
> (Heidegger 1977: 217)

Heidegger implies that acting has more importance than its utility effect. Even if that importance cannot be calculated, action is motivated to accomplish something based on a sense of ordinary life. Heidegger claims that *Dasein*'s resolution to anticipate its possibility is the motive of action and implies a criticism against a utilitarian decision theory that is typical of economics.

Third, if one does not take into account the future utility effect of action, is action random and without discretion? No, past experience will act as a guide. *Dasein* as Being-in-the-world is under the restraint of history, tradition, and custom, and it has acquired a certain experience and knowledge about the self, others, and the world. Insofar as past data are considered to persist, the conventional mode of action will be more or less maintained today. This is how *Dasein* conceives and practices its mode of action, under "thrownness," in the world.

Neoclassical economic theory is often criticized for being an atemporal system with a focus on equilibrium, subject to given data. However, as far as the data remain constant through time and the past mode of action is maintained, neoclassical theory is not an unrealistic fiction; rather, it describes the static reality. In explaining the core of neoclassical economics, Schumpeter did not follow the method of describing a static economy in terms of an atemporal state of "equilibrium," but in terms of a process of "circular flow" (*Kreislauf*) in which an economy repeats itself on the same scale with the same structure, year after year (1912: ch. 1). This is an excellent idea, and it represents the decision making of economic agents in a real static economy with an explicit time axis; it is also comparable to Marx's scheme of simple reproduction. While a characteristic of the Austrian School of economics is its concern with the market process rather than market equilibrium, Schumpeter practiced it in an idiosyncratic way.

To use a hermeneutical term, while in the static economic world all economic agents are "thrown" into the circular flow, Schumpeter defined an innovative entrepreneur as one who destroys the customary path of the economy by "projecting" a new lifestyle of economy on the basis of strong will and penetrating foresight, not calculating prudence. This is a clear answer to Heidegger's anti-utilitarian question.

Fourth, in terms of temporality, agents stand at the intersection of "projection" of Being into the future and "thrownness" of Being by the past, in Heidegger's usage, or of "innovation" and "routine," in Schumpeter's usage. Their pairs of terms are exactly comparable in meaning and implication. For Heidegger, when agents content themselves with "thrownness" as the Being-in-the-world and do not face the "anxiety" of the future seriously, their attitude serves as an easy escape to the everyday world and facilitates a "degradation" or "falling" into inauthentic life. For Schumpeter, when agents are content with a "circular flow" and do not challenge the uncertain world of the future, their attitude leads to a static economy that is inauthentic to capitalism, from a macroscopic perspective, and a dominance of average people with an adaptive propensity, from a microscopic perspective. To be free of the conventional world, one needs to make super-human efforts; in other words, a predicting ground for supporting innovative activity is nil in the context of decision making under uncertainty.

Fifth, Heidegger has no notion of innovation, other than "jump or leap" (*Sprung*). He observes: "Jump is an utmost projection of the nature of Being in the sense that, in an open space cleared by projection, we place ourselves in an internally tense situation and become ourselves only through a combination with the emerging truth of Being" (Heidegger 1989: 230, my translation). It can be argued that the "jump" is the key to the critical problem of his "turn" (*Kehre*), namely, the turn from the earlier Heidegger to the later Heidegger, which refers to the relationship between the conferring of Being by "projection" and the emergence of the truth of Being from the state of "thrownness." The "jump" implies that only a small number of people can go into the crucial truth of Being; it is the projection to grasp the "culture, ideal, value, and meaning" in light of the truth of Being. The hermeneutical circles between the projection of Being and the emergence of its truth constitute the method of ontology. The "jump or leap" is not a mere projection into the future but a rare resolution to come across the truth of Being in the space thrown by a series of past conventions. The rarity of "jump" is comparable to the extraordinary nature of creative activities in Schumpeter.

In developing the conceptual framework of economic dynamics in comparison to statics, Schumpeter starts by contrasting a hedonistic person and an energetic person. The motives for innovation by energetic persons are not the calculation of profits, utility, and pleasure reduced to a certainty equivalent of uncertainty and risks, but the exercise of capability and the realization of ambition, dreams, and the will to cope with the unknown future. In other words, the motivating power of innovation is the aspiration to realize the meaning of Being as a bundle of possibilities, and it differs from the notion of rationality implied by the maximizing principles of profits and utility.

Schumpeter neither affirms the man of innovation nor dismisses the man of adaptation; both of them carry out necessary functions in society: "creative destruction" and "order maintenance," respectively. In other words, they are the necessary agents for performing Heidegger's functions of "projection and thrownness" to integrate the three dimensions of temporality, that is, the past, present, and future. Schumpeter was the subconscious and rare practitioner of ontological hermeneutics in economics; thus, in his system of thought are the moments of ontology for social science, which are difficult to find in standard economics based on *homo economicus*.

A dialogue on the prestructure of science

It is worthwhile to summarize the consequences of the preceding discussion of the ontological decision making of *Dasein* on the construction and philosophy of science. In understanding the results of "projection and thrownness" Heidegger (2006: 150–1; 1962: 191) defines what he calls the "hermeneutical situation" in terms of the "prestructure" (*Vor-struktur*) of knowledge, consisting of three aspects: "fore-having" (*Vorhabe*), for what we have in advance; "foresight" (*Vorsicht*), for what we see in advance; and "fore-conception" (*Vorgriff*), for what we grasp in advance. In other words, the "prestructure" of knowledge or pre-theory comprises the precedent definition of research objects, a viewpoint, and concept formation. The "goal" (*Woraufhin*) of interpretation, which is imagined by the total gadget of "prestructure," is no less than the meaning of Being, which must be laid at the foundations of a particular science. Heidegger's definition of the "prestructure" of science is more detailed than that of Schumpeter's which is well known as "vision and ideology" (Schumpeter 1949).

The epistemological significance of Heidegger's prestructure of science should be emphasized. The contrasting concepts of "projection and thrownness" or "innovation and routine," which are constitutive of the paradigm of ontological hermeneutics, nullify the validity of the traditional counter concepts of "subjectivity and objectivity" in epistemology, for the ontological antithesis in "hermeneutical circles" lies behind the epistemological conflict of "subjectivity and objectivity." Thus, Rorty (1979: ch. 7), attempting a reconstruction of modern philosophy, expresses his direction through the catchphrase "from epistemology to hermeneutics." In the paradigm of ontological hermeneutics, both "projection and thrownness" provide a prejudice or preunderstanding of the entities in question: "projection" is a prejudice to see the world new, while "thrownness" is a prejudice to see the world as conceived previously.

In spite of the turn "from epistemology to hermeneutics," the consequences on the epistemological context of hermeneutical work have yet to be clarified. Schumpeter (1947) cites three points that the essential characteristics of creative activities impose on epistemology, as follows. (1) Creative activities cannot be predicted by applying the ordinary rules of inference from pre-existing facts; they are so unique that their mechanisms must be investigated in each case. (2) Creative activities, if seen *ex post*, shape the whole course of subsequent events and their long-run outcome; there is no bridge between the incommensurable situations before and after the innovation. (3) Creative activities have something to do with the quality, roles, and leadership of human beings in a society. Schumpeter insists that the sources of energy for creative activities and the ensuing social mechanism should be the highest-priority foci of the social sciences, and that they might be best explored by sociological studies. Schumpeter (2005) summed up the fundamental issues of creative activities as the interrelationship between "novelty, indeterminacy, and discontinuity."

The reference to Schumpeter sheds light on both the social and epistemological aspects of "projection," neither of which had been touched upon by Heidegger's philosophical inquiry. Just as philosophers of romanticism have tended to allocate artistic creativity outside cognitive knowledge, so the issues of economic creativity and innovation also await analysis by economists, because the "novelty, indeterminacy, and discontinuity" of social phenomena are difficult to handle.

Although Schumpeter's view was originally proffered in the early period of the twentieth century, its significance has not declined, even after a century. This chapter concerns itself with Schumpeter's social science from the ontological viewpoint, but elsewhere I have dealt with his epistemological structure, characterized as a system of "economic sociology, instrumentalism, and rhetoric" in light of the broad framework of "theory, meta-theory, and pre-theory" (Shionoya 2004).

The Heidegger=Schumpeter theses

We can sum up what might be called the Heidegger=Schumpeter ontological theses with an emphasis on *Dasein*. The integration of philosophy and economics is based on the idea that while Heidegger no doubt contributed to the construction of philosophical hermeneutics, it was Schumpeter, among others, who could incorporate the substantive content of the social science into the framework of hermeneutics, given the shared background of Austrian subjectivism, which emphasizes the role of human factors in association with social organisms in understanding interdependent social phenomena. Let us examine these theses in greater detail under the following eight headings.

Isomorphic duality

Both Heidegger and Schumpeter share a dualism of human nature and its consequences: "projection and thrownness" and "jump and degradation" (in Heidegger's usage) and "innovation and routine," "creation and adaptation," and "vision and ideology" (in Schumpeter's usage). These antitheses appear repeatedly in various fields of social life, often with different forms and names. They may be part of what is termed in ontology as an "isomorphic duality." The cause of the duality is basically the tension between the romantic and historicist worldviews.

Dasein *as the thrown projector*

The dual elements in the antithesis are linked and mediated by an understanding of *Dasein* as the Being-in-the-world, who is the agent of "thrown projection" and is faced with the time horizon of the past, present, and future. The bilateral interaction between the dual elements in *Dasein* is created by "hermeneutical circles" in constructing the knowledge in question, and it contrasts with foundationalist logic. While the objects of interpretation are manifold, including text, literature, ideology, experience, and institution, the interpretation itself always relates to the existential characteristics of human beings. Schumpeter defines the typology of "energetic and hedonistic" persons as the presupposition of social science, while Heidegger distinguishes between "authentic and inauthentic" persons: both of them depend on the full scope of human nature.

Understanding of Being as the prestructure of knowledge

Dasein is not an abstract rational individual, but a full person with a set of "reason, feeling, and will" that is historically conditioned and oriented in the lifeworld. *Dasein*'s understanding of Being is to project the possibilities of human beings with a full mindset into the future. The projection involves the process of the "hermeneutical circle" that is concerned with not only the time horizon of the past, present, and future, but also the social horizon of different areas of human activity. Thus, hermeneutics provides the prestructure of social and historical sciences from the viewpoint of integrating diverse perspectives or horizons. The prestructure (*Vor-struktur*) consists of a preliminary provision of the object (*Vorhabe*), a viewpoint (*Vorsicht*), and concept formation (*Vorgriff*) for constructing knowledge. The "goal" (*Woraufhin*) of interpretation presumed by the totality of the prestructure is the meaning of Being that should underlie the science in question. The world of historical relativity and plurality demands understanding and interpretation in terms of full, living individuals.

Nature of projection

The decision making and action at present would disclose and develop the possible future as the reality. This is the role of the "projection" of the authentic *Dasein* in anticipation of his possibility in the future. "Projection" is the irradiation of light into the dark future and the formation of knowledge with regard to the emerging future. Its motive is the resolution to anticipate possibility, and its essence is accomplishment: the exertion of the capacity and realization of the ambition, dreams, and will. Projection is a non-utilitarian act that is not based on a utilitarian calculation of its effects. The predictive basis to support projection and innovation is nil in the context of decision making under uncertainty: indeed, the creative act of projection is characterized by "novelty, indeterminacy, and discontinuity."

Nature of thrownness

Thrownness refers to *Dasein* that remains within the given world under the constraints of history, tradition, and custom. The adaptive and average person maintains a given lifestyle, leading to statics and the degradation of life. The removal of the constraints of custom requires gigantic energy. There is no concept of innovation in Heidegger but that of "jump" (*Sprung*), or the utmost projection of the essence of Being in which a limited number of people could join. However, thrownness and adaptation are not dismissed; they play a necessary function in a society no less than its opposite, projection, and innovation. "Creative destruction" and "order maintenance" are complementary; in other words, the two types of human being are necessary agencies for integrating three dimensions of temporality: the past, present, and future.

The social-science implications of an understanding of Being

Philosophically speaking, the world into which we are thrown is a compulsory framework combining the selves and others (*Ge-Stell*, in Heidegger's idiosyncrasy); it consists of "institutions and values" from the viewpoint of social science, which are concerned with the interaction between the "mind and society" according to the moral-philosophical view of the eighteenth century. If the crystallization of the mind is "values," and if the crystallization of society is "institutions," "institutions and values" are the result of a historical typification of particular and contingent social phenomena. Moreover, while "institutions" are a fixation of "values," "values" are an extraction of "institutions": thus, "institutions and values" constitute the "hermeneutical circle" addressed to the "mind and society."

It follows that both "institutions and values" are the historical and social strata and form a network of intersubjective meaning and communication. The "projection and thrownness" take place on this structural network or stratum of a society. In other words, "projection and thrownness" do not stand in counterpoint without mediation, but are combined through the medium of "institutions and values." The effects of thrownness depend on the conservative function of institutions in maintaining the order; the creative effects of projection represent possible changes in the institutional framework of normative values, and are expected to be absorbed into new institutions.

The capacity of a society to innovate is dependent on the institutions that work as repositories of technical knowledge and human values. "Institutions and values" in a society are the legacy of its past and affect its developmental path into the future either positively or negatively, depending on the understanding of *Dasein*. The modus operandi of the understanding of *Dasein* in general is what constitutes fundamental ontology, but it does not reach the particular ontology addressed to social science. The particular ontology is facilitated by locating the ontological modus operandi upon "institutions and values" as the historical and social strata. The object of social science is thus partially path dependent and partially path breaking.

Relevance of the history of science

Heidegger's famous topic of *Kehre* (turn) relates to the special relationship between the time horizons of the past and future. According to the thesis of *Kehre*, the truth of Being would appear out of "thrownness" in such a way that the supremacy of "projection" would be limited, and that "projection" should meet the call from the past. For Schumpeter, the totality of the history of thought has the possibility of rebirth, and would generate a "filiation of scientific ideas" when a past-buried theory is combined with a forward-looking vision (Schumpeter 1954: 6). Despite apparent scientific revolutions, science would achieve continuity by the discovery of a "filiation of scientific ideas" that serves to contribute to the true totality and systemic nature of science. The materials of hermeneutics are found in the history of science; the implications of the history of economics to hermeneutics are discussed elsewhere (Shionoya 2009b).

Unsettled problem

The central issue suggested from the analysis of "projection and thrownness" with regard to a specific social process is to reconsider the relationship between "rationality and time." Modern science has typically developed under the presumption of an end–means rationality, from an ahistorical and present-centered viewpoint; in economics, human beings are regarded as the rational maximizers of the targeted present values. A reconsideration of "rationality and time" from the viewpoint of the lifeworld is the strategy suggested by hermeneutics for social science. In view of the fact that institutions, customs, and values shape individual behavior and beliefs, rationality should be conceived not as the norm of abstract individuals, but as that of the society that is at once path dependent and path breaking. The theme of "rationality and time" may be comparable to that of Heidegger's *Sein und Zeit*.

Conclusion

We have interpreted hermeneutics as the development of Austrian subjectivism, the seminal core of which is Brentano's concept of intentionality; it has been formulated with respect to the relationship between the projection and thrownness of acting agents. We have created a paraphrase of Heidegger by Schumpeter, to position hermeneutics closer to economics. The unique accomplishments of the economist Schumpeter with regard to economic theory, economic sociology, and the history of economics are properly interpreted from his ontological commitments (Shionoya 2009a). Hermeneutical insight is transmitted to economics through Schumpeter's broad conception of the mind and society. I conclude that if the Enlightenment was about the philosophy of social science modeled after natural science, the Heidegger=Schumpeter theses represent an alternative philosophy of social science, based on a different philosophical worldview.

References

Böhm-Bawerk, E. von ([1889] 1921) *Kapital und Kapitalzins*, Part 2, *Positive Theorie des Kapitales*, Vol. 2, *Exkurse zur "Positive Theorie des Kapitales,"* 4th edition, Jena: Gustav Fischer.

Brentano, F. (1874) *Psychologie vom empirischen Standpunkt*; trans. A.C. Rancurello, D.B. Terrell, and Linda L. McAlister (1973) *Psychology from an Empirical Standpoint*, London: Routledge.

Dilthey, W. ([1883] 1922) *Einleitung in die Geisteswissenschaften*, in *Gesammelte Schriften*, Vol. I, Stuttgart & Göttingen: Vandenhoeck & Ruprecht.

Dilthey, W. ([1910] 1927) *Aufbau der geschichtlichen Welt in den Geisteswissenschaften*, in *Gesammelte Schriften*, Vol. VII, Stuttgart & Göttingen: Vandenhoeck & Ruprecht.

Ebeling, R. (1986) "Toward a hermeneutical economics: expectations, prices, and the role of interpretation in a theory of the market process," in I.M. Kirzner (ed.) *Subjectivism, Intelligibility and Economic Understanding*, London: Macmillan.

Gadamer, H.G. (1960) *Wahrheit und Methode: Grundzüge einer philosophischen Hermeneutik*; trans. J. Weinsheimer and D.G. Marshall (2nd revised edition, 2004) *Truth and Method*, London: Continuum.

Heidegger, M. ([1927, 2006] 1962) *Sein und Zeit*, 19th edition; trans. J. Macquarrie and E. Robinson (1962) *Being and Time*, Oxford: Blackwell.

Heidegger, M. ([1947] 1977) "Letter on humanism," in D.F. Krell (ed.) *Martin Heidegger, Basic Writings*, New York: Harper Collins.

Heidegger, M. (1989) *Beiträge zur Philosophie (Vom Ereignis)*, Frankfurt am Main: Vittorio Klostermann.

Horwitz, S. (1994) "Subjectivism," in P.J. Boettke (ed.) *The Elgar Companion to Austrian Economics*, Cheltenham: Edward Elgar.

Husserl, E. ([1913] 1950) *Ideen zu einer reinen Phänomenologie und phänomenologischen Philosophie*, Vol. 1; trans. F. Kersten (1982) *Ideas Pertaining to a Pure Phenomeology and to a Phenomenological Philosophy*, vol. 1, The Hague: Nijhoff.

Hutchison, T.W. (1981) "Carl Menger on philosophy and method," in *The Politics and Philosophy of Economics: Marxians, Keynesians and Austrians*, Oxford: Basil Blackwell.

Kauder, E. (1957) "Intellectual and political roots of the older Austrian school," *Zeitschrift für Nationalökonomie*, 17: 411–25.

Lachmann, L.M. (1990) "Austrian economics: a hermeneutic approach," in D. Lavoie (ed.) *Economics and Hermeneutics*, London: Routledge.

Lavoie, D. (1990) "Understanding differently: hermeneutics and the spontaneous order of communicative processes," in B.J. Caldwell (ed.) *Carl Menger and His Legacy in Economics*, Durham, NC: Duke University Press.

Menger, C. (1871; 2nd edition, 1923) *Grundsätze der Volkswirtschaftslehre*, 2nd edition; trans. of 1st edition, J. Dingwall and B.F. Hoselitz (1981) *Principles of Economics*, New York: New York University Press.

Menger, C. (1883) *Untersuchungen über die Methode der Socialwissenschaften, und der politischen Oekonomie insbesondere*; trans. F.J. Nock (1985) *Investigation into the Method of the Social Sciences with Special Reference to Economics*, New York: New York University Press.

Nakayama, I. ([1926] 1973) "Two forms of marginal utility theory: Austrian school and Lausanne school," (in Japanese) in *Collected Works of Ichiro Nakayama*, Vol. 2, Tokyo: Kodansha.

Polanyi, K. (1971) "Carl Menger's two meanings of economic," *Studies in Economic Anthropology*, 7: 16–24.

Polanyi, K. (1977) ed. by H.W. Pearson, *The Livelihood of Man*, New York: Academic Press.

Rescher, N. (1969) *Introduction to Value Theory*, Englewood Cliffs, NJ: Prentice-Hall.

Rorty, R. (1979) *Philosophy and the Mirror of Nature*, Princeton, NJ: Princeton University Press.

Schumpeter, J.A. (1912; 2nd edition, 1926) *Theorie der wirtschaftlichen Entwicklung*; abridged trans. of 2nd edition, R. Opie (1934) *The Theory of Economic Development*, Cambridge, MA: Harvard University Press.

Schumpeter, J.A. (1947) "The creative response in economic history," *Journal of Economic History*, 7: 149–59.

Schumpeter, J.A. (1949) "Science and ideology," *American Economic Review*, 39: 345–59.

Schumpeter, J.A. (1954) *History of Economic Analysis*, New York: Oxford University Press.

Schumpeter, J.A. (2005) "Development," *Journal of Economic Literature*, 43: 108–20.

Shionoya, Y. (1997) *Schumpeter and the Idea of Social Science: A Metatheoretical Study*, Cambridge: Cambridge University Press.

Shionoya, Y. (2004) "Scope and method of Schumpeter's universal social science: economic sociology, instrumentalism, and rhetoric," *Journal of the History of Economic Thought*, 26: 331–47.

Shionoya, Y. (2009a) "Schumpeter and evolution: an ontological exploration," in Y. Shionoya and T. Nishizawa (eds.) *Marshall and Schumpeter on Evolution: Economic Sociology of Capitalist Development*, Cheltenham: Edward Elgar.

Shionoya, Y. (2009b) "The history of economics as economics?" *European Journal of the History of Economic Thought*, 16: 575–97.

Shionoya, Y. (2010) "Hermeneutics and the Heidegger = Schumpeter theses," in W.S. Ho and F.S. Lee (eds.) *Laurence S. Moss 1944–2009: Academic Iconoclast, Economist, and Magician*, Malden, MA: Wiley-Blackwell.

Smith, B. (1994) *Austrian Philosophy: The Legacy of Franz Brentano*, Chicago, IL: Open Court.

6 Carl Menger's subjectivism

"Types," economic subjects, and microfoundation

Yukihiro Ikeda[1]

Introduction

In this chapter, I present my critique of the methodological arguments of Carl Menger, the founder of the Austrian School of Economics, with special attention paid to his subjectivism, the general theme of the entire volume. Menger has been widely viewed as a mentor of the school, and although his subjectivism plays an important role in the arguments of later Austrians, his methodology is not always well founded. My thesis statements are that: (1) Menger failed to apply his own methodology to *Grundsätze* (1871), one of his main works, which contributed a great deal to the foundation of microeconomics in the broader sense of the term. (2) Menger attempted to provide the foundations of his methodology in his 1883 book, but he was not successful in doing so. He failed to persuade the reader that an economic analysis based on each individual subject and economic behavior is more relevant than other vantages in understanding economic phenomena.

In order to preclude the possibility of misinterpretations and facilitate understanding in the reader, the provision of rather simple but formal definitions of the two terms is in order. First, "subjectivism" refers to a way of understanding social phenomena, in which one relies upon subjects with unified personalities.[2] In economics, it is generally the case that subjects are supposed to have a consistent preference ordering. Second, if analysis is based upon individuals and not on society, a community, or a nation, it is said to be founded on *individualism*; herein, we refer to methodological individualism, a term coined by Joseph Alois Schumpeter, a later Austrian.

A number of publications address Menger's methodology. Alter (1990) devotes a substantial part of his book to it. Among the papers read at the Menger conference in 1989 at Duke University, four papers concerned themselves with it. Whether Menger was an Aristotelian continues to be an important and attractive issue among Menger scholars who investigate his methodology. For instance, Alter (1990) and Smith (1990) each attempt to interpret Mengerian methodology in the context of Aristotelian philosophy. Milford (2010) denies an Aristotelian interpretation of Menger's economic thought; rather, he attempts to read Menger's text by relying upon Popperian terminology.[3] I refrain from participating in this debate, as deriving an answer depends completely on the interpretations of the great ancient philosopher. This necessitates a deep scholarship of the philosopher himself, to be sure. Menger was an economist with some philosophical background, yet it is not possible to compare his arguments directly to those of Aristotle or Kant. I do not share the standpoint of those who believe that Menger's text can be better understood when viewed through the lens of an Aristotelian or some other philosophical context. I prefer to interpret Menger's text in itself, without relying on specific philosophical frameworks.

As is well known, Menger's 1883 book continues to be a valuable source of thought, from which some of the important ideas of modern Austrians are drawn. Among the few contributions that attempt to take a critical look at Menger's methodology, Lawson (1996) deserves to be mentioned here. From the standpoint of critical realism, Lawson shows persuasively that Menger's methodological individualism is simply baseless. Indeed, this is a new contribution to Menger's methodology. My analysis below draws heavily upon Lawson's penetrating critical analysis.

My chapter is divided into two parts. First, I examine Menger's 1871 book, as far as it relates to methodological issues. After addressing Menger's arguments in the Preface of *Grundsätze*, I analyze Menger's characteristic definition of "imaginary goods," followed by a section in which concrete models are examined from a methodological viewpoint. I argue that some statements in *Grundsätze* cannot be justified by his attempt to establish his economics methodology in its Preface – an attempt that leads to his detailed analysis in the second book. Then, the second part of this chapter undertakes a critical understanding of his methodological book. First, I will take a close look at the methodological foundation in *Untersuchungen* (1883); I then go on to the critical arguments made by the German Historical School against the English Classical School. I will follow Menger's counterarguments against the former, showing that not all the points he raises can be adequately supported. This might lead to a serious breakdown of both methodological individualism and subjectivism. In conclusion, this chapter summarizes and makes critical remarks on Mengerian methodology.

Methodological foundations of *Grundsätze*

As is well known, *Grundsätze* was written as a *Habilitationsschrift* to be submitted to Vienna University. This is basically a book of economic theories with a scant explanation of economics methodology per se. However, the following passage in the Preface of the book is concerned with the methodological justification of economics. In fact, he refers to the "simplest elements" for the first time in his publication:

> In what follows I have endeavored to reduce the complex phenomena of human economic activity to the simplest elements that can still be subjected to accurate observation, to apply to these elements the measure corresponding to their nature, and constantly adhering to this measure, to investigate

the manner in which the more complex economic phenomena evolve from their elements according to definite principles.

(Menger 1871: 46)

From this quote, we can garner no detailed explanation of what these "simplest elements" are. We are told only that these elements are "subjected to accurate observation" and that every economic phenomenon can be explained by reducing it to the "simplest elements." Considering the arguments in *Untersuchungen* (1883) seen below, the historical development of his thought can be neatly summarized as follows: from the outset, Menger had a reductionist viewpoint vis-à-vis economic methodology. He attempts to analyze economic phenomena by reducing them to certain basic elements, which he calls "simplest elements." Although he does not provide in the Preface concrete examples of such elements, it is certain that what he had in mind was individual economic agents and their maximizing behavior. All who have ever read the 1871 book will agree with the widely accepted opinion that the entire edifice is an attempt to reduce economic phenomena to the behavior of individual economic subjects. Then, in his later work on methodology, he begins his argument by defining the concept of "types"; he then goes on to combine the concept of "strict types," a derivative of the latter, with the "simplest elements." Thus, chronologically, the concept of the "simplest elements" came first, and he supplemented it with a new idea in 1883. Nonetheless, as seen below, Menger did not succeed in persuading others with different "types" of economic analysis that his "types" were superior.

Although Menger maintains his aforementioned methodological viewpoint in his 1871 book, he sometimes does develop arguments that can be interpreted within the framework of neither subjectivism nor methodological individualism. In what follows, I introduce some cases that ultimately show the inconsistency of his arguments in the Preface and in his own interpretations of the economic models he extended.

Imaginary goods[4]

In *Grundsätze*, Menger basically argues within the frameworks of subjectivism and methodological individualism; however, in some cases, he transcends these areas, as seen in some examples. In this section, I deal with the concept of "imaginary goods." The following quote is taken from the Goods Theory, found in the beginning of the 1871 book:

> A special situation can be observed whenever things that are incapable of being placed in any kind of causal connection with the satisfaction of human needs are nevertheless treated by men as goods. This occurs (1) when attributes, and therefore capacities, are erroneously ascribed to things that do not really possess them, or (2) when non-existent human needs are mistakenly assumed to exist. In both cases we have to deal with things that do not, in reality, stand in the relationship already described as determining the

goods-character of things, but do so only in the opinions of people. Among things of the first class are most cosmetics, all charms, the majority of medicines administered to the sick by peoples of early civilizations and by primitives even today, divining rods, love potions, etc. For all these things are incapable of actually satisfying the needs they are supposed to serve. Among things of the second class are medicines for diseases that do not actually exist, the implements, statues, buildings, etc., used by pagan people for the worship of idols, instruments of torture, and the like. Such things, therefore, as derive their goods-character merely from properties they are imagined to possess or from needs merely imagined by men may appropriately be called *imaginary* goods.

(Menger 1871: 53)

Certain things are said to be goods, but "only in the opinions of people." Here, Menger differentiates two cases. The first refers to the case in which a certain thing is erroneously thought by some agents to be a good: that good does not serve human wants, although it is believed to. This demarcation is based on the second condition of goods. Let us examine a concrete example from Menger: cosmetics. He seems to argue that they are useless in making women look beautiful. However, is it not conceivable that women continue to use cosmetics, simply because they really make them pretty, and thus attract men? In a nutshell, it is arguable that cosmetics belong to the first category of imaginary goods. It is highly possible that it does belong to the category of "goods," in the true sense of the word.

The second case is even more problematic, from my standpoint. In Menger's own words, it refers to the case "where non-existent human needs are mistakenly assumed to exist." Human need is the first condition for things to be considered goods, and since human need does not really exist in the above case, the good loses its quality as such. The problem here is obvious: who decides whether a certain human need is real, whereas others are not? According to the subjectivist framework from which Menger argues, this should remain unanswered. Thus, the strict framework of subjectivism is alien to the above passage, to say the least.

As I showed elsewhere, one finds the concept of "imaginary goods" in Wilhelm Roscher's *Grundlagen der Nationaloekonomie* (1854).[5] And we encounter another use in Peter Mischler's *Grundsätze der National-Oekonomie* (1857).[6] Menger was deeply involved in the German tradition of economic thought, from the introduction of Smithian doctrines to Germany to the work of textbook writers such as Heinrich Rau and Roscher. It is debatable whether the above definition of "imaginary goods" leads to the breakdown of subjectivism. It can be interpreted as a "residue" of German discourse in economic thought, which is more or less normative-biased compared to the doctrines of other countries. The concept does not play any substantial role in further arguments in *Grundsätze*.

Economic models in *Grundsätze*

As Menger paved the way for the later development of the Austrian School of Economics, which included a relatively new group of heterodox economists called "the modern Austrians" in the United States, most of the models in *Grundsätze* can be interpreted within the framework of individualism. However, there appear to be some cases where his analysis goes beyond the limitations implied by his viewpoint, as suggested in the Preface.

First, I follow the arguments in Chapter 2, entitled "Economic Goods and Economy." The third section of this chapter begins with the following characterization of economy:

> In the two preceding sections we have seen how separate individuals, as well as the inhabitants of whole countries and groups of countries united by trade, attempt to form a judgment on the one hand about their requirements for future time periods and, on the other, about the quantities of goods available to them for meeting these requirements, in order to gain in this way the indispensable foundation for activity directed to the satisfaction of their needs.
>
> (Menger 1871: 94)

Menger indicates two different cases to which the concept of economy can be applied. First, each individual decides to consume, based on his or her judgment of the economic subject. This is what he calls "the indispensable foundation for activity directed to the satisfaction of their needs," which can be aptly translated as "economy." The second case deals with "inhabitants of whole countries and groups of countries united by trade." In emphasizing his opinion that the value phenomena are not limited to exchange economy, he says: "Hence economic and noneconomic goods also exist for an isolated individual. The cause of the economic character of a good cannot therefore be the fact that it is either an 'object of exchange' or an 'object of property'" (Menger 1871: 101). It is true enough that Menger emphasizes the methodological point that the concept can be applied to each economic player without considering whether or not the goods are objects of exchange. It is, as we have seen already, faithful to his original idea. Nonetheless, this is not the only case to which the concept of economy can be applied. It must be underscored that Menger also applies it to the case where there are plural economic subjects united by exchange. It is straightforward that the first case, involving only one economic player, can be interpreted within the framework of methodological individualism; however, in what way can we interpret the second? In order to understand Menger's intention more thoroughly, we need to examine this chapter more thoroughly.

Menger gives us timber and land as examples of goods that began to be included in economic goods as civilization developed, although they were free goods in older times. School education and drinking water are given as examples of goods that are now provided by the state or similar institutions, although they are economic goods of value. Obviously, these cases are based on social economy, in which there are plural economic subjects. Thus, the economic or noneconomic character of goods is evaluated within a society consisting of different economic subjects.

From the Mengerian perspective, the problem here is the aggregation of the preference ordering of each individual. What we need is a social utility function that decides the importance of each commodity. If we maintain the Mengerian framework proposed in the Preface of *Grundsätze*, we must begin our arguments with individual economic players, each of whom has a utility function, leading then to the configuration of social utility. To the best of my knowledge, Menger does not offer any ways of executing this procedure. One possible remedy, in the absence of such direction, is to assume that the utility functions of all individuals are the same, which implies that there is only one representative person. Then, and only then, would the problem of the aggregation procedure disappear.

Now let us turn to the exchange model offered in Chapter 4. In this exchange model, after dealing with a model with two frontiersmen, Menger interprets his own model, this time through the use of two nations. In his own words:

> A social economy is made up of individual economies, and what has been said above is therefore just as valid for the trade of entire peoples as it is for single economizing individuals. Two nations, one chiefly engaged in agriculture and the other primarily in industry, will be in a position to satisfy their needs much more completely if each exchanges a portion of its produce for the produce of the other (the first nation a portion of its agricultural produce and the second a portion of its manufactures).
>
> (Menger 1871: 187)

Without going into the model itself, it is not difficult to understand this quote, especially with regard to his intention to interpret it as an exchange model between two nations. This is a procedure that one encounters quite often in economics textbooks, even to this day. Now the problem here is as follows: if we were to interpret the above quote very strictly, it definitely contradicts his own methodology, which was extended later in his 1883 book. In his methodological book, he consistently maintains his thesis that economic models should be built on individual economic subjects with unified personalities. They consume, and exchange if necessary, based on their preference ordering. He was against those who attempted to construct economic models of nations, communities, and some other institutions that had no definite preference ordering. Later, Menger would have criticized the above quote, perhaps with the following queries: How is it possible to know the utility functions of each nation? How is it possible to construct the preferences of two nations from those of the people who live there?

"Types," "strict types," and "simplest elements"

We now turn to his second book, which allegedly opened a way to the famous *Methodenstreit* between the two schools. Let us begin with Part 1, Chapter 1 of

Menger's *Untersuchungen*. In what follows, Menger explains a basic concept inherent in his methodological analysis, the concept of "type." This deserves close attention, since it is a fundamental pillar on which his later arguments are based. In his own words:

> In spite of the great variety of concrete phenomena, we are able, even with cursory observation, to perceive that not every single phenomenon exhibits a particular empirical form differing from that of all the others. Experience teaches us, rather, that definite phenomena are repeated, now with greater exactitude, now with lesser, and recur in the variation of things. We call these empirical forms *types*.
>
> (Menger [1883] 1996: 2)

This is a starting point of the methodological arguments found in his 1883 book. The description is based on our daily experiences, beginning from childhood. Not all experiences differ but, as Menger says, certain experiences can be placed into certain categories, each of which he defines as a "type." As examples, Menger mentions purchases, money, supplies, demands, prices, capital, and interest rates, all of which are familiar categories in economics. Here, Menger does not enter the famous debate as to whether these categories are products of our thinking, or if they simply exist independent of our recognition.[7] Thus, we are left uninformed as to whether certain "types" can be reduced to the active function of our minds. Also, he says nothing of whether these "types" depend on the persons involved or whether they are shared among them, if they are found within the same community. His description is quite natural, in that it corresponds to daily life; nonetheless, there are certain inherent ambiguities that contribute to problems in his later analysis.[8]

Based upon this typology, he proceeds with his account of laws in economic science:

> On the other hand the regular drop in price of a commodity as a result of an increase in supply, the rise in price of a commodity as a result of an increase in currency, the lowering of the rate of interest as a result of considerable accumulation of capital, etc., present themselves to us as typical relationships among economic phenomena.
>
> (Menger [1883] 1996: 2)

After defining "types," Menger defines "typical relationships," or the relationships among types. According to the above quote, these relationships are basically quantitative. In the first example given, Menger mentions the possible effect of an increase in supply on price; the other two examples are well known in the history of economic theory, at least since the English Classical School. Let me summarize: the basic elements of our analysis are "types" and "typical relationships," and all analyses in economics can be reduced to these two elements.

I now turn to the concept of "strict types," which is derived from the concept of "types." Menger explains the relationship between "strict types" and "simplest elements" thus:

> But the way by which theoretical research arrived at the above goal, a way essentially different from Bacon's empirical-realistic induction, is the following: it seeks to ascertain the *simplest elements* of everything real, elements which must be thought of as strictly typical just because they are the simplest.
>
> (Menger [1883] 1996: 29)

In Menger's view, theoretical research should determine the simplest elements of real things, without providing any definite terminological meanings. With respect to the quote above, Menger uses the latter concept as early as 1871; it was used in a succinct explanation of his methodology in the Preface of *Grundsätze*. In this sense, it is older than the concept of "strict types." Then, abruptly, he relates this older concept to "strict types" in the above quote. Menger says very briefly that "the *simplest elements* of everything real, elements which must be thought of as strictly typical," without providing any detailed account of the relationships between the two concepts.[9]

Based upon the concept of "simplest elements," without giving a clear definition of the term, Menger attempts to clarify his methodological point of view. In what follows, he adds the adjective "original" to the noun "factors," that is, "elements":

> The nature of this exact orientation of *theoretical* research in the realm of ethical phenomena, however, consists in the fact that we reduce human phenomena to their most original and simplest constitutive factors. We join to the latter the measure corresponding to their nature, and finally try to investigate the laws by which *more complicated* human phenomena are formed from those simplest elements, thought of in their isolation.
>
> (Menger [1883] 1996: 31)

Thus, in Menger's view, economic phenomena can be reduced to the "simplest elements," by which "more complicated human phenomena" can be explained. Still, we have no information whatsoever regarding the nature of the "most original and simplest constitutive factors." Note that the adjectives "original" and "simple" are used almost interchangeably.

At this point, Menger provides concrete examples of the "simplest elements":

> The most original factors of human economy are the needs, the goods offered directly to humans by nature (both the consumption goods and the means of production concerned), and the desire for the most complete satisfaction of needs possible (for the most complete covering of material needs possible).
>
> (Menger [1883] 1996: 32)

Here, Menger gives us three "simplest elements" of economics: needs, goods already existing on earth, and the maximization of utility. Obviously, these correspond to the standard description of resource allocation often found in microeconomics textbooks. His viewpoint is restricted to the exchange model; he does not include among the "simplest elements" the moment of production.

Beginning with his arguments in Chapter 1 vis-à-vis "types," Menger arrives at the concept of the "simplest elements" of economics – a concept that is substantially similar to the basic idea of microeconomic analysis, based on the exchange model. Why are these three elements so important in economic science? To address this question, let us start by posing some other questions. Why is the maximization of utility essential in economic analysis? Is it not possible to construct economic models without depending upon utility maximization or maximization itself? Furthermore, is it possible to omit the production model and instead specialize in exchange phenomena? All these queries remain unanswered.

German Historical School vs. English Classical School

Members of the German Historical School have criticized the English Classical School from several different perspectives. In my view, there are three important points with regard to this schism, and I will scrutinize them one by one below. They are scattered here and there in the book, but I will take up all of them, in a comprehensive fashion, in this section, since they are not only related to the relationships between the German Historical School and Menger but also essential to understanding the methodological standpoint of the latter.

First, let us examine the dogma relating to self-interest. After quoting Karl Knies's *Die politische Oekonomie vom Standpunkte der geschichtlichen Methode* (1853), Menger attempts to clarify the meaning of that dogma:

> By the "dogma of self-interest" some economists understand the basic principle that the pursuit of private interest on the part of single economic individuals, uninfluenced by politico-economic government measures, must have as a consequence the highest degree of common welfare which a society can attain, considering its spatial and temporal conditions. However, we do not intend to deal here with this opinion, which is erroneous at least in its general form, for it has no immediate connection with those methodological questions which will occupy us in this section.
>
> (Menger [1883] 1996: 55)

This definition is a proviso of the following discussion. Menger introduces here one possible interpretation of the dogma: economic liberalism. Since he has something different in mind in this section, he ceases to follow this argument in this section. An alternative interpretation is as follows:

> What claims our interest at this point is, rather, the thesis, known under the above designation, that humans truly are guided in their economic activity

exclusively by consideration of their individual interests. This is a thesis which, as the representatives of the historical school of German economists assume, is placed like a basic axiom of the "unhistorical" schools of our science, at least.

(Menger [1883] 1996: 55)

This definition differs from the previous one. The point is that, in economics, economic agents are supposed to be led by self-interest. Obviously, as the argument of the German Historical School goes, people do not act solely on the basis of self-interest. It is true enough that most of the arguments of economic science, including those of the English Classical School, are based on self-interest; however, Menger does not accept the critique, for the following reason:

> The circumstance that people are not guided exclusively by self-interest prohibits, in the above sense, the strict regularity of human action in general, and of economic action in particular – and thereby eliminates the possibility of a rigorous economic theory. But there is another factor, equally important, that does the same thing. I mean *error*, a factor which surely can be separated still less from human action than custom, public spirit, feeling for justice, and love of one's fellow can be separated from economy. Even if economic humans always and everywhere let themselves be guided exclusively by their self-interest, the strict regularity of economic phenomena would nonetheless have to be considered impossible because of the fact given by experience that in innumerable cases they are in error about their economic interest, or in ignorance of the economic state of affairs.
>
> (Menger [1883] 1996: 56)

Although the hypothesis of "self-interest" continues to play an important role in economics, we also have other postulates. In this quote, Menger emphasizes that economic agents are supposed to have enough information vis-à-vis economic variables, and it is assumed that they will behave correctly, based on that information. Menger argues that this is another equally important hypothesis of economic science, along with that of "self-interest." Today, we do have economic theories that deal with uncertainty, but in the 1880s, all existing economic theory was based on the assumption of "complete information," if one is allowed to use modern terminology here.

Menger continues:

> We are far from asserting that with the above dogmas the entirety of presuppositions of a rigorous theory of economic phenomena, in the sense in which our historians think of it, is already exhausted. Rather, it is clear to anyone not completely inexperienced in methodological investigations that they would have to be complemented by a series of other similar dogmas (in the realm of economic phenomena especially *the dogma of complete freedom from external compulsion*, among others).
>
> ([1883] 1996: 57)

Thus, Menger argues, there are many postulates in economics whose reality are debatable. One cannot envisage any economic theories that correspond exactly to reality. In this way, in Menger's opinion, the critique of the German Historical School is not well founded.

Following dogma, let us examine perpetualism and cosmopolitism, both of which have a long history in the interpretation of the English Classical School in German-speaking regions. Menger summarizes the argument as follows:

> A similar statement is true of the charge of "cosmopolitism." Simultaneous phenomena belonging to the same empirical form exhibit not only international or interlocal differences, but also differences in the same place and at the same time. This is a circumstance which, as scarcely needs to be noted, likewise cannot remain without influences on the more or less universal validity of theoretical knowledge. If anyone declares general economic laws inadmissible because economic phenomena exhibit *interlocal* differences, if he considers a modification of them necessary according to spatial conditions, he cannot at any rate help coming to similar conclusions in respect to the *local* differences of homogeneous economic phenomena. Also with the mere effort to avoid the charge of "cosmopolitism" in economic theory the mistake of excessive generalization of the theory is by no means removed. The conception of so-called "perpetualism" and "cosmopolitism" which the historical school of German economists has had is thus inadequate.
>
> ([1883] 1996: 86)

To be sure, many differences in terms of human character, climate, nationality, and social institutions are reflected in the economic phenomena of each nation. Members of the German Historical School argue that these differences must necessarily lead to different economic theories among different nations. As is well known, the critique has a long tradition that goes back at least as far as Friedrich List, a forerunner of the German Historical School. While basically admitting to the correctness of the critique, Menger simultaneously emphasizes that there are differences among various regions of a country – say, between the southern and northern parts of Germany. The same can be said of "perpetualism." Thus, all in all, Menger does not accept the critique of the German Historical School, in terms of these two points.

In this section, I introduced two points made by the German Historical School versus the English Classical School and how Menger defends the latter. I am certain that Menger at least succeeds in persuading the reader that the efficacy of a critique of the German Historical School is still debatable. I now turn to the third point: the critique of atomism, made also by German economists of Menger's time.

Menger says that their critique derives from the Historical School of Jurists, represented by Fr. Savigny. In his own words:

> The dogma under discussion here also owes its origin above all to the historical school of jurists, from whose methods it was borrowed mechanically

> like many another part of the methodology of our historical school of economists. "There is," says Savigny, "no completely separate and isolated human existence. Rather, whatever can be viewed as separate is, when considered from another side, a member of a larger unit. Thus each separate human is of necessity to be considered at the same time as a member of a family, of a nation, as the continuation and development of all previous time." Savigny then speaks of the higher nature of a nation as a unit which is constantly growing, constantly developing, of which "higher nation," indeed, the present age too is but one member, etc.
>
> (Menger [1883] 1996: 64)

As one can see, Menger here quotes from Savigny's article. Savigny emphasizes that each individual is part of a larger community, such as a family, a regional community, or a nation; this, argues Savigny, makes it difficult for one to analyze individuals in isolation from their communities. In Menger's opinion, critiques of the atomistic method did not derive originally from German economists, but were instead borrowed from the Historical School of Jurists.

Menger then goes on to discuss the basic difference in political ideology between the German Historical School of Jurists and the German Historical School of Economics. While the former emphasizes the organic development of social institutions, the latter tends to be an ardent supporter of social policies. This distinction is curious, Menger argues, considering that the German Historical School of Economics attempted to convey the message that they are true successors of their forerunners of law. Note that Menger's own view of social institutions can be interpreted within a historical line of thought that comprises Burke, Savigny, and himself. Following this detour of sorts, he defends the use of the so-called "atomistic method" in the social sciences:

> The error of this doctrine, more immediately occasioned by the confusion of historical and theoretical points of view and more ultimately caused by the failure to recognize the real character of "national economy" in its relations to the singular economic phenomena out of which it is constituted – the error of this doctrine is obvious. The *nation* as such is not a large subject that has needs, that works, practices economy, and consumes; and what is called the true sense of the word.
>
> (Menger [1883] 1996: 66)

Each economic subject, then, can save, but the nation itself cannot. Each economic subject can decide whether he or she will use this part of the product for direct consumption or for investment. To put it more formally: while each individual has a coherent order of preference, the nation does not. Furthermore, it would difficult to aggregate individual preferences in order to achieve a coherent body of preference for the whole of the nation. Thus, the nation is not an economic subject, per se – at least not as Menger envisages the term.

Several comments are in order. In the modern usage of the term, an "economic subject" is expected to have a preference that satisfies the following conditions. (1) The preference is complete; that is, x is better than y or indifferent to y, or y is better than x or indifferent to x. (2) A preference is reflexive; that is, x is better than x or indifferent to x. (3) A preference is transitive; that is, if x is better than y or indifferent to y, and y is better than z or indifferent to z, then x is better than z or indifferent to z. While the second condition is a rather formal request, from an analytical viewpoint, the other conditions reveal a certain rationality of economic subject. If Menger's aforementioned characterization roughly corresponds here to the rationality of economic subject, his concept is a typical example of modern subjectivism, to be sure. Each personality is rational in the sense that his or her behavior can be analyzed through the use of preference-ordering, as described above.

However, it is still debatable as to why his analysis must stop here. The nation is far from being an economic subject in the sense of Menger; so far, so good. However, why must an economist start with an analysis of individual subjects that satisfy, say, the above characterization of rationality? Why would an economist not go deeper into an analysis of behavior – something that can be accomplished by using methods borrowed from other social and natural sciences? Menger provides no satisfactory answers to these questions.

A microfoundation of economics: do we really need one?

Let me briefly summarize and make conclusions vis-à-vis the thesis statements of the chapter. First, I have shown that Menger frequently goes beyond the framework he proposes in his 1871 and later book on methodology. In interpreting his own models, he envisages the value phenomena of society, as well as those of each economic subject. Although methodological individualism is seen as one of the most important hallmarks of the Austrian School of Economics, one encounters arguments among its proponents that are not necessarily based on this tradition. Menger's arguments, as seen here, are examples, and they might be taken as a starting point. Later, Friedrich von Wieser introduced the concept of "simple economy" in *Der natürliche Wert* (1889).[10] Moreover, von Wieser's concept was taken up by Friedrich Hayek in his *Pure Theory of Capital* (1941).[11] Although it is thought to be a first approximation of reality for Hayek, it certainly plays an important role in his analysis. One finds here the historical development of the concept of social evaluation, beginning with Menger and leading through von Wieser to Hayek. This is reminiscent of the fact that von Wieser was Menger's successor as the chair of economics at Vienna University, and also a mentor of Hayek. Thus, some arguments relating to the representative figures of the School are based on an analysis of the value phenomena of society – an analysis that is diametrically opposed to the formal methodology of the founder, if we adhere strictly to his standpoint. While mainstream Austrians tend to deny the concept of social value, Menger's arguments above, paradoxically, make it possible to analyze economic phenomena in a communist society.

In the second part of my chapter and while paying special attention to Menger's 1883 book, I scrutinize the Mengerian foundation of economics methodology and come to the conclusion that it is not always strong. He does not succeed, for example, in demonstrating that economics must start with an analysis of individual players, rather than of society itself.

In general, a focus on individual subjects is thought to be characteristic of the social sciences, at least within the context of the nineteenth century. Individual subjects, after all, have certain characteristics that demonstrate their unified personalities in their own ways. In terms of having this focus, Menger's economic thought is no exception. In his economic models in *Grundsätze*, an economic agent feels, chooses, and decides. Let me provide a very brief example: a person feels hungry and, faced with a given volume of commodities, he or she attempts to satisfy his or her needs. (The famous Menger Table is often interpreted as illustrating the maximizing behavior of economic subjects.) These matters clearly show that Menger's economic model can be reduced to a unified personality – a concept he shares with many contemporary thinkers. Thus, Menger's thought can be interpreted within the framework of subjectivism, in the general sense of the term.

As shown above, Menger provides no justifications for his subjectivism. Why not go deeper into the analysis of brain matter, as has been done recently in neuroeconomics? Why must we stop at the subject level, without researching further the *elements* of a subject – research that might provide more fundamental ways of understanding economic phenomena?

Closely related to subjectivism is the methodological justification of individualism. Does Menger provide any? The answer is never. Nowhere in his published works does he provide a detailed justification for methodological individualism.

As is well known, the two other "stars" of the Marginal Revolution also based their analyses on methodological individualism. Their children and grandchildren continue to play the same game to this day, without delving deeply into the methodological accounts of their standpoints. In the 1970s, we saw an abundance of publications in the field of the microfoundation of Keynesian economics, including those of Barro and Grossman (1971), Benassy (1975), and Drèze (1975). Nonetheless, were there any economists among these who were seriously taxed with justifying the microfoundation of Keynesian economics in particular and economics in general? What is the *raison d'être* of this research program, apart from attempting to identify the microfoundation of Keynesian economics? If they were to say that it is worthwhile to compare it with the general equilibrium model of Walrasian economics, it simply begs the question: a comparison of two models based on microeconomics is important only if the procedure of methodological reduction to individuals can be justified. Later, in the 1980s, we no longer encountered articles of this genre in the top journals. Indeed, it might be high time to seriously reconsider the importance of the microfoundation of economics. Ultimately, the question we must ask is: do we really need one?

Notes

1 Comments from Naoki Haraya, Mikio Ito, and Masahiro Kawamata are gratefully acknowledged. They helped push me to consider economics methodology and assisted also in clarifying the previously weak points of this chapter. The usual disclaimers apply.
2 Boehm (1983) points out that there are several different definitions of "subjectivism."
3 Milford's comment on Menger's "Wesen" deserves to be quoted: "It is indeed true that Menger frequently uses the term das 'Wesen.' But it is quite impossible to infer any philosophical theory defended by Menger from the frequency of his using this term" (Milford 2010: 174). This is a typical example of misunderstanding by those eager to read some profound message among the German words, whatever they are. It is true that Germany and Austria are so-called philosophers' countries, but this does not mean that every word from them bears a deep philosophical meaning. I am certain that this "profound" interpretation contributed to the popularization of Aristotelian readings of Menger's texts.
4 For a detailed analysis of the methodological differences between Menger and Ludwig Mises, see Okon (Chapter 8) in this volume. Okon also mentions the concept of "imaginary wants" in the second edition of *Grundsätze*. One can well imagine that it was totally ridiculous from the standpoint of radical subjectivism, as represented by Mises: obviously, Mises's subjectivism is much more radical than that of Menger, as Okon emphasizes in his chapter. In Mises's own words:

> Die Wissenschaft vom Handeln hat das Handeln zu betrachten und zu erforschen, nicht aber werten und zu richten. Sie kennt nichts gutes und schlechtes, richtiges und unrichtiges, vernünftiges und unvernünftiges Handeln; für sie ist alles keine Wertmasstäbe, um das Handeln an ihnen zu messen. Sie erforscht das Sein des Handelns und fragt nicht danach, wie gehandel werden soll.
>
> ([1940] 1980: 14)

To be sure, this can be interpreted as a critique against the moderate subjectivism of Menger, who did not deny the normative aspect of human behavior. In fact, it was Mises who first criticized the subjectivism in Menger's economics as being insufficient. See Mises ([1933] 2003), Chapter 5. For this information, I owe a debt of gratitude to Hiroyuki Okon.
5 See Ikeda (1995: 211–12).
6 For Mischler's economics in general and his relationship with Menger, see Ikeda (1997: 90–116). Mischler was a professor of economics at Prague University when Menger was a student there.
7 This ambiguity has led to a dispute among Menger scholars, as to whether his methodology can be interpreted within the Aristotelian or Kantian framework. Smith indicates seven points of Aristotelian philosophy that are, in his view, vitally important in analyzing Menger in particular and the Austrian School of Economics in general. The first point is that "the world exists, independently of our thinking and reasoning activities" (Smith 1990: 266). Mäki also emphasizes the realist aspect of the Austrian School of Economics when he says that "If it is correct to say that many Austrian economists are realists in the above sense, then it is also correct to say that they are objectivists" (1990: 294). Even after considering these passages and checking the relevant portions of *Untersuchungen*, I am not quite certain whether Menger vindicated or challenged this point. As far as we know from his arguments in 1883, his standpoint is far from clear.
8 I believe that the following remark might be a good description of what Menger was thinking of:

> Austrian economics is entirely comparable in this respect to the more recent "universals of language" research program in linguistics. Here too the assumption is

made that there are structures in (linguistic) reality which are universal to all languages. Such structures are at least tacitly familiar to everyone who has dealings with the objects concerned (i.e., to every speaker of a language).

(Smith 1990: 278–9)

As I wrote in the text, Menger was far from aware of the delicate problem of how possible it is for us to see, interpret, and analyze natural and social phenomena by using the same types.

9 Lawson's pertinent comments must be quoted here: "Now, Menger at no stage explains why the simplest elements must be thought of as strictly typical" (1996: 451). Furthermore, "That theory must start with the simplest elements is simply asserted by Menger" (1996: 452). The description in this section draws heavily on Lawson.

10 For a detailed analysis of von Wieser's economics, see Arena (2010).

11 See the following note in *Pure Theory of Capital*, in which Hayek explains the origins of his concept:

This device was used most systematically by Friedrich von Wieser, first in his Natural Value [London: Macmillan, 1893; first German edition 1889] and later in his Social Economics [London: George Allen & Unwin, 1927; first German edition 1914], where he prefixed his theory of the social economy with an elaborate theory of what he called 'simple economy,' i.e., a centrally directed economy.

(Hayek [1941] 2008: 50, n. 16)

Bibliography

Alter, M. (1990) *Carl Menger and the Origins of Austrian Economics*, Boulder, CO: Westview Press.

Arena, R. (2010) "Friedrich von Wieser on institutions and social economics," in E. Hagemann, T. Nishizawa, and Y. Ikeda (eds.) *Austrian Economics in Transition: From Carl Menger to Friedrich Hayek*, London: Palgrave Macmillan.

Barro, R.J. and Grossman, H.I. (1971) "A general disequilibrium model of income and employment," *American Economic Review*, 61(1): 82–93.

Benassy, J.P. (1975) "Neo-Keynesian disequilibrium theory in a monetary economy," *Review of Economic Studies*, 42(4): 503–23.

Boehm, S. (1983) "The ambiguous notion of subjectivism: Comment on Lachmann," in I.M. Kirzner (ed.) *Method, Process, and Austrian Economics: Essays in Honor of Ludwig von Mises*, Lexington, MA: D.C. Heath and Company.

Caldwell, B. (ed.) (1990) *Carl Menger and His Legacy in Economics* (Annual Supplement to volume 22, History of Political Economy), Durham, NC, and London: Duke University Press.

Drèze, J.H. (1975) "Existence of an exchange equilibrium under price rigidities," *International Economic Review*, 16(2): 301–20.

Hagemann, H., Nishizawa, T., and Ikeda, Y. (eds.) (2010) *Austrian Economics in Transition: From Carl Menger to Friedrich Hayek*, London: Palgrave Macmillan.

Hayek, F. (1941) *Pure Theory of Capital*; reprinted in L. White (ed.) (2008) *The Collected Works of F.A. Hayek*, vol. XII, *Pure Theory of Capital*, New York and London: Routledge.

Ikeda, Y. (1995) "Roscher's *Grundlagen* in the history of economic thought," *Journal of Economic Studies*, 22(3/4/5): 209–20.

Ikeda, Y. (1997) *Die Enstehungsgeschichte der "Grundsätze" Carl Mengers*, St. Katharinen: Scripta Mercaturae Verlag.

Kauder, E. (1965) *A History of Marginal Utility*, Princeton, NJ: Princeton University Press.
Knies, K. (1853) *Die politische Oekonomie vom Standpunkte der geschichtlichen Methode*, Braunschweig: C.S. Schwetschke und Sohn.
Lawson, C. (1996) "Realism, theory, and individualism in the work of Carl Menger," *Review of Social Economy*, 54(4): 445–64.
Mäki, U. (1990) "Mengerian economics in a realist perspective," in B. Caldwell (ed.) *Carl Menger and His Legacy in Economics* (Annual Supplement to volume 22, History of Political Economy), Durham, NC, and London: Duke University Press.
Menger, C. (1871; 2nd edn., 1923) *Grundsätze der Volkswirtschaftslehre*, trans. James Dingwall and Bert F. Hoselitz, *Principles of Economics*, Ludwig von Mises Institute. Online, available at: http://mises.org/etexts/menger/principles.asp (accessed July 2011).
Menger, C. (1883) *Untersuchungen über die Methode der Socialwissenschaften und der politischen Oekonomie insbesondere*, trans. Francis J. Nock (1996), *Investigations into the Method of the Social Sciences*, Grove City, PN: Libertarian Press.
Milford, K. (1990) "Menger's methodology," in B. Caldwell (ed.) *Carl Menger and His Legacy in Economics* (Annual Supplement to volume 22, History of Political Economy), Durham, NC, and London: Duke University Press.
Milford, K. (2010) "A note on Menger's problem situation and non-essentialist approach to economics," in E. Hagemann, T. Nishizawa, and Y. Ikeda (eds.) *Austrian Economics in Transition: From Carl Menger to Friedrich Hayek*, London: Palgrave Macmillan.
Mischler, P. (1857) *Grundsätze der National-Oekonomie*, Vienna: Verlag von Friedrich Manz.
Mises, L. (1933) *Grundprobleme der Nationalökonomie: Untersuchungen über Verfahren, Aufgaben und Inhalt der Wirtschafts- und Gesellschaftslehre*, trans. George Reisman (2003), *Epistemological Problems of Economics*, 3rd edn., Ludwig von Mises Institute. Online, available at: http://mises.org/resources/116/Epistemological-Problems-of-Economics (accessed August 2011).
Mises, L. (1940) *Nationalökonomie: Theorie des Handelns und Wirtschaftens*, reprinted as L. Mises (1980) *Nationalökonomie: Theorie des Handelns und Wirtschaftens*, Munich: Philosophia Verlag.
Roscher, W. (1854) *Grundlagen der Nationaloekonomie*, Stuttgart and Tübingen: J.G. Cotta'scher Verlag.
Smith, B. (1990) "Aristotle, Menger, Mises: an essay in the metaphysics of economics," in B. Caldwell (ed.) *Carl Menger and His Legacy in Economics* (Annual Supplement to volume 22, History of Political Economy), Durham, NC, and London: Duke University Press.
von Wieser, F. (1889) *Der natürliche Wert*, Vienna: Alfred Hölder.

7 Böhm-Bawerk's objectivism beyond Menger's subjectivism

Shigeki Tomo[1]

If Böhm-Bawerk had entirely agreed with Menger's subjectivism, there would be no need for this chapter. It would be sufficient for those who want to know about Böhm-Bawerk's subjectivism to read Menger's *Grundsätze der Volkswirtschaftslehre*. In fact, at Innsbruck University during the early 1880s, Böhm-Bawerk repeatedly taught almost all of the essential ideas that appeared in the first five chapters of Menger's work: the four conditions for a thing to be a good for an economizing individual (Menger 1871, ch. 1),[2] the condition for a good to be an economic good (ibid., ch. 2),[3] the subjective definition of value on the basis of the loss principle (ibid., ch. 3),[4] the conditions for exchange (ibid., ch. 4),[5] and the formation of prices in the isolated and competitive markets (ibid., ch. 5).[6]

By contrast with the contents of those unpublished Innsbruck lectures on economics, *Nationalökonomie*, his famous *Economic Journal* article on the Austrian Economists in 1891, Böhm-Bawerk's objectivism in the understanding price is evident.[7] He stated that, according to Austrian-Economists' conclusions:

> the price or "*objective value*" of goods is a sort of resultant of the different subjective estimates of the goods which the buyers and sellers make in accordance with the law of final utility; and, indeed, the price coincides very nearly with the estimate of the "last buyer."[8]
>
> (Böhm-Bawerk 1891, p. 362)

It was not in the 1891 article that Böhm-Bawerk's way of thinking, which perceived price as an objective entity, made its first appearance, even though the phenomenon of market price resulted from subjective evaluations of market participants.

Already as early as 1886, Böhm-Bawerk presented his objectivist interpretation of price in "Grundzüge der Theorie des wirtschaftlichen Güterwerts." One of the major purposes of that paper was to divide Menger's theory of value and price into two parts: the theory of subjective value and that of price as objective exchange value. This division led to its two-part publication in the German economics journal, *Conrad Jahrbücher*: the first part in pp. 1–88, and the second in pp. 477–541. The latter is entitled "Theorie des objecktiven Tauschwertes."

Of course, Böhm-Bawerk replaced the title of the second part with "Price" when incorporating it into *Positive Theorie des Kapitales* in 1888.[9] However, this does not mean that he withdrew his conceptualization of price as objective exchange value. On the contrary, he maintained it almost until his death. In his later lectures on economics at Vienna University, which he prepared as an emeritus professor after having resigned from the office of third Financial Minister under Körber's cabinet in 1905, Böhm-Bawerk assigned four pages of his lecture notebooks on economics to repeating his objectivist explanation. He titled these pages, "Preis u. objektiver Tauschwert."[10]

To characterize Austrian subjectivism properly, it is necessary to consider not only Böhm-Bawerk's long-lasting objectivism, but also its serious violation of Menger's second subjectivism. Such consideration would make it possible to explain the reason Menger told Schumpeter, "the time will come when people will realize that Böhm-Bawerk's theory is one of the greatest errors ever committed."[11] If one assumes "Böhm-Bawerk's theory" in this statement refers his theory of interest because Böhm-Bawerk criticized Menger's use theory of interest, then Schumpeter's recollection would deserve no attention from the modern microeconomics viewpoint, which adopts the Böhm-Bawerk–Fisher intertemporal discount theory of interest. However, a major divide existed between the Austrian Grandmaster Menger and the Master Böhm-Bawerk with respect to the nature of market price.

In what follows, this chapter will argue that the divide did not remain at this high mastery level, but involved at least three eminent Austrians: Wieser, Schumpeter, and Mises. Their attitudes toward Böhm-Bawerk's transformation from atemporal to intertemporal kinds of objectivism eventually introduced certain major analytic conceptions to the history of economic thought: namely, natural value, the view of money as a veil, the historically transmitted purchasing power of money, and the indispensability of money in economic calculation. The last two are, attributable to Mises, in chronological order, but characterized as by-products of Mises' regression from intertemporal to atemporal objectivism, proposed by the older Master Böhm-Bawerk.

Menger's second subjectivism[12]

The first three conditions for a thing to be a good – including subjective elements, human need, and the recognition of a thing's capacity for satisfying said need – presented in the opening chapter of Menger's *Grundsätze* had already been mentioned by Wilhelm Roscher,[13] and the fourth condition – namely, whether an economizing individual has the thing in command or not – is to be objectively judged.[14] Therefore, Menger's new subjectivism, which Hayek later confessed to have acquired from Menger, must be located outside the definition of goods. One could detect it in the next chapter, where the fourth objective command (*Verfügung*) concept of goods is subjectified by Menger. To be sure, what one has in command seems to be objective as a numerical quantity, but Menger finds the available quantity (*verfügbare Quantität*) as a piece of subjective knowledge regarding the acquisitive possibilities of trade, production, or other means in the inequality of scarcity condition for a good to be economic, namely, the demanded quantity > the available quantity. Any economizing behavior would not be required for what are known to be things that are easily obtained, even though, at present, there is not enough in command.

The subjectification of the command concept as knowledge is Menger's first expression of the new subjectivism. The second is found in Chapters V and VI of Menger's *Grundsätze*. It is fully compatible with the assertion he made when criticizing Eberhard Friedländer in the longest footnote in Chapter III, in which he argued that objective value does not exist.[15]

In the beginning of Chapter V of *Grundsätze*, entitled "Price," Menger claims that price does not represent anything objective, like the equivalent quantity of labor embodied in the commodities exchanged at the market. This assertion so much impressed almost all historians of economics that they have been moved to interpret Menger as a revolutionary who opposed the classical labor theory of value.

Furthermore, from his journalist observation of the Vienna stock market,[16] Menger came to be aware of the non-objectiveness of market price: a stock's price can assure neither its purchase nor sale in the future, because it can serve as the rate of exchange only for those who could achieve transaction. That is why he asserted that, "if goods were equivalents in this sense, there would be no reason, market conditions remaining unchanged, why every exchange should not be capable of reversal."[17] To underscore the point that there are no objective equivalents in price, Menger relied on the historical fact that there had never existed a market in which any buyer could resell his purchased commodity at the same price at will. In addition, he demonstrated, by constructing his famous horse-trading model, the fact that, even in a competitive market, there are often traders excluded from achieving actual transactions due to their irrelevant quoted prices. The realized price is economically meaningful only for those who could execute their transaction; it has little meaning for those excluded.

The exclusion of some participants from actual transactions due to his/her quoted price means that the market price could be the rate of exchange only for those market participants able to realize their purchases and sales at the market price, because they were not excluded from the transaction. For the buyers and sellers excluded from transactions, the market price is not their exchange rate, but only a part of their knowledge. Furthermore, market price would not be knowledge for many non-participants in market transactions, since they did not concern themselves with that market price. In this sense, market price, as a rate of exchange, is not objective, but an exclusively subjective phenomenon by nature.

The chapter following the "Price" chapter of *Grundsätze*, entitled "Value in Use and Value in Exchange," is where Menger subjectifies the concept of value in exchange by introducing the distinction between direct and indirect manners, which can be used by economizing individuals to ensure need-satisfaction. Use for one's own purposes is direct, whereas exchange is indirect. From this individualist point of view, Menger saw this distinction as "the two forms of the one general value phenomenon,"[18] and defined exchange value as "the importance that goods acquire for us because their possession assures the same result indirectly."[19] This definition must be interpreted as a foundation for Menger's subjectivist understanding of the nature of price.

Static or atemporal objectiveness

Menger's second subjectivism denied any objective meaning in the nature of market price even after its formation. Böhm-Bawerk, surely following Menger's subjectivism, agreed with the idea that, before price formation, namely, the market process of price formation, was inherently subjective, but went further than Menger to suggest the objective role played by the finally established price system. We have to distinguish the situation before and after the occurrence of price formation to fully understand Böhm-Bawerk's objectivism and its departure from Menger's subjectivism. In this sense, it would be misleading to accept the following statement by Hennings: "the theory of objective value is the attempt to explain the formation of prices in markets."[20]

Once the level of prices has been determined, regardless of whether the determination has been embraced by market competitors, or the role of government policies, it should have some kind of objective meaning. If two goods, A and B, have their own definite prices, it needs to be numerically shown how much A would correspond to a unit of B in terms of price. Böhm-Bawerk called this the power of exchange (*Tauschkraft*)[21] and regarded it as an objective property of goods. After the formation of prices, in which subjective valuations resulted, the new objective function of the price system emerges: the indication for quantity relations between goods in terms of their prices.

Whenever a price list is displayed in a shop, everyone can objectively know the equivalent-rate of one commodity to another that the shop is providing and determine how dear each commodity is in comparison with others. In addition, in microeconomics, the competitive equilibrium price has a certain theoretical objectiveness. Under the assumption of a given price known to all the members of the economy, everyone can optimally allocate his/her resources. Otherwise, nobody could maximize his/her utility and profit in equilibrium. From the viewpoint of microeconomics, it could be possible to interpret Böhm-Bawerk's life-long adherence to price objectiveness as being motivated by the need to represent the static or atemporal meaning of equilibrium price in competitive economies.

Nevertheless, the equilibrium market price provides no guarantee to any future exchanges: all the transactions at that price must be completely cleared at the same time the price is established. Only during periods in which the price system known to everyone in an economy remains unchanged can price objectiveness be maintained.

The road to objectivism

In his 1876 seminar paper at Heidelberg, Böhm-Bawerk had already come to a modern reinterpretation of the legal conception of loan (mutuum) as an exchange of present and the future goods. Accordingly, it was thus natural for him to apply his philosophy of price objectiveness to the rate of interest as an intertemporal price phenomenon.[22] For this application, Böhm-Bawerk devoted "Book V. Present and Future"[23] of *Positive Theorie*, which contains the three famous reasons for the existence of positive interest rates, to "show how the ratio that obtains between present and future goods in subjective valuations is transferred to their *objective exchange value*."[24] Moreover, the regular existence of certain positive rates of interest as macro-economic valuables or properties of economic communities is indicated by the historical prohibition of interest-taking by the Catholic Church. Karl Knies provided his twenty-five-year-old seminarian, Böhm-Bawerk, with historical information on the controversies over the prohibition of interest-taking through the scholarship he did on credit in 1876. This scholarship reveals the existence of positive interest rates even in the stationary state of the middle ages, and might have led Böhm-Bawerk to presuppose the existence of objective interest rates. By using the expression "the interest rate particular to the country" (*der landesübliche Zinsfuß*) three times in the opening chapter on the problem of interest in *Geschichte und Kritik der Kapitalzinstheorien*,[25] he appeared to be recognizing a kind of objectiveness in the interest rates at the macro-economic level in society as a whole.

Because of the way he understood the historical nature of interest rates and his need to clarify the methodological assumption for his macroeconomic model of distribution, namely the period-of-production model, Böhm-Bawerk was obliged to consciously maintain the idea of price objectiveness in 1886. Since the main theoretical structure of that model involved choosing the average period of production subject to the maximization of profit under a given product price and wages, "price and wages" objectiveness must be assumed for its construction. The assumption that prices are "given" means that they are objectively known to every optimizing member of the economy.

Böhm-Bawerk took a detour in publishing *Positive Theorie*, probably to underline the assumption of price objectiveness. In his letter to Carl Menger, dated December 24, 1884, just after the publication of the first part of *Kapital and Kapitalzins, Geschichte und Kritik*, he announced that Part II, *Positive Theorie*, would appear within half a year.[26] However, this did not occur. Instead of rushing its publication, Böhm-Bawerk had an opportunity to reformulate Menger's subjective theory of value and price. From another letter from Böhm-Bawerk to Menger dated July 13, 1886, one could see that it was not by Menger's recommendation, but by Böhm-Bawerk's own independent decision that *Grundzüge* was prepared and published.[27] Since almost all the content of *Grundzüge* was later incorporated into the beginning of Book III of *Positive Theorie*, Böhm-Bawerk's detour must have been motivated by his theoretical agenda to construct his macroeconomic distribution model.

However, another three-year postponement of the publication of *Positive Theorie* following that of *Grundzüge* in 1886[28] would have had nothing to do with Böhm-Bawerk's objectivism. Rather, it can be explained otherwise: the conceptualization of the average period of production. To be sure, this concept is a serious violation of Böhm-Bawerk's earlier intertemporal viewpoint, because, without any qualifications, it adds the labor amounts existing at different periods of time, which should theoretically be regarded as different economic goods and thus incapable of simple summation. As far as its atemporalization is concerned, the concept of the average production period may belong to the same category as price objectiveness. However, since the latter was clearly presented in 1886, it cannot be the main reason for the postponement of Böhm-Bawerk's publication.

The transformation of Böhm-Bawerk's objectivism

Böhm-Bawerk's atemporal objectivism has transformed into an intertemporal kind of objectivism over the course of two decades. The first step was marked by Wieser's support with a slight improvement in nomenclature. To clarify what had been left unanswered by Böhm-Bawerk regarding the relation between subjective evaluations in a competitive market and price objectiveness, Wieser coined the concept of natural value. Then, after inspiring Schumpeter's instant conception of money as a veil as a way of evading the marginal-utility problem of the value of money, Böhm-Bawerk finally introduced his old perspective of intertemporality as a means for revising price objectiveness. After Mises applied his mentor's revised idea to reach his concept of the historically transmitted objective exchange value of money, Mises restarted the quest for the reinterpretation of older atemporal objectiveness. One of the major results for Mises was to identify the indispensability of money in economic calculation.

Wieser

The objective function of a given price system, which Böhm-Bawerk called the power of exchange, does not necessarily secure any other exchanges at those price levels – quite the contrary with respect to goods in general in real life. Even when the price of a snack is $10, it is very hard for the possessor of the same snack to secure $10 at will in exchange for it. In this sense, the term "the power of exchange" or "purchasing power" is not as suitable for expressing the price objectiveness of goods in general as money. Though he shared the idea of price objectiveness with Böhm-Bawerk in his publication of *Der natürliche Werth* in 1889, Friedrich von Wieser did not adopt Böhm-Bawerk's 1886 term *Tauschkraft*, and instead introduced the much better expression, "the ranking of goods in the economic transaction" (*der Rang der Güter im volkswirtschaftlichen Verkehre*) (1889, S. 49). Needless to say, the connotation of the phrase does not contain any possibility for or assumption of another exchange.

Of course, Wieser did not ostensibly point out that he thought it would be better to escape from the limited qualification of "exchange" in the explanation of price objectiveness. However, if one looks, not at the English translation, but at the German original of *Der natürliche Werth*, especially the title of §. 14 of Chapter II (1889, S. 48),[29] one can easily detect Wieser's intention: he added "transaction value" (*Verkehrswert*)[30] after the main title, "Exchange value in the objective sense." This addition can be read as Wieser's positive proposal for the dismissal of the exchange qualification. Nevertheless, the English translation unfortunately failed to reveal this dismissal properly for English-speaking readers, as it omitted Wieser's original German term *Verkehrswert*.[31] The reason for this omission is very simple: the translator identified it with exchange value (*Tauschwert*). Still, since exchange (*Tausch*) is literally only a part of transactions (*Verkehr*), this identification could not differentiate Wieser's from Böhm-Bawerk's expression for price objectiveness.

Wieser's concept of natural value was originally a theoretical apparatus; it was not an effort to adopt any kind of general equilibrium,[32] but rather to underline that price objectiveness has nothing to do with the market process of subjective valuation, and that it is impossible to systematically explain price objectiveness by using the principle of marginal utility. It should be added that Wieser acknowledged the objectiveness of already-established market prices. On one hand, the price formation or the formation of transaction value (*Verkehrswert*):

> is disturbed by human imperfection, by error, fraud, force, chance; and on the other, by the present order of society, by the existence of private property, and by the differences between rich and poor, as a consequence of which latter a second element mingles itself in the formation of exchange value, namely, purchasing power.
>
> (Malloch tr. 1893, pp. 61–62)

In order to direct the readers' attention to the subjective principle of marginal utility before price formation, or "in a community at a high stage of development carrying on its economic life without price or exchange,"[33] Wieser coined the concept of natural value, and asserted that "the value which we looked at in the first book, under the elementary theory, is natural value."[34] The first book of *Der natürliche Wert* contains his elaboration on the theory of marginal utility. It is, therefore, impossible for Wieser's natural value to be objective in manner of price objectiveness or *Verkehrswert*.

Schumpeter

According to his above-mentioned recollection of Menger, as well as his participation in Böhm-Bawerk's seminar *Volkswirtschaftliche Übungen* in the summer[35] semester of 1905, Schumpeter surely would have had an opportunity to consider deeply the difference between Menger's subjectivist and Böhm-Bawerk's objectivist understandings of the nature of market price and money. Nevertheless, all we can find in *Das Wesen und Hauptinhalt der theoretischen*

Nationalökonomie regarding price objectiveness are several superficial sentences indicating Schumpeter's mere concern:

> to recognize something objective in the exchange value would be as if it tried to sinfully pity something different from the use value, even after having given up the embedded quantity of labor for the explanation of the exchange value.[36]
>
> (Schumpeter 1908, pp. 109-110)

Schumpeter, as a proponent of Walras, did not recognize the theoretical importance of the objective exchange value or purchasing power of money or numéraire from the static viewpoint. After equilibrium price formation occurred in competitive markets, the purchasing power of money or numéraire can be objectively calculated using these formed prices, and can never influence the monetary price determination itself in a static economy.

Whether Schumpeter had this idea in mind before or after writing *Das Wesen* is still an open question. However, it is very likely that it was before, since Böhm-Bawerk and Wieser served as the examiners for Schumpeter's habilitation, which was finally acknowledged at a faculty meeting held on February 15, 1909 (Yagi 1993, p. 73). In any case, in moving from the static to the dynamic worlds in his second book on economic development in 1911, he tried to transplant the atemporal objectiveness of money value by referring to the static concept of money as a mere veil (*Schleier*) for exchanging economy (Schumpeter 1911, 6th ed. [1934], S. 66). As a result, Schumpeter failed to theoretically grasp the intertemporal unneutrality of money in a developing economy, although he could evade the bane of marginal utility in explaining the objective exchange value of money.

Intertemporality

Clearly, even when Good A is priced at $10 and Good B priced at $5, it is almost impossible to directly exchange one A for two Bs in the real world. Only money, rather than goods in general, has the objective power of actual exchange, namely, the purchasing power under a given price system. This fundamental understanding might have later brought about Böhm-Bawerk's transformation regarding the notion of price objectiveness: he purged his older 1886 explanation with the term "exchange power" (*Tauschkraft*) of goods,[37] and developed another explanation for the support of the idea of price objectiveness in the special section "*Preis u. objektiver Tauschwert*" in his 1912 Viennese lectures on economics.

For the atemporal concept "power of exchange" (*Tauschkraft*),[38] Böhm-Bawerk substituted an intertemporal element to maintain his philosophy of price objectiveness: expectation based on previously executed payment. At the beginning of that section, he made the following proposition:

> In terms of the price one can measure the exchange value of a good by how much was paid for the good under the situation similar to that of the past,

and expect according to the exchange value how much one can exchange for the good at present and in the future.

(1912, p. 193)[39]

He stated, "The situation similar to that in the past," which was not further described in those lectures, could be interpreted as a necessary condition for everyone to be able to objectively anticipate the price and thence exchange value at present and in future. Although Böhm-Bawerk did not derive any sufficient conditions for price objectiveness, the notion of intertemporality was still a breakthrough not only for Böhm-Bawerk's theory of interest, but also for the maintenance of his price objectivism in general.

The breakthrough should have been extended to the explanation of the objective exchange-value or purchasing power of money. However, Böhm-Bawerk could not liberate himself from his ardent life-long belief in metallic standard currency.[40] At Vienna as well as at Innsbruck, he taught that, under the institution of free coinage, the purchasing power of money must be subject to that of the precious metal used for coinage, which follows the marginal principle of demand and supply (Böhm-Bawerk 1912, p. 253, para. 72).[41] However, this cannot explain how the objective value or purchasing power of money emerges from the subjective use value of money, which both Böhm-Bawerk and Wieser identified with the subjective exchange value of money, because money is used fundamentally as the medium of exchange.

In explaining the objective purchasing power of money, the precious-metal-value principle probably would not have satisfied Böhm-Bawerk, because it has no linkage with the basic function of money in exchange. Of course, both gold and silver have their physical superiorities, but they are not the cause and effect of exchange. The prices of gold and silver are determined by their market, not by their physical properties.

So far, it appears no direct evidence has survived that shows Böhm-Bawerk's discontent with the explanation based on the precious-metal-value principle. Still, it is at least known that he instructed Mises to solve the theoretical imperfection of the precious-metal-value principle in his habilitation paper, which was published as *Theorie des Geldes und der Umlaufsmittel* in 1912 and acknowledged at a faculty meeting held on February 27, 1913, according to referee reports by Wieser and Philippovich.[42]

Mises

In its preface, which unfortunately remains untranslated in English, Mises referred to Böhm-Bawerk as the first who had introduced him to a theory of money and banking, although he himself likely had not chosen to pay attention to the problems of money and banking (Mises 1912, p. IV).[43] Since Böhm-Bawerk had actually published nothing on money and banking, Mises' evaluation of Böhm-Bawerk must have come from his own experiences in the old Master's seminars at Vienna University.

Unlike Schumpeter, Mises regularly attended Böhm-Bawerk's seminars before his habilitation (Mises 1978, S. 24). The extensive knowledge (*Belesenheit*)[44] of his mentor equipped Mises to examine critically the static Walrasian understanding of price objectiveness. Mises concentrated on equilibrium price: individual "exchange-ratios are determined within that range where both supply and demand are in exact quantitative equilibrium" (Batson 1934, p. 108). Once these exchange-ratios have been established, the "objective exchange value [of goods] is expressed in terms of money" (p. 48), whereas:

> The objective exchange-value of the monetary unit can be expressed in units of any individual commodity. Just as we are in the habit of speaking of a money price of the other exchangeable goods, so we may conversely speak of the commodity price of money, and have then so many expressions for the objective exchange-value of money as there are commercial commodities that are exchanged for money.
>
> (p. 188)

This equilibrium-theoretic indifferent classification of goods and money as mere numéraire "tell[s] us little" (p. 188); Mises called it the outer (*äußere*) objective exchange-value of money, and distinguished it from the inner (*innere*) one,[45] represented by the price of the precious metal used for coinage. It is obvious that the outer value is of no use for explaining the phenomenon of inflation, because it merely reflects a timeless or photographic relationship between goods and money; furthermore, the inner one attributes inflation to the increasing amounts of precious metal.

In order to explain the objective exchange-value of money with some consistency in terms of price movement, Mises returned to his mentor's application of intertemporality:

> Once an exchange-ratio between money and commodities has been established in the market, it continues to exercise an influence beyond the period during which it is maintained; it provides the basis for the further valuation of money. Thus the past objective exchange-value of money has a certain significance for its present and future valuation. The money-prices of to-day are linked with those of yesterday and before, and with those of to-morrow and after.
>
> (Mises 1912, S. 108; Batson tr. 1934, p. 109)

Here, it is evident that Böhm-Bawerk's past-present-future point of view on price objectiveness led Mises to develop his idea of the historically transmitted objective exchange-value of money (*der geschichtlich überkommene objektive Tauschwert des Geldes*).[46] This is Mises' answer to the critical question: what are the determinants of the objective exchange-value or purchasing power of money? Although Mises did not succeed in fully elaborating on the "historically transmitting" process influencing the formation of the objective exchange-value, one can see the above quotation as indicating Mises' deeply serious confrontation with Böhm-Bawerk's stubborn philosophy regarding price objectiveness and his dissatisfaction with the precious-metal-value principle.

Another major way in which Mises profited through the objectiveness discourse together with Böhm-Bawerk was his notice of the indispensability of money for economic calculation. This is usually understood as the kernel of Mises' critique of the socialist economic system. To be sure, in his 1920 paper, published just after the establishment of the Soviet Union, he discussed this issue for the first time. Eight years had passed since Mises had adopted Böhm-Bawerk's intertemporal perspective as his own understanding of price objectiveness. However, Mises' discovery of the special role of money in economic calculation did not come from any further development of the idea of intertemporality, but was rather one of successful consequences by retracing of his mentor's intellectual development with respect to the concepts of exchange and wealth computation.

When Böhm-Bawerk was twenty-five years old, he had been so radical that he had reduced the legal concept of loan to the concept of exchange: in economics, loan should be interpreted as an intertemporal exchange between present and future goods. This was repeated in the Master's late Viennese lectures on economics: according to Böhm-Bawerk, "Economists understand the concept of exchange much wider than the jurists do. Exchange in economics includes onerous transferences like purchase, rent, leasehold, loan, and employment contract, etc."[47]

Böhm-Bawerk's economic teaching that the various transactions should be reduced to exchange reflects his fundamental understanding that economics should treat exchange as the starting point for the explanation of all economic phenomena. This philosophy might lead Mises to the emphasis of economics as the science of exchange, namely, catallactics. His first application of this idea can be seen in his classification of the theories of money in a 1917 paper, where he utilizes the dichotomy between catallactic and acatallactic theories (1912, p. 191).[48] The catallactic theory of money should have been investigated from the viewpoint of atemporal or intertemporal distinction. The fact of its absence in that paper may be interpreted as a prelude for Mises to return to the atemporal objectiveness of price.

The main purpose of Böhm-Bawerk's reference to the concept of wealth computation in his 1879 habilitation paper[49] was to criticize Menger's use theory of interest. If one assumes the existence of the use of money as an economic good, for which interest is paid, then the forbidden double-counting should take place in wealth computation. This assertion would later be refuted with respect to credit obligation (*Forderungsrecht*) by Menger in the single footnote of the obituary he wrote for Böhm-Bawerk (Hayek 1934, p. 301). Mises knew this controversy well (1912, p. 33), and probably understood the general premise of wealth computation, which used the objective exchange-values of goods as the unit for computation. Unless prices were objectively given, one could not compute the economic value of his own possessions or wealth at all.

This perspective crystallized itself in a sentence from Mises' 1920 paper: "In an exchange economy, the objective exchange-value of commodities enters as the unit of economic calculation" (S. 94; Hayek 1935, p. 97). It is not any physical units, such as kilogram, meter, or liter, but the prices or the objective exchange-values that are indispensable to economic calculation. These are expressed in terms of money. Money is, therefore, indispensable for indirect exchange as well as the expression of the objective exchange-value as the unit of economic calculation. Here, we can see that the student has surpassed the master by presenting a new interpretation of price objectiveness. Whereas Böhm-Bawerk clearly mentioned nothing about the economic function of price objectiveness and introduced the idea of intertemporality to revise price objectiveness, Mises, after following Böhm-Bawerk's conversion to an intertemporal perspective, returned to the previous atemporal conception of price objectiveness, and then resurrected it in the form of the fundamental proposition of money: money or the monetary expression of the objective exchange-value of goods is indispensable to economic calculation.

Although Mises' achievement must be seen as establishing the foundation for criticism of the socialist economic system, it is not compatible with Menger's second subjectivism with respect to the temporal nature of market price since it is still in line with Böhm-Bawerk's atemporal conception of price objectiveness.

Mises called market prices "exchange-relations" (*Austauschverhältnisse*) at least thirteen times in his 1920 paper, just as Böhm-Bawerk had referred to the "exchange power" (*Tauschkraft*) of goods. Both expressions represent these thinkers' atemporal view of exchange and price. Of course, all market prices are the results of exchange, but the act of exchange that determines price always belongs to the past, never to the future. Market prices in our actual lives do not tell us what money can or will be able to buy, but what it did in fact buy. Therefore, the equilibrium market price can represent neither exchange power nor exchange relation in the future. In the future, the price must be determined again catallactically, namely, in another market process of exchange or transaction. There is no guarantee that the price of a good will remain the same in future.

Concluding remarks

The philosophy of price objectiveness supported by Böhm-Bawerk and Wieser (1889, p. 53)[50] in opposition to Menger in the late 1880s merely represented an atemporal understanding of a theoretical characterization of the price system in an economy at a certain time and place. Both disciples of Menger did not give any theoretical elucidation to the process of how price objectiveness emerges through the market integration of subjective evaluations, at least not in their work during the nineteenth century. However, in the first decade of the subsequent century, Böhm-Bawerk did locate the intertemporal condition that allowed price to be objective: a same or similar economic situation in which everyone expects no change in the relative prices. In the sense that this idea survived in Mises' concept of the historically transmitted objective exchange value of money, and that Böhm-Bawerk's atemporal objectivism brought Mises to the idea of the indispensability of money in economic calculation, it was not Menger–Böhm-Bawerk's subjectivism, but rather Böhm-Bawerk's objectivism that could more fully explain the various continuities in the doctrinal developments of later generations of the Austrian School.

Since the transformation of Böhm-Bawerk's objectivism is evidenced in his lecture notebooks of 1912, it seemed that Menger was not aware of Böhm-Bawerk's intertemporal objectivism. In the same year, 1914, when Böhm-Bawerk suddenly died at Kramsach Achenrain in Tirol due to pulmonary thromboembolism, Wieser acknowledged in his *Theorie der gesellschaftlichen Wirtschaft* that there is no objective exchange-value. Returning to Menger's subjectivist understanding of market, Wieser gave his reasoning behind the non-objectiveness of market price: "It [objective exchange-value] never holds for those persons who do not wish to take part in the exchange because the price, as it stands, is either too high or too low for their personal valuation" (Hinrichs 1927, p. 235).

This statement is surely ambiguous with respect to the automatic exclusion of participants from transactions due to the offers they make in the competitive market, but Wieser was fully aware of the point Menger had mentioned regarding the non-objectivity of market price in Chapter V of *Grundsätze*. No evidence survives to indicate whether Menger and Wieser were discussing price objectiveness on the day of Böhm-Bawerk's funeral. At any rate, Wieser could escape Menger's blame for seeing prices as being objective.

Menger was so clear-minded that he could unconsciously follow Frege–Popper's definition of objective knowledge (Popper 1979, ch. 3). Menger found that market price could have economic meaning only for those who could achieve a transaction at that price. The knowledge of market price is not economically meaningful for all members of society. Its economic meaning as an exchange rate depends on whether market participants, as knowing subjects, could realize the transaction or not. In this sense, a market price is not any kind of objective knowledge, because it does not fulfill the Frege–Popper criterion of "knowledge without a knowing subject."

Money must be objective according to the Frege–Popper criterion: everyone has it because he/she knows it is generally accepted in exchange for those goods that he/she wants to obtain. Surely, the salability of commodities in general is not objective because it depends on their market situation. However, the highest salability, marketability, or liquidity among commodities must be objective, because it is so fully known to all members of an economy as the commodity possessing the highest salability functions as the medium of economic exchange.

Nevertheless, the last chapter of Menger's *Grundsätze* on money does not have any statements of the objectiveness of money in terms of its origin. This may not be because he tenaciously maintained his subjectivist position, but rather because the spontaneousness of some social institution (such as money) is not equivalent to its objectiveness and Menger might have been concerned with the former much more than the latter. This point also remains an open question for future research.

Notes

1. My thanks go to Professor Endres who kindly gave me helpful comments to the former version.
2. Tomo (1998, p. 86). Böhm-Bawerk omitted the fifth condition, "knowledge," which he had introduced in *Rechte und Verhältnisse*.
3. Tomo (1998, p. 89f.).
4. Ibid. (p. 92f.).
5. Ibid. (p. 178f.).
6. Ibid. (p. 184f.).
7. Böhm-Bawerk's earlier Innsbruck lectures did not refer to the objectivist understanding of price. However, it would be dangerous to assume that he did not have any objectivist thoughts with respect to price in the preparation period of his lectures, simply because Böhm-Bawerk did not mention his own time-discount theory of interest. He did refer to the Mengerian use theory of interest in his university lectures. Yet he had pronounced against Knies' use theory in his 1876 report on interest theory in Knies' Seminar at Heidelberg University. See Yagi (1983).
8. Italics inserted by the present author.
9. This book appeared in December 1888, although its title page lists 1889 as its publication year.
10. Böhm-Bawerk (1912, S. 193, in para. 54). Of price and price formation in general, Chapter 1, "Theory of Price," in *Book III Economic Transaction*. The New York Public Library gives no date for Böhm-Bawerk's *National-Oekonomie* because no information is included on its title page. However, according to the 1911 gold production data appearing on page 266, one can estimate the sale of the texts began after 1911 at the earliest.
11. Schumpeter (1954, p. 847). Endres (1987, p. 291) properly cited Streissler's suggestion regarding Menger's apparent dislike of Böhm-Bawerk's objectivism. Hennings attributed Böhm-Bawerk's dichotomy between subjective and objective values to "the older Continental tradition." Kurz (1997, p. 74).
12. The present author previously read this argument as part of a conference presentation. Tomo (2009).
13. Menger himself referred to this fact in the footnote. Menger (1871, S. 2).
14. Mises recognized the fourth as objective.
15. Menger (1871, S. 110): "Fr. gelangt denn auch lediglich zur Bestimmung des Masses für 'den objectiven Werth' der einzelnen Güter (S. 68), während *ein solcher* in Wahrheit doch gar nicht vorhanden ist." The reader must be careful to detect the error in the corresponding English translation: "Friedländer therefore arrives merely at the definition of a measure of the 'objective value' of different goods, although *a measure of this sort* does not, in reality, exist" Dingwall and Hoselitz (1981, p. 299). It is just because "ein solcher" in the German original points to the masculine noun "der objective Werth," and the German "Mass," meaning measure, is neutral.
16. See Yagi (2011, ch. 2).
17. Menger (1871, S. 174), Dingwall and Hoselitz (1981, p. 193).
18. Dingwall and Hoselitz (1981, p. 228).
19. Ibid. (p. 228).
20. Kurz (1997, p. 75).
21. Böhm-Bawerk (1886, the LSE edition, SS. 5–7, 54–55, 84, 86, and passim).
22. Böhm-Bawerk's *Jugendarbeit* and three Menger-Böhm letters were transcribed and republished by Yagi (1983), and detailed accounts on the background of these are found in Yagi (2011, p. 66f.).
23. W. Smart's translation modified the original chapter structure. Here, it corresponds to *III. Buch, III. Abschnitt, Gegenwart und Zukunft in der Wirtschaft* of the first edition.
24. Smart (1891, p. 278 [Böhm-Bawerk (1889) S. 295]). The italics were added by the present author.

25. Smart differentiated between his translations of those words: "the usual rate of interest" or "the customary rate of interest" (1890, p. 9); "the rate of interest usual in the country" Böhm-Bawerk (1884a, S. 394); Smart (1890, p. 344).
26. Yagi (1983, p. 39).
27. The author's transcription is partly available in Tomo (1994, p. 122).
28. Some more detailed accounts of the postponement are available in my English explanatory introduction "Eugen von Böhm-Bawerk's Innsbruck Lectures on Economics" to the reconstruction of Böhm-Bawerk's lectures at Innsbruck, Tomo (1998, p. 30ff.), which is essentially based on Tomo (1994, p. 110f.).
29. Wieser (1889, p. 48) titled the chapter, "*Tauschwerth im objectiven Sinne (Verkehrswerth).*"
30. Batson translated it as "value in business transaction" (1934, p. 100).
31. Chapter III of Book II of Malloch's translation.
32. A general interpretation of Wieser's similarity to Walras' theory of general equilibrium is given in Yagi (2011, p. 98).
33. Malloch (1893, p. 39).
34. Ibid. (p. 60).
35. The mistake of this term as "winter" by Haberler (1950, p. 337) and Allen (1991, p. 39) was corrected by Yagi (1993, p. 63).
36. Schumpeter described,

> Bebauptet man z. B. daß der Tauschwert eines Gutes gleich der in ihm enthaltenen Arbeitsmenge sei, dann ist er etwas sehr Festes, quantitativ Bestimmtes. Sieht man in ihm ferner etwas vom Gebrauchswerte Verschiedenes, dann hat er große Wichtigkeit. Hat man aber diese Auffassungen verlassen, so wäre es eine übel angebrachte Pietät, diesen Begriff, der ganz ihr Kind ist, zu schonen.

37. On the contrary, Menger acknowledged from the practical point of view that those conceptions like "money equivalents" or the "exchange power" of goods could not simply be called unrealistic. Latzer and Schmitz (2002, p. 61). But, of course, this acknowledgment is related not to the understanding of price, but to the conception of money as a standard of the exchange value of goods.
38. Earlier, on page 96, which included the part of his lecture that discussed kinds of values, Böhm-Bawerk defines value in the objective sense as the capability of a good to bring a thing in return to its owner in an exchange transaction (*das Fähigkeit eines Gutes, in Tauschverkehr ihrem Eigentümer eine Gegengabe zu verschaffen*).
39. Böhm-Bawerk taught,

> Man bemißt den Tauschwert nach der Höhe des Preis, der für ein Gut in ähnlicher Situation in der Vergangenheit gegeben wurde u. von dem man erwartet, daß man ihn auch in der Gegenwart u. in der Zukunft wird erlangen können.

40. See Böhm-Bawerk's earlier lectures, Tomo (1998, p. 216).
41. The lithographically reproduced texts were sold for the convenience of the overpopulated student body at Vienna University. To be sure, he did not publish any works on money, as pointed out by Anderson (1917, p. 48), but the chapter on money of his Viennese lectures must be the key surviving source for understanding Böhm-Bawerk's own thoughts on money and its value from the standpoint of marginal utility and his influence on contemporary Austrians like Schumpeter, Hilferding, Bauer, and Mises.
42. Personal records (*Personalakte*), Ludwig von Mises at *das allgemeine Verwaltungsarchiv* in Vienna.
43. Mises wrote, "In der Tat hat erst Böhm, mag er selbst auch den Problemen der Geld- und Banktheorie keinerlei Beachtung geschenkt haben, den Weg freigelegt, der zu ihnen führt."

44 This is a term used by Menger (1915). Hayek (1934, p. 299).
45 Batson ignored Mises' distinction and left two terms untranslated in English, indicating his own justification in the footnote on page 124.
46 The English translation of the phrase can be found on page 124 of Batson (1934), which translates it into "continuity"; this concept appears for the first time in the title of Chapter II.
47 Böhm-Bawerk taught, "Die Nationalökonomen fassen den Begriff des Tausches viel weiter als die Juristen. Er umfaßt jede entgeltl. Übertragung, sei es Kauf, Miete, Pacht, Darlehen, Dienstvertrag etc."
48 This paper was reproduced in Batson's English translation as Appendix A. I was kindly informed of this by Professor Okon.
49 This was acknowledged at the faculty meeting held on February 24, 1880, and the revised version was published in 1881.
50 Wieser pointed out, "Menger dagegen bringt eine vollendete Theorie des subjectiven Werthes, ohne aber den objectiven Werthbegriff zu entwickeln."

References

Allen, Robert Loring (1991) *Opening Doors: The Life and Work of Joseph Schumpeter*, New Brunswick: Transaction Publishers.
Anderson, B. M. Jr. (1917) *The Value of Money*, New York: Macmillan.
Batson, H. E. tr. (1934) *The Theory of Money and Credit by Ludwig von Mises*, London: J. Cape.
Böhm-Bawerk, Eugen von (1876) Zinstheorie, housed at the library of Salzburg University, a manuscript of the Report on Interest in the Seminar of Karl Knies, in: Yagi, Kiichiro ed. (1983) *Böhm-Bawerk's First Interest Theory with C. Menger–Böhm-Bawerk Correspondence 1884–5, Study Series*, vol. 3, Tokyo: Center for Historical Social Science Literature at Hitotsubashi University, pp. 15–35.
Böhm-Bawerk, Eugen von (1881) *Rechte und Verhältältnisse vom Standpunkt der Volkswirtschaftlichen Güterlehre*, Innsbruck: Verlag der Wagner'schen Universitäts-Buchhandlung. In: Weiss, F. X. ed. (1924) *Gesammelte Schriften von Eugen von Böhm-Bawerk*, Wien: Hölder-Pichler-Tempsky A. G., SS. 1–126, tr. in English by Huncke, George D., "Whether Legal Rights and Relationships are Economic Goods," in: Nymeyer, Frederick ed. (1961) *Shorter Classics of Eugen von Böhm-Bawerk*, Vol. I, South Holland, IL: Libertarian Press, pp. 25–138.
Böhm-Bawerk, Eugen von (1881–1884) Lectures on Economics at Innsbruck University, in: Tomo, S. ed. (1998) *Eugen von Böhm-Bawerks Innsbrucker Vorlesungen über Nationalökonomie: Wiedergabe aufgrund zweier Mitschriften*, Marburg: Metropolis Verlag, pp. 39–308.
Böhm-Bawerk, Eugen von (1884a) *Kapital und Kapitalzins, 1. Abt. Geschichte und Kritik der Kapitalzins-theorieen*, 1. Aufl. Innsbruck: Verlag der Wagner'schen Universitäts-Buchhandlung, tr. in English by Smart, William tr. (1890) *Capital and Interest: A Critical History of Economical Theory*, London: Macmillan.
Böhm-Bawerk, Eugen von (1884b) 12/29 Letter to Carl Menger in: Yagi ed. (1983) *Böhm-Bawerk's First Interest Theory with C. Menger-Böhm-Bawerk Correspondence 1884–5, Study Series*, vol. 3, Tokyo: Center for Historical Social Science Literature at Hitotsubashi University, pp. 38–39.
Böhm-Bawerk, Eugen von (1886a) 7/13 Letter to Carl Menger, housed with the Menger papers at the Perkins Library of Duke University.

Böhm-Bawerk, Eugen von (1886b) Grundzüge der Theorie des wirtschaftlichen Güterwerts, *Jahrbücher für Nationalökonomie und Statistik*, Neue Folge Bd. 13 rep. by the London School of Economics in 1932.

Böhm-Bawerk, Eugen von (1889) *Kapital und Kapitalzins*. 2. Abt. *Positive Theorie des Kapitals*, 1. Aufl. Innsbruck: Verlag der Wagner'schen Universitäts-Buchhandlung, tr. into English by Smart, William (1891) *Capital and Interest: Positive Theory of Capital*, London: Macmillan.

Böhm-Bawerk, Eugen von (1891) The Austrian Economists, *Annals of the American Academy of Political and Social Science*, vol. 1, pp. 361–384, reproduced in: Weiss, F. X. ed. (1924) *Gesammelte Schriften von Eugen von Böhm-Bawerk*, Wien: Hölder-Pichler-Tempsky A. G., SS. 205–29; Nymeyer F. ed. (1961) *Shorter Classics of Eugen von Böhm-Bawerk*, Vol. I, South Holland, IL: Libertarian Press, pp. 1–24.

Böhm-Bawerk, Eugen von (1912) *National-Oekonomie*, 412 p., a lithographic manuscript of lectures on economics. Housed at the Kokushoh Library at Okayama University as well as at the New York Public Library, and privately bought in 1928 by Seiichi Tohhata at a secondhand bookseller in Berlin. One Xeroxed duplication of Tohhata's copy was kindly given to the present author by Takuma Yasui in 1986.

Dingwall, James and Hoselitz, B. F. tr., with an Introduction by F. A. Hayek (1981) *Principles of Economics*, New York: New York University Press.

Endres, Anthony M. (1987) The Origins of Böhm-Bawerk's "Greatest Error": Theoretical Points of Separation from Menger, *Zeitschrift für die gesammte Staatswissenschaft*, vol. 143, pp. 291–309.

Haberler, Gottfried (1950) Joseph Alois Schumpeter, 1883–1950, *Quarterly Journal of Economics*, vol. 64, 333–372.

Hayek, Friedrich August von ed. (1934) *The Collected Works of Carl Menger III*, London: London School of Economics and Political Science.

Hayek, Friedrich August von ed. (1935) *Collectivist Economic Planning: Critical Studies on the Possibilities of Socialism*, with an Introduction and a Concluding Essay, London: G. Routledge.

Hinrichs, A. Ford tr., with a Preface by Wesley Clair Mitchell (1927) *Social Economics by Friedrich von Wieser*, London: George Allen & Unwin.

Knies, Karl Gustav Adolf (1876) *Der Credit*, 2. Abt. 1, Hälfte von *Geld und Credit*, Berlin: Weidmann.

Kurz, Heinz D. ed. (1997) *Hennings, K. H.: The Austrian Theory of Value and Capital, Studies in the Life and Work of Eugen von Böhm-Bawerk*, Cheltenham: Edward Elgar.

Latzer, Michael and Schmitz, Stefan W. ed. (2002) *Carl Menger and the Evolution of Payments System from Barter to Electronic Money*, Cheltenham: Edward Elgar.

Malloch, Christian A. tr. (1893) Edited with a Preface and Analysis by William Smart, *Natural Value by Friedrich von Wieser*, London: Macmillan.

Menger, C. (1871) *Grundsätze der Volkswirtschaftslehre*, Vienna: Wilhelm Braumüller.

Menger, C. (1915) Eugen von Böhm-Bawerk, *Almanach der Kaiserlichen Akademie der Wissenschaften in Wien*. Jahrgang 1915.

Mises, Ludwig Edler von (1912) *Theorie des Geldes und der Umlaufsmittel*, 1. Aufl. München, Leipzig: Duncker & Humblot.

Mises, Ludwig Edler von (1917) Zur Klassifikation der Geldtheorien, *Archiv für Sozialwissenschaft u. Sozialpolitik*, Bd. 44, SS. 198–213. English tr. in: Appendix A of Batson, H. E. tr. (1934) *The Theory of Money and Credit by Ludwig von Mises*, London: J. Cape.

Mises, Ludwig Edler von (1920) Die Wirtschaftsrechnung im sozialistischen Gemeinwesen, *Archiv für Sozialwissenschaft u. Sozialpolitik*, Bd. 47, SS. 86–121 in: Hayek, Friedrich August von ed. (1935) pp. 87–130.

Mises, Margit von ed. (1978) *Erinnerungen von Ludwig v. Mises*, Stuttgart: Gustav Fischer Verlag.

Popper, Karl Raimund (1979) *Objective Knowledge: An Evolutionary Approach*, revised edn., Oxford: Oxford University Press.

Schumpeter, Joseph Alois (1908) *Das Wesen und der Hauptinhalt der theoretischen Nationalökonomie*, Leipzig: Duncker & Humblot.

Schumpeter, Joseph Alois (1911) *Die Theorie der Wirtschaftlichen Entwicklung*, 1 Aufl., Leipzig: Duncker & Humblot.

Schumpeter, Joseph Alois (1954) *History of Economic Analysis*, ed. from manuscript by Elizabeth Boody Schumpeter, London: Allen & Unwin.

Smart, William tr. (1890) *Capital and Interest: A Critical History of Economical Theory*, London: Macmillan.

Smart, William tr. (1891) *Capital and Interest: Positive Theory of Capital* [Böhm-Bawerk, Eugen von (1889)], London: Macmillan.

Tomo, Shigeki (1994) *Eugen von Böhm-Bawerk: Ein großer österreichischer Nationalökonom zwischen Theorie und Praxis*, Marburg: Metropolis Verlag.

Tomo, Shigeki ed. (1998) *Eugen von Böhm-Bawerks Innsbrucker Vorlesungen über Nationalökonomie: Wiedergabe aufgrund zweier Mitschriften*, Marburg: Metropolis Verlag.

Tomo, Shigeki (2009) An Incomplete Temporalization: The Reason for Böhm-Bawerk's Regression, read at the annual tenth conference of the HETSA, held in Perth.

Yagi, Kiichiro ed. (1983) *Böhm-Bawerk's First Interest Theory with C. Menger-Böhm-Bawerk Correspondence 1884–5*, *Study Series*, vol. 3 [Böhm-Bawerk, Eugen von (1876) and letters].

Yagi, Kiichiro (1993) Schumpeter and Vienna University (in Japanese), *Supplement of the Kyoto Economic Review*, vol. 5, pp. 63–83.

Yagi, Kiichiro (2011) *Austrian and German Economic Thought: From Subjectivism to Social Evolution*, London: Routledge.

Wieser, Friedrich Freiherr von (1889) *Der natürliche Werth*, Wien: Alfred Hölder k. k. Universitäts-Buchhändler.

8 Ludwig von Mises as a pure subjectivist

Hiroyuki Okon[1]

Introduction

Subjectivism has been the hallmark of Austrian economics tradition from Carl Menger and Eugen von Böhm-Bawerk to the present-day Austrian economists.[2] However, economists of Austrian school pursued the subjectivist position with varying degrees of thoroughness. Among them, the most consistent and complete subjectivist was Ludwig von Mises.[3] Indeed, he had pointed out the shortcomings of Menger's and Böhm-Bawerk's subjectivism and tried to fill the gaps by providing the fundamental insight that there is no such thing as value calculation.

This chapter will demonstrate that Mises was not merely a subjectivist but a pure subjectivist. Here the term "pure" should be understood to mean consistent, logical, thorough, and coherent. In this sense, Mises's subjectivism is much purer than any of his predecessors in the Austrian tradition, such as Menger, Böhm-Bawerk, and Friedrich von Wieser, or even subsequent ones like Friedrich Hayek and Fritz Machlup. Furthermore, it will also be shown that, for Mises himself, subjectivism was the driving force of his scholarship.

In the chapter entitled "The Austrian School of Economics" of his *Notes and Recollections* (Mises 1978: 33–41), Mises reflected on his first reading of Menger's *Grundsätze der Volkswirtshaftlehre* (*Principles of Economics*) around Christmas of 1903 when he was twenty. He confessed that, "[i]t was the reading of this book that made an 'economist' of me" (ibid.: 33). In the publication, Mises mentioned an "economist," not an "Austrian economist." The reason for this lack of qualification must be that, for Mises, there was only one correct type of economics, so it is sufficient to refer to himself as an economist.

However, substantively Mises identified himself as a continuator in the tradition of Austrian economics, which had begun with Menger's *Principles*. Since the essence of *Principles* lays in its subjectivist orientation, we might qualify Mises's recollection as "it was the reading of Menger's *Principles* that made a subjectivist of me." For Mises, economics meant only that which was based on subjectivism and the Austrian school of economics was nothing but a subjectivist school of economics.

Subjectivism is not only the fundamental starting point but also the driving force of Mises's quest to enhance the science of human action. It is true that economics is a whole and an integral science based on the logical, step-by-step analysis of individual human action. However, a logical, step-by-step analysis is never an autonomous or a mechanical process. It needs something to stimulate the analyst and subjectivism provides just that. The result of Mises's subjectivist enterprise is a theoretical edifice of human action where his purely subjective theory of value, theory of economic calculation, theory of market and pricing process, theory of money or indirect exchange, and applications of those theories to various fields, including socialism and welfare state, are systematically explained.

This chapter is structured as follows. The first and second sections trace Mises's refinement of subjectivism, which started with a critical scrutiny of the school's founding fathers' impure subjectivism in his 1912 book *Theorie des Geldes und der Umlaufsmittel* (*The Theory of Money and Credit*) (Mises 1934/1980), followed by several papers written during the late 1920s and the early 1930s and his book *Grundprobleme der Nationalökonomie: Untersuchungen über Verfahren, Aufgaben und Inhalt der Wirtschafts-und Gesellschaftslehre* (*Epistemological Problems of Economics*) (Mises 1960/2003). The third section will discuss the third part of *Nationalökonomie: Theorie des Handels und Wirtschaften* (Mises 1940), the German-language predecessor of *Human Action: A Treatise on Economics* (Mises 2007), where Mises completed his theory of money or indirect exchange. The theory of monetary calculation will be specifically examined in this section, from the perspective of Mises's pure subjectivism. In the fourth section, the relationship between Mises's science of human action and his pure subjectivism will be explained. Finally, we will make two concluding remarks about his pure subjectivism. First, we will discuss briefly the question of how Mises's subjectivism is related to the radical subjectivism of Ludwig Lachmann. Second, the possibility of further purification of Mises's subjectivism will be suggested in terms of a theory of interest.

Elimination of the inconsistencies with subjectivism

Connected to Menger's and Böhm-Bawerk's subjectivism, Mises who had already become a self-conscious subjectivist, decided to construct his own theory of money after finishing two articles on the foreign exchange policy of the Austro-Hungarian central bank. It was initially projected as the first part of his grand theory, which would integrate the theories of direct and indirect exchanges into his own science of human action.

However, because he did not have sufficient time to launch his project by constructing a theory of direct exchange, Mises decided to first develop a theory of indirect exchange. The result was *The Theory of Money and Credit*, which was published in 1912.[4] As he recollected in his memoir, Mises attempted to explore the essence of value and valuation in the first and the second chapter of that book (Mises 1934/1980: 29–49). In other words, he articulated the gist of subjectivism along with the function of money and the impossibility of the measurement of value. First, Mises elucidates the general conditions for the use of money or indirect exchange, the prime function of money as a common medium of exchange, and the origin of money as the most marketable commodity. Then, he demonstrates that there are no measurements of value or value calculations and that it is an illusion to assume that total value can be calculated from partial value. He also asserted that money, the common medium of exchange, is a price index. In writing this book, however, Mises faced some difficulties relating to the deficiencies of his predecessor's subjectivism.

> I could not use any of the existing comprehensive theories. *The systems of Menger and Böhm-Bawerk were no longer wholly satisfactory to me.* I was ready to proceed further on the road these old masters had discovered. But I could not use their treatment of those problems with which monetary theory must begin.
>
> (Mises 1978: 55–6, emphasis added)

It is true that Mises followed the tradition of subjectivism inaugurated by Menger and Böhm-Bawerk. However, it is also true that Mises was uneasy with their subjectivism and felt the necessity to rectify its defect and develop it further to its logical conclusion.

His mentors had attempted to explain how real prices emerge in real-world markets and they recognized that we could make economic calculation only with money prices. Thus, they argued that a realistic theory of money prices must be a theory of indirect exchange with money prices. However, their approach failed to provide a theory of money prices and logically this implied that a theory of monetary calculation and of indirect exchange with the use of money was not possible. The reason for their failure to provide a theory of indirect exchange was the approach's inability "to overcome the seemingly irremediable split between monetary and value theory" (Salerno 1999: 56). Thus, their theory of prices remained a theory of barter exchange.

Then, what part of their explanation did Mises find unsatisfactory? He explains as follows:

> One point which I could not silently ignore, although it belongs to the general value theory, was *the problem of assumed measurement of value*, and the related problem of total value. In order to develop the theory of money I had to refute the notion that there was such a thing as (1) value calculation or even measurement; (2) that the "value" of a total supply could be calculated from the known "value" of a part; or, (3) inversely that the "value" of any part could be obtained from the known "value" of a total. I had to explore the hypothesis of "value" and to demonstrate that there is an activity of valuing and acts of valuation, but that the term "value" is permissible only when limited to denoting an individually valued object, or to designate the result of a valuation process.
>
> (Mises 1978: 57, emphasis added)

Mises as a pure subjectivist 129

According to Mises, the decisive flaw or the logical inconsistency of their subjectivism was that the measurement of value and value calculations were thought to be possible. This impurity precluded their recognition of the necessity of developing the theory of indirect exchange with the use of money. In his arguments, Mises openly contradicts his own teacher Böhm-Bawerk's impure subjectivism.

> On the subject of the measurement of value, as on a series of further subjects that are very closely bound up with it, the founders of the subjective theory of value refrained from the consistent development of their own doctrines. *This is especially true of Böhm-Bawerk.*
>
> (Mises 1934/1980: 40, emphasis added)

Mises detected the same impurity also in the works of Wieser, who he was even more critical of than Menger and Böhm-Bawerk. In fact, Mises never classified Wieser as a subjectivist, and even believed that he was by and large "more harmful than useful" (Mises 1978: 36).[5]

> [Wieser] never really understood the gist of the idea of Subjectivism in the Austrian School of thought, which limitation caused him to make many unfortunate mistakes. His imputation theory is untenable. His ideas on value calculation justify the conclusion that he could not be called a member of the Austrian School, but rather was a member of the Lausanne School, which in Austria was represented brilliantly by Rudolf Auspitz and Richard Lieben.
>
> (Ibid.)

Unlike his predecessors, Mises defines value in a "trilateral relationship" (Hülsmann 2003: xxxvi) between one individual and at least two different economic goods as "the significance attributed to individual commodity by a human being who wishes to consume or otherwise dispose of various commodities to the best advantage" (Mises 1934/1980: 51).[6] Thus, for Mises, value or valuation is inseparably linked to the comparison of plural goods by acting individuals. In this strict definition, as far as value is concerned, we can only speak of ordinal nature and not cardinal nature.

As was stated earlier, Mises had intended to develop a theory of indirect exchange in *The Theory of Money and Credit*. Nevertheless, the book became a halfway product because the problem of monetary calculation, the explanation of which is the essence of a theory of indirect exchange, was addressed only in terms of very restricted questions of the social consequences of monetary depreciation. That is, he excluded other considerations related to the theory of direct exchange. However, as far as subjectivism is concerned, the basic thought was already explained. "[T]here are values and value calculations, but no measurements of value and no valuations; the market economy calculates with money prices. This was not new; it was merely a logical conclusion from the theory of subjective value" (Mises 1978: 111). After the publication of *The Theory of Money and Credit*, the most important issue for Mises, who intended to complete his theory of indirect exchange and to explore the problems of monetary calculation, was to thoroughly and or logically purify subjectivism as it had developed under Menger and Böhm-Bawerk. It cannot be overstressed that Mises himself believed that the complete prevalence of subjectivism, or the purification of subjectivism, had to be of prime significance for the systematization of a science of human action. However, the historical environment did not allow him to do so and he had to content himself with writing papers and several books not on general systematic themes but on such specific subjects as socialism, interventionism, and epistemology.[7]

The further persistence of subjectivism

During the 1920s, Mises published several articles and books, which in his own words, "offer a comprehensive analysis of the problem of social cooperation" and "investigate all conceivable system of cooperation and examine their feasibility" (Mises 1978: 113). The most famous among them are his 1920 paper "Economic Calculation in the Socialist Commonwealth" (Mises 1920/1990) and *Die Gemeinwirtschaft: Untersuchungen über den Sozialismus* (*Socialism: An Economic and Sociological Analysis*) (Mises 1936/1981), which stirred the so-called socialist calculation debate.[8] At first glance, it is seemingly unrelated to the theory of subjective value. However, this could not be further from the truth. "The existence of this important problem [of economic calculation] could be revealed only by the methods of the modern subjective theory of Value" (Mises 1936/1981: 186). "All attempts at disproving the cogency of my thesis were destined to fail because they did not delve into the value-theoretical center of the problem" (Mises 1978: 112).[9]

As these quotations show, Mises's argument that rational economic calculation was impossible under socialism should be simply understood as a logical consequence of the fundamental theorem of the subjective theory of value – there is no such thing as value calculation. This fundamental theorem also implies the logical necessity of monetary calculation or calculation with money prices in an advanced economy. Subsequently, the theory of monetary calculation was to become the most important part of the theory of money and credit or of indirect exchange, the development of which continued to be Mises's prime purpose until 1940.

From 1928 to 1932, Mises wrote several essays to demonstrate positively the logical character of the propositions of economics and sociology and to critically evaluate the doctrines of historicism, empiricism, and irrationalism. Although these can be read independently from one another, according to Mises, "[f]rom the outset, however, they were conceived and planned as parts of a whole" (Mises 1960/2003: 79). This whole is the book *Epistemological Problems of Economics* published in 1933 (ibid.).[10]

Among the articles in the *Epistemological Problem of Economics*, two expressly take up the subjective theory of value and, in them, Mises once again exposits the doctrine of subjectivism. In "Remarks on the Fundamental Problem of the Subjective Theory of Value" (Mises 1928/2003), Mises sought to "put an end to the serious misunderstandings that modern (subjective) economic theory repeatedly encounters" (Mises 1960/2003: 177), which appears as a distinction between economic and noneconomic action. According to Mises, these misunderstandings could be attributed to "stylish faults in the presentation" of the subjectivist theories by Menger and Böhm-Bawerk; their writings "include propositions and concepts carried over from the objective theory of value and therefore utterly incompatible with the subjectivism of the modern school" (ibid.).

Menger introduced a distinction between real and imaginary wants in the posthumous second edition of *Principles*. Böhm-Bawerk differentiated between economic and noneconomic motives, expressing his opinion that, when reflecting on each motive, there should be two different theories of price determination. Based on the premise that the task of the subjective theory of price determination is "explaining the formation of the exchange ratios of economic goods that are actually observed in the market," Mises critically demonstrated that all of these distinctions are never compatible with the doctrine of subjectivism.[11]

In his 1931 paper "On the Development of the Subjectivist Theory of Value," Mises again traces the origin and the process of diffusion of the absurd thought of distinguishing between economic and noneconomic or uneconomic action, which is irreconcilable with the subjective theory of value. Mises also articulates the meaning of the changes in data, the role of time, and the concept of cost from a purely subjectivist standpoint. However, what is most striking in the paper is his account of "monetary calculation" in the sixth and seventh sections. There, based on the subjective theory of value and valuation by an acting individual, Mises demonstrated the nature of monetary calculation.

> Monetary calculation is not the calculation, and certainly not the measurement, of value. Its basis is the comparison of the more important and the less important [by the acting individual]. It is an ordering according rank [by the acting individual], an [individual] act of grading (Čuhel), and not an act of measuring. It was a mistake to search for a measure of the value of goods. In the last analysis, economic calculation does not rest on the measurement of values, but on their arrangement in an order of ranks [by the acting individual].
>
> (Ibid.: 169, parenthetic added except for that of "Čuhel" which is Mises's own)

As is clearly noticeable in the above citation and several other places in his writings,[12] Mises mentions the name of Čuhel time and again. In fact, as he himself confessed, his subjectivism was built on an important insight of the Czech economist Franz Čuhel,[13] a student at Böhm-Bawerk's graduate seminar, on the subjective nature of ordinal utility. In fact, Mises gives him rare praise by extolling his pioneering book *Zur Lehre von den Bedürfnissen* (*On the Theory of Needs*) published in 1907[14] by saying that "there cannot be any doubt that, in the end, Čuhel will occupy a deservedly honored place in the history of our science" (Mises 1978: 57). In fact, Čuhel had emphasized that value was nothing but a purely ordinal relationship between economic goods and this relationship was always bound up with an actual context of concrete time and place of a particular individual. Thus, it is safe to say that Mises's subjectivism was the same as that of Čuhel.

From this Čuhel–Mises insight into ordinal valuation, Mises deduced the fundamental theorem of subjectivism. The essence of subjective use-value is a human action preferring one thing to other things or choosing one thing and setting aside other things. It is never a measurement of anything. Rather, it is a subjective ordering of things or a subjective comparison among things from the perspective of the party whose desire is to relieve discomfort and uneasiness and get more satisfaction. Since value is within the consciousness of men, it depends on the time, place, and conditions of the action of valuation. If they change, valuation also changes and leads to a different ordering of things.

Mises categorically denies the illusion of "value calculation," saying that there is no scale of measurement of value. Since there is no such thing as value calculation, therefore there are no general principles for the same. He stressed that valuation is never a measurement of value as it is definitely impossible to measure value. These fundamental theorems are nothing but the logical implications of the subjectivism of the founding fathers of the Austrian school of economic thought. Thus, Mises can assert that the Austrian school "has never suffered from the illusion that values can be measured" (ibid.: 36).

Subjectivist theory of indirect exchange

As Mises himself explained in his memoir *Notes and Recollections*, his theory of money (or theory of indirect exchange), whose essential part is the economic calculation with the use of money prices, had not been completely discussed in *The Theory of Money and Credit* or in his subsequent articles and books. It was finally completed in his *Nationalökonomie*, which was published in 1940 when Mises was in Geneva.

> My *Nationalökonomie* finally afforded me the opportunity to present the problems of economic calculation in their full significance. Meanwhile, I had to content myself with demonstrating fallacies and contradictions of proposals for socialist economic calculation. Only in the explanations offered in the third part of my *Nationalökonomie* did my theory of money achieve completion [1940]. Thus I accomplished the project that had presented itself to me thirty-five years earlier. I had merged the theory of indirect exchange with that of direct exchange into a coherent system of human action.
>
> (Mises 1978: 112)

These retrospections should be read with great care because they show Mises's grand project and its historical process very clearly. What we must note is that his monetary theory was completed in the "third part" of *Nationalökonomie*, which comprised only thirty-six pages.[15] Furthermore, in that book, Mises attained his ideal, which was the construction of a science of human action through merging the theory of indirect and direct exchanges.

The title of this "third part" is *Rechnen im Handel* (*Calculation in Action*), and it consists of three chapters: "Wertung Ohne Rechnen" (Valuation without Calculation), "Die Geldrechnung, ihre Voraussetzungen und die Grenzen ihres Bereiches" (Monetary Calculation, its requisites and limits), and "Die Geldrechnung, ihre Voraussetzungen und die Grenzen ihres Bereiches" (Monetary Calculation as a Tool of Thinking in Action).[16] Thus, we can convince ourselves that the gist of Mises's theory of indirect exchange is the notion of calculation with money prices. As Jörg Guido Hülsmann notes, "what set Mises apart from his contemporaries and what, to present day, sets his followers apart from virtually all other economist, is the issue of economic calculation" (2003: xxxiii).

Mises starts this part with the simple but decisively important explanation of valuation by an acting man from his trilateral point of view. As we saw before, valuation is nothing but the universal category of human action in preferring *a* to *b*. Based on this strictly ordinal nature of value and valuation, Mises says, "It does not open a field for economic calculation and the mental operations based upon such calculation" (Mises 2007: 200).

Keeping consistency with this recognition, we have to explain real monetary prices in real markets or, to put it the other way around, we have to trace real monetary prices in the market to the ultimate category of valuation as preferring *a* to *b*. According to Mises, some imaginary construction of the market in which all transactions are made in direct exchange without money must be used for this problem (ibid.: 201–2).[17] However, the use of this imaginary construction can and did lead to two types of errors. First, it is believed that money is neutral and therefore there is no significant difference between direct exchange and indirect exchange. Those who commit this error do not feel the necessity to explore the nature of indirect exchange further. The second, more harmful, error is to suppose that value is objective, measurable, having some kind of unit, extensive quantity, or cardinal number. It is easy to see that this error leads to the belief that value calculation is possible and that economic calculation can be performed as value calculation.

However, as Mises insists, pure subjectivism implies that money is not neutral. It offers that indirect exchange is decisively different from direct exchange and the former must be analyzed as an independent subject. Furthermore, valuation means only preferring *a* to *b* and there is no such thing as value calculation of objective realities. Consequently, there exists in fact only money price calculation and it can come into existence only in the economy of indirect exchange.

> In the market society there are money prices. Economic calculation is calculation in terms of money prices. The various quantities of goods and services

enter into this calculation with the amount of money for which they are bought and sold on the market or for which they could prospectively be bought and sold. It is a fictitious assumption that an isolated self-sufficient individual or the general manager of a socialist system, i.e., a system in which there is no market for means of production, could calculate. There is no way which could lead one from the money computation of a market economy to any kind of computation in a nonmarket system.

(Ibid.: 205)

Following these penetrating insights into the money price calculation and the discussion of the sphere and limitation of economic calculation,[18] Mises further explored the nature of monetary calculation as a mental tool of action. According to him, under the complex social system of division of labor, this was "the guiding star of action," "the compass of the man embarking upon production," "a device of acting individual," or "arithmetic tool in the struggle for a better" (ibid.: 229–30).

Monetary calculation is never a universal system. It is conditional; that is to say, it can only appear in a society in which the means of production are privately owned or only in the free market economy.

The system of economic calculation in monetary terms is conditioned by certain social institutions. It can operate only in an institutional setting of the division of labor and private ownership of the means of production in which goods and services of all orders are bought and sold against a generally used medium of exchange, i.e., money.

(Ibid.: 229)

As the above citation clearly shows, Mises's theory of monetary calculation based on his pure subjectivism leads us to an understanding of the institutional importance of capitalist free market economy. As a matter of fact, only with the possibility of monetary calculation, can some important measurable accounting notions be developed through the individual's mental desire to know the prospects and the results of purposeful activities. These include mental categories such as costs and proceeds, profit and loss, and most importantly "capital."

Every single step of entrepreneurial activities is subject to scrutiny by monetary calculation. The premeditation of planned action becomes commercial pre-calculation of expected costs and expected proceeds. The retrospective establishment of the outcome of past action becomes accounting of profit and loss.

(Ibid.)

Monetary calculation reaches its full perfection in capital accounting. It establishes the money prices of the available means and confronts this total with the changes brought about by action and by the operation of other factors. This confrontation shows what changes occurred in the state of acting men's affairs and the magnitude of those changes; it makes success and failure, profit and loss ascertainable. The system of free enterprise has been dubbed capitalism in order to deprecate and to smear it. However, this term can be considered very pertinent. It refers to the most characteristic feature of the system, its main eminence, viz., the role the notion of capital plays in its conduct.

(Ibid.: 230)

Mises recognizes that the accounting categories, which we use in our daily activities, are firmly dependent on monetary calculations whose indispensable nature is derived from the theorem of pure subjectivism. Mises's pure subjectivism makes him look at and understand the real world from this institutional perspective.

Mises's theory of pricing process based on subjectivism

In *Nationalökonomie*, the discussion of "economic calculation" in the third part is followed by that of "Die Marktwirtschaft" (The Market Economy),[19] which can be undoubtedly thought of as the core of the book. This part is much longer than any other sections of the book, consisting of eleven chapters and comprising more than 400 pages. There, for the first time, Mises presented the explanation of how the actual money prices of goods and services – as they are really asked for and paid – in real market transactions are determined based on his pure subjectivism. We can see Mises's subjectivism most clearly in his explanation of the pricing process of goods of higher order. He postulates that, although the ultimate source of the determination of prices is the value judgments of consumers and prices are the outcome of the valuation preferring *a* to *b*, the pricing process as social phenomena depends on activity other than valuation. Rather, it depends on an appraisement based on economic calculation with money prices. Thus, according to Mises,

> Appraisement must be clearly distinguished from valuation. Appraisement in no way depends upon the subjective valuation of the man who appraises. ... Appraisement is the anticipation of an expected fact. It aims at establishing what prices will be paid on the market for a particular commodity or what amount of money will be required for the purchase of a definite commodity.
>
> (Mises 2007: 332)

However, in the pricing process, valuation and appraisement are intimately connected because the individual must scrutinize the structure of market prices and rely on the appraisement when he makes valuation. In this sense, "[t]he valuation makes a detour, it goes via the appraisement of the structure of market prices" (ibid.). Then we can describe the pricing process as social market process as follows.

In the market, which has the existing structure of market prices, men appraise the future prices by economic calculations with money prices and make subjective valuations. Based on their valuations, they bid money prices in the markets. This results in there emerging the new structure of market prices from these bidding activities. Then the men evaluate their activity, or calculate profit and loss, through another economic calculation with money prices. Again, in the market that has the newly emerging structure of market prices, men appraise the future prices by doing economic calculations with money prices and make subjective valuations for their bidding activities. Mises made the following observation on the nature of this unending pricing process.

> The pricing process is a social process. It is consummated by an interaction of all members of the society. All collaborate and cooperate, each in the particular role he has chosen for himself in the framework of the division of labor.
>
> (Ibid.: 338)

The prices of the goods of higher orders are also determined in the same way.

> The prices of the goods of higher orders are ultimately determined by the prices of the goods of the first order, that is, the consumers' goods. As a consequence of this dependence they are ultimately determined by the subjective valuations of all members of the market society. It is, however, important to realize that we are faced with a connection of prices, not with a connection of valuations. ... The factors of production are appraised with regard to the prices of the products, and from this appraisement their prices emerge. Not the valuations but the appraisements are transferred from the goods of the first order to those of higher orders. The prices of the consumers' goods engender the action resulting in the determination of the prices of the factor of production.
>
> (Ibid.: 333–4)[20]

The central problem of economics, or Catallactics to use Mises's term, is the explanation of the formation of the money prices of goods and services as they are really asked for and paid in the real market transactions at a specific place on a specific date. Therefore, it constitutes the core of Mises's science of human action. Based on these comprehensive considerations, we can say that the whole edifice of Mises's systematic theory of human action stands on the single a priori true axiom of pure subjectivism that an acting individual's valuation means nothing beyond preferring *a* to *b*.

Concluding remarks: Mises as a pure subjectivist

In this concluding section, two main remarks about Mises's pure subjectivism are presented. These remarks at first glance appear to be unrelated, but they are in fact intimately connected. The first remark concerns the relationship between Mises's pure subjectivism and the radical subjectivism[21] of certain modern Austrians economists, the leading representative of which is Ludwig Lachmann. Second, we will introduce an example of further purification of Mises's subjectivism in a theory of interest.

In his paper entitled *From Mises to Shackle* (Lachmann 1976/1994),[22] Ludwig Lachmann examined the similarities and differences between the works of Mises and George L.S. Shackle. In doing so, he confirmed that "our two authors are completely at one" (ibid.: 235) on the nature of human action. However, Lachmann is of the opinion that Shackle stands ahead of Mises in the subjectivist movement.

According to Lachmann (1990/1994), we can identify three stages in the history of subjectivism. The first stage was the subjectivism of want, as marked by Menger's *Principles*. Mises, who advocated the subjectivism of means and ends, realized the second stage. However, Lachmann alleges, the end is still given in his subjectivism. According to him, Shackle had progressed beyond the traditional value subjectivism of the Austrian school and had moved subjectivism to the third and a more "radical" stage. In this stage, the subjective nature of the active mind was recognized and the role of the imagination of expectations was analyzed.[23] Is there really a relationship between Mises's pure subjectivism and the radical subjectivism of knowledge, expectation, and imagination? Can we take the radical subjectivism as the next stage or natural extension of Mises's subjectivism? Is it a logically necessary step to move "from Mises to Shackle?"

In his discussion of "the temporal relation between actions" (Mises 2007: 102–4), Mises reveals a kind of the "radical" nature of his understanding of human action that "[t]wo actions of an individual are never synchronous" (ibid.: 102).

> The attempt has been made to attain the notion of a non-rational action by this reasoning: If a is preferred to b and b to c, logically a should be preferred to c. But if actually c is preferred to a, we are faced with a mode of acting to which we cannot ascribe consistency and rationality. This reasoning disregards the fact that two acts of an individual can never be synchronous. If in one action a is preferred to b and in another action b to c, it is, however short the interval between the two actions may be, not permissible to construct a uniform scale of value in which a precedes b and b precedes c. Nor is it permissible to consider a later third action as coincident with the two previous actions. All that the example proves is that value judgments are not immutable and that therefore a scale of value, which is abstracted from various, necessarily nonsynchronous actions of an individual, may be self-contradictory.
>
> (Ibid.: 103)

"If the valuations change, acting must change also" (ibid.). "Acting must be suited to purpose, and purposefulness requires adjustment to changing conditions" (ibid.). If Mises appears as a "radical" subjectivist it is because we assume the subjectivism of neoclassical economics, which expressed itself in notions such as the utility function and the indifference curve as our standards. When we recall Mises's definition of valuation, even non-rational, nonsynchronous, and seemingly self-contradictory actions should be thought of as just "human action" from which we have to explain the real market money prices.

While, on the one hand, Mises insists that a change in the conditions necessitate adjustment actions, on the other hand, he also argues the opposite relationship between actions and conditions: "Man himself changes from moment to moment and his valuations, volitions, and acts change with him. In the realm of action there is nothing perpetual but change" (ibid.: 219).

Changes come from both human actions and the conditions under which individuals act. For Mises as a pure subjectivist, change is one of the essential features of our society. Thus, how can we answer the question posed above on the relationship between Mises's subjectivism and radical subjectivism? Although the author of this chapter will leave the question open, it should be pointed out that, while Mises's pure subjectivism does not exclude radical subjectivism of "knowledge, expectation, and the imagination," it does not seem appropriate to consider his subjectivism "less radical" than Lachmann's subjectivism.[24]

The second remark on Mises's pure subjectivism concerns the necessity of still further purification of his subjectivism. Although Mises started his work by eliminating the logical inconsistencies with true subjectivism, which exist in the works of his predecessors, when it came to the fundamental thought of his subjectivism that there is no measurement of value and value calculation, there is still an area that could not be detached from their errors. Therefore, further consideration is needed in analyzing a subjectivist theory of interest. A theory of interest is to explain the cause of the observable spread between selling proceeds and cost expenditure in the market.

As is well known, Mises believed that his own notion of time preference[25] could explain the phenomenon of interest. However, as Jörg Guido Hülsmann demonstrates convincingly, Mises's time preference theory, even though it accounts for the value differential between two different uses of the same good, cannot explain the price spread between selling proceeds and expending costs. That is to say, it is unrelated to interest in the market.[26] Therefore, Mises's contention that "[t]ime preference manifests itself in the phenomenon of originary interest, i.e., the discount of future goods as against present goods" (Mises 2007: 524) is untenable. Then, what causes originary interest?

According to Hülsmann, it is the simplest and plainest fact that, the end that an acting individual pursues is inherently more valuable than the means to be used for the attainment of the same end. Further, we can define originary interest realistically: "*Originary interest is the fundamental spread between the value of an end and the value of the means that serve to attain this end*" (Hülsmann 2002: 87, emphasis original).

Original interest thus defined can explain the observable spread between selling proceeds and cost expenditure in the market, that is, market interest.

However, we are mainly concerned with the question of why Mises did not notice this simplest fact and develop the idea of originary interest as a value spread between means and end. According to Hülsmann, this was due to "the weight of tradition" (2002: 88) of the Austrian school, which, until Mises, was part of mainstream thinking to the extent that they both assumed the cardinality of value, value calculation, and value imputation. We should note here that on one hand, even for Mises, the completion of subjectivism to its ultimate form was not an easy task. At the same time, there is still the room for Mises's subjectivism to be made much purer than done by the man himself.

On reviewing Mises's *Nationalökonomie* in 1941, Hayek tried to understand, with some sympathy, his performance but was confused by the fact that Mises "seems to have been little affected by the general evolution of our subject during the period over which his work extends," and that "[w]hat growth there is appears to be decidedly *autonomous*" (Hayek 1941/1992: 150, emphasis added).

Regarding this "autonomy," however, Joseph Salerno correctly points out that, "*Nationalökonomie* represented Mises's deliberate attempt to 'autonomously' reconstruct a paradigm that could not be reconciled with the 'general evolution' of economics in the direction of the Walrasian–Marshallian fusion" (Salerno 1999: 58). Based on the arguments presented in the previous sections, we can understand Mises's autonomy as the operation of his thoroughgoing subjectivism. Without doubt, *Nationalökonomie*, especially its part three on economic calculation with money prices, should be appreciated as an admirable scientific achievement of *Ludwig von Mises as a pure subjectivist*.[27]

Notes

1 Faculty of Economics, Kokugakuin University, Tokyo, Japan.
2 Horwitz (1994) gives a concise account for subjectivism of the Austrian school.
3 For Mises's life and works, see Butler (1988, 2010), Hülsmann (2007), Kirzner (2001), or Rothbard (1988).
4 First German edition was published in 1912, second German edition in 1924, and the English translation of the second German edition was printed in 1934.
5 It should be noted that this very critical attitude to Wieser by Mises is starkly different from the evaluations by Hayek and Oskar Morgenstern. In fact, for Wieser's *Theorie der gesellschaftlichen Wirtschaft* (*Social Economics*), Hayek wrote in 1926 that it "offers not only the sole consistent treatment of economic theory produced by the modern subjectivist school, but it also constitutes, above all, what may well be the greatest synthesis achieved by economic theory in our time" (Hayek 1926/1992: 119). In the same vein, Morgenstern acclaims it as "the greatest systematic treatise that has been written by an Austrian in which *the principle of marginal utility is analyzed in all its ramifications*" (Morgenstern 1976: 482–3, emphasis added).
6 In contrast, Carl Menger defines value in a "bilateral relationship" as "the importance that individual goods or quantities of goods attain for us because we are conscious of being dependent on command of them for the satisfaction of our needs" (Menger 1994: 115). According to Hülsmann (2003: xxxvi–xxxvii), the bilateral definition of value of Menger and the mainstream economists implies "the common denominator for the economic significance of all goods" and therefore the possibility of value calculation.

7 It is not the intention of this author to imply in any way that these papers and books are not important. In fact, all of them should be appreciated as part of his great contribution to social science in general and to economics in particular.

8 When we keep in mind that, for Mises, the most important work was to complete subjectivism, we should say that there were "two" different but mutually intimately related debates on the possibility of rational economic calculation under socialism. One was the "open" debate between Mises and Hayek on the one hand and between Otto Neurath, Karl Polanyi, *et al.*, and socialists on the other. The other, which was much more important to Mises, was the "hidden" debate, in which he criticized the thought of many scholars that led logically and ultimately to the absurd opinion that economic calculation was possible even in the socialist society. Therefore, in truth, it was to Friedrich von Wieser, an economist from the Austrian school, on whom Mises shifted his criticism. For these reasons, Mises who fired the charge did not participate in the open discussion with the explicit socialists. See Mises (1940: 192–4) and Mises (2007: 204–5). For the history of the open debate, see, for example, Hoff (1949).

9 We can find the same wordings by Mises in *Human Action*.

> If it were true that the value of things is determined by the quantity of labor required for their production or reproduction, then there is no further problem of economic calculation. The supporters of the labor theory of value cannot be blamed for having misconstrued the problem of a socialist system. *Their fateful failure was their untenable doctrine of value*.... The illusion that a rational order of economic management is possible in a society based on public ownership of the means production owed its origin to *the value theory of the classical economists* and its tenacity to the failure of many modern economists to think through consistently to *its ultimate conclusions the fundamental theorem of the subjectivist theory*.
>
> (Mises 2007: 205–6, emphasis added)

Yet, it was Dominick Armentano who noticed and pointed out this decisive point of Mises's argument on the impossibility of the rational economic calculation under socialism: "To comprehend Mises' remark concerning the efficiency of resource allocation in a socialist community, it is necessary to review briefly his general theories of value and the nature of economic calculation" (Armentano 1969: 128).

10 As Jörg Guido Hülsmann correctly points out (2003: xi), the original German title of the book can be translated into "Fundamental Problems of Economics," reflects Mises's thought that, in order to develop the general theory of human action, two foundational areas should be dealt with: epistemology and subjective theory of value.

11 While criticizing Menger and Böhm-Bawerk of inconsistent ideas in subjectivism, Mises points out that these impurities never diminish the great merit of their pioneering works to explain the determination of real prices in terms of the subjective theory of value. See Mises (1960/2003: 184, 189, and 192–3).

12 Mises (1934/1980: 41; 1920/1990: 12, fn. 4; 1960/2003: 169 and 224; 1969/1984: 42; and 1978: 57).

13 For Franz Čuhel, see Hudík (2007).

14 Franz Čuhel, *Zur Lehre von den Bedürfnissen. Theoretische Untersuchungen über das Grenzgebiet der Ökonomik und der Psychologie*, Innsbruck: Wagner'ssche universität-Buchhandlung, 1907. Čuhel (1907/1994) provides an English translation of chapter six of the original German text. Čuhel (2007) offers an English translation of his own summary of that German text.

15 That is, from pp. 188–223. The corresponding part of *Human Action* is even shorter, just thirty-one pages from pp. 200–31.

16 The subparts in *Human Action* are, respectively, *Economic Calculation* as the title of the third part, *Valuation without Calculation* as chapter eleven, *The Sphere of Economic Calculation* as chapter twelve, and the thirteenth chapter of *Monetary Calculation and the Science of Human Action*.

17 Because money is nothing but a medium of exchange, "what is ultimately exchanged are always economic goods of the first order against other such goods" (Mises 2007: 202).
18 Mises (2007: 212–28).
19 Mises (1940: 224–627). Corresponding part of *Human Action* can be found in Mises (2007: 232–688).
20 Based on these insights into the pricing process of the goods of higher orders, Mises criticizes Schumpeter's proposition on the possibility of the rational economic planning under socialism that consumers in evaluating consumers' goods *ipso facto* also evaluate the means of production which enter into the production of these goods as being "hardly possible to construe the market process in a more erroneous way" (Mises 2007: 357).
21 According to Jack Wiseman, "[t]he essence of the radical subjectivist position is that the future is not simply 'unknown,' but is 'nonexistent' or 'indeterminate' at the point of decision" (1989: 230). Given this position, radical subjectivism implies that economic theory cannot provide knowledge of future contingents, and must abandon prediction of the future.
22 See also Lachmann (1978/1994; 1990/1994).
23 What is striking in Lachmann's "kaleidic" view of markets in which imaginative and creative nature of choice and its diversity is recognized is his rejection of any equilibrating tendencies of market processes.
24 According to John O'Neill (2000) who comments on the debate in the Austrian school between radical subjectivists and their conservative opponents from the standpoint of logic and philosophy, radical subjectivism is neither radical nor subjectivist. As far as economics is concerned, the debate "is an argument about proffered modes of speech" (ibid.: 28).
25 It should be differentiated from Böhm-Bawerk's notion of time preference. On the one hand, the term is concerned with "an observable value differential between two physically similar goods existing at two different points of time." On the other hand, Mises's time preference refers to "the value differential between that use of the good that comes to be realized in the present, and an alternative future use of this good that could have been realized if a different choice had been made" (Hülsmann 2002: 83).
26 According to Hülsmann, the reason for this inability is that, while Mises's time preference can explain only one action which prefers the realized end to an unrealized one, the interest emerges from at least two different actions: buying action of means of production and selling action of product (Hülsmann 2002: 84).
27 We can still deepen our understanding of Mises's autonomy by referring to Mises's explanation of the beginning of "the Austrian School of Economics" in his *The Historical Setting of the Austrian School of Economics*.

> Whatever this method [i.e., ascribing the exploits of a man of genius to the operation of his environment and to the climate of opinion of his age and his country] may accomplish in some cases, there is no doubt that it is inapplicable with regard to those Austrians whose thoughts, ideas and doctrines matter for mankind. Bernard Bolzano, Gregor Mendel and Sigmund Freud were not stimulated by their relatives, teachers, colleagues or friends.... Bolzano and Mendel carried on their main work in surroundings which, as far as their special fields are concerned, could be called an intellectual desert.... Freud was laughed at when he first made public his doctrines in the Vienna Medical Association.
>
> (Mises 1969/1984: 9–10)

References

Armentano, D.T. (1969) "Resource Allocation Problem under Socialism," in W.P. Snavely, *Theory of Economic Systems: Capitalism, Socialism and Corporatism*, Columbus, OH: Charles E. Merrill Publishing Co.: 127–39.

Butler, E. (1988) *Ludwig von Mises: Fountainhead of the Modern Microeconomics Revolution*, Aldershot, UK and Vermont, USA: Gower Publishing Company.

Butler, E. (2010) *Ludwig von Mises: A Primer*, London: Institute of Economic Affairs.

Čuhel, F. (1907/1994) "On the Theory of Needs: Theoretical Studies of the Border Area between Economics and Psychology," translated by William Kirby, in Israel M. Kirzner ed. (1994) *Classics in Austrian Economics: A Sampling in the History of a Tradition, Vol. I, The Founding Era*, London: William Pickering: 305–38.

Čuhel, F. (2007) "On the Theory of Needs," *New Perspectives on Political Economy*, 3(1): 27–56.

Hayek, F.A. (1926/1992) "Friedrich von Wieser (1851–1926)," in Peter G. Klein, ed. (1992) *The Collected Works of F. A. Hayek, vol. 4, The Fortune of Liberalism: Essays on Austrian Economics and the Ideal of Freedom*, Chicago, IL: University of Chicago Press: 108–25.

Hayek, F.A. (1941/1992) "Review of Mises's Nationalökonomie," in Peter G. Klein, ed. (1992) *The Collected Works of F. A. Hayek, vol. 4, The Fortune of Liberalism: Essays on Austrian Economics and the Ideal of Freedom*, Chicago, IL: University of Chicago Press: 149–52.

Hoff, T.J.B. (1949) *Economic Calculation in the Socialist Society*, London/Edinburgh/Glasgow: William Hodge.

Horwitz, S. (1994) "Subjectivism," in Peter J. Boettke, *The Elgar Companion to Austrian Economics*, Cheltenham: Edward Elgar: 17–22.

Hudík, M. (2007) "František Čhuhel (1862–1914)," *New Perspectives on Political Economy*, 3(1): 3–14.

Hülsmann, J.G. (2002) "A Theory of Interest," *Quarterly Journal of Austrian Economics*, 5(4): 77–110.

Hülsmann, J.G. (2003) "Introduction to the Third Edition: From Value Theory to Praxeology," in L. von Mises (1960/2003) *Epistemological Problems of Economics*, 3rd edn., Auburn: Ludwig von Mises Institute: ix–lv.

Hülsmann, J.G. (2007) *Mises: The Last Knight of Liberalism*, Auburn: Ludwig von Mises Institute.

Kirzner, I.M. (2001) *Ludwig von Mises: The Man and His Economics*, Wilmington, DE: ISI Books.

Lachmann, L.M. (1976/1994) "From Mises to Shackle: An Essay on Austrian Economics and the Kaleidoscopic Society," in L.M. Lachmann (1994) *Expectations and the Meaning of Institutions: Essays in Economics by Ludwig Lachmann*, London and New York: Routledge: 229–40.

Lachmann, L.M. (1978/1994) "Carl Menger and the Incomplete Revolution of Subjectivism," in L.M. Lachmann (1994) *Expectations and the Meaning of Institutions: Essays in Economics by Ludwig Lachmann*, London and New York: Routledge: 213–17.

Lachmann, L.M. (1990/1994) "G. L. S. Shackle's Place in the History of Subjectivist Thought," in L.M. Lachmann (1994) *Expectations and the Meaning of Institutions: Essays in Economics by Ludwig Lachmann*, London and New York: Routledge: 241–8.

Menger, C. (1994) *Principles of Economics*, translated by James Dingwall and Bert F. Hoselitz, Grove City, PA: Libertarian Press.

Mises, L. von (1920/1990) *Economic Calculation in the Socialist Commonwealth*, Auburn: Ludwig von Mises Institute.

Mises, L. von (1928/2003) "Remarks on the Fundamental Problem of the Subjective Theory of Value," in L. von Mises (1960/2003) *Epistemological Problems of Economics*, 3rd edn., Auburn: Ludwig von Mises Institute: 177–93.

Mises, L. von (1931/2003) "On the Development of the Subjectivist Theory of Value," in L. von Mises (1960/2003) *Epistemological Problems of Economics*, 3rd edn., Auburn: Ludwig von Mises Institute: 155–75.

Mises, L. von (1934/1980) *The Theory of Money and Credit*, Indianapolis, IN: Liberty Classics.

Mises, L. von (1936/1981) *Socialism: An Economic and Sociological Analysis*, Indianapolis, IN: Liberty Classics.

Mises, L. von (1940) *Nationalökonomie: Theorie des Handelns und Wirtschaftens*, Geneva, Switzerland: Editions Union Genf.

Mises, L. von (1960/2003) *Epistemological Problems of Economics*, 3rd edn., Auburn: Ludwig von Mises Institute.

Mises, L. von (1969/1984) *The Historical Setting of the Austrian School of Economics*, Auburn: Ludwig von Mises Institute.

Mises, L. von (1978) *Ludwig von Mises, Notes and Recollections*, translated by Hans F. Sennholz, South Holland: Libertarian Press.

Mises, L. von (2007) *Human Action: A Treatise on Economics*, Indianapolis, IN: Liberty Fund.

Morgenstern, Oskar (1976) "Friedrich von Wieser, 1851–1925," in *Selected Economic Writings of Oskar Morgenstern*, edited by Andrew Schotter, New York: New York University Press.

O'Neil, J. (2000) "Radical Subjectivism: Not Radical, Not Subjectivist," *Quarterly Journal of Austrian Economics*, 3(2): 21–30.

Rothbard, M.N. (1988) *Ludwig von Mises: Scholar, Creator, Hero*, Auburn: Ludwig von Mises Institute.

Salerno, J.T. (1999) "The Place of Mises's *Human Action* in the Development of Modern Economic Thought," *Quarterly Journal of Austrian Economics*, 2(1): 35–65.

Wiseman, J. (1989) *Cost, Choice, and Political Economy*, Cheltenham: Edward Elgar.

9 Uncertainty and strategic interdependence in the interwar Viennese milieu

Chikako Nakayama

Introduction

Recently, Robert Boyer analyzed the financialization phenomenon in recent decades and explained that it had culminated in a crisis involving financial institutions, wherein prices cease to function as the bearer of necessary information. In his words, "having intentionally concealed risks and distorted the integrity of the system of asset prices, the finance has itself engendered the crisis of its institution of the basis: that is, the market as the disseminator of pertinent information" (Boyer 2011: 71; Japanese version: 137). He then cites this Hayekian component of the crisis:

> If we dare to utilize irony, we could assert this crisis as the triumph of Hayek's conception of prices as the vector of information (Hayek 1945). Having them perverted constantly, the Wall Street itself collapses, as the organizational model and the unquestionable hegemonic power in the definition of economic priority of the United States.
> (Boyer 2011: 115; Japanese version: 191)

This was Boyer's unique way of "utilizing irony": it was not a manifestation of support, but rather a critique of a belief in the function of markets, as shown explicitly in the subtitle of his book, "the crisis of the absolutism of markets." However, his idea, in itself, is not our target of investigation. What deserves attention here is the issue whether markets could be the disseminator of pertinent information through prices credited to Hayek's article in 1945, where he writes that

> in a system in which the knowledge of the relevant facts is dispersed among many people, prices can act to coordinate the separate actions of different people in the same way as subjective values help the individual to coordinate the parts of his plan.
> (Hayek 1945: 526)

Then, in confronting market crises, could subjective values be the alternative that takes over the function of prices, as Hayek contrastingly suggests? This has been the thrust of the discussion vis-à-vis the efficient market model versus behavioral finance theory, since the 1980s. However, if we return to Boyer, we find that he believes that "the behavioral finance which had provided an interesting and useful contribution to the comprehension of the functioning of financial markets proved to be very disappointing, facing the crises which repeated themselves and in some cases became systemic" (Boyer 2011: 26; Japanese version: 63). In the conception of behavioral finance theory, we can see some implication of subjectivity that could also be dated back, like the Hayekian component, to the interwar Viennese milieu. This half-forgotten contribution of subjectivity to financial markets is our focus of interest here.

Morgenstern on subjectivity and foresight

Subjective value, as has been written in the "Whig" – the textbook type of historical narrative – was taken into consideration in the latter half of the nineteenth century, especially by the Austrian School of Economists. Friedrich von Wieser, one of two early followers of Carl Menger, the School's founder, contributed to the precise formulation of subjective value. Von Wieser describes it as follows: "both exchange value and use value are subjective and vary according to personal circumstances. And everyone needs to have an exact subjective estimate of the value of money to oneself," but "this personal attitude can have no effect on the movement of goods in the great economic exchange between one economy and another" (von Wieser 1889/1893: 50). He then emphasizes that "the word value alters its original sense somewhat, when transferred from the subjective relation to wants to the objective relation to price" (von Wieser 1889/1893: 51).

This was, in reality, roughly the common understanding of the term "subjectivity" until the beginning of the twentieth century. Subjectivity, in this understanding, vanishes into the process of price-building, when respective individuals come to some market and show their valuations and bargain with sellers or buyers. In other words, prices in the markets bear information and absorb all the possible subjective values of the participatory individuals in their change. Neither von Wieser nor other Austrians inquired further, into whether this definition would hold true regardless of the number of participants in the market, or of the specific characteristics of some particular markets; they focused instead on formulating the general function of markets within the framework of equilibrium.

Hayek, typically, defined this function thus:

> it [the foresight of the different members of the society] must be correct in the sense that every person's plan is based on the expectation of just those actions of other people which those other people intend to perform and that all these plans are based on the expectation of the same set of external facts, so that under certain conditions nobody will have any reason to change his plans.[1]
>
> (Hayek 1937: 41)

Hayek held to this definition, despite his admission within the same article that assumptions about foresight and anticipation play an important role in thinking with regard to dynamics (Hayek 1937: 34). He could not really confront the question of "why the subjective data to the different persons correspond to the objective facts," which he had posed there (Hayek 1937: 50).

In contrast, Morgenstern, who was also trained within the tradition of the Austrian School of that generation, paid attention to economic individuals hidden behind subjective value theory, and he attempted to determine their influence on fluctuations. This focus caused some intellectual friction between him and Hayek. Hayek's version of market analysis became much more popular than that of Morgenstern; in fact, it survived for several decades and later developed into the efficient market model for financial markets, around the beginning of the 1970s. Now, however, the time has come for us to re-examine Morgenstern's rather heterodox idea of subjectivity.

The place of subjectivity in economic foresight

The literature has frequently pointed out Morgenstern's emphasis of the role of time in economic theory; with that emphasis – as I myself once pointed out (Nakayama 2010: 238) – Morgenstern made clear his intention to connect business-cycle theory with the concept of a general equilibrium, thereby following the idea of Böhm-Bawerk. This intention was sometimes explained in terms of his institutional motivations, referring to his directorship of the Institute of Business Cycle Research (Institut für Konjunkturforschung) in Vienna since 1928.[2] However, Morgenstern had interest in the research area already around the middle of the 1920s, going to the United States and European countries, meeting and having discussions with several economists. One outcome was his publication of an article in 1928, in which he deals mainly with Mitchell, Pigou, and Snyder and discusses methodological issues concerning business-cycle theory (Morgenstern 1928b):[3] he claims therein, for example, that both qualitative and quantitative studies were needed to generate business-cycle theory. At the end of this article, he concludes that there lay a vast area of research to be investigated, but that this was not surprising "if one understands the business-cycle theory rightly, with Böhm-Bawerk as the final part of a whole theoretical system" (Morgenstern 1928b: 86).[4] Thus far, Morgenstern's stance might not have been remarkably different from Hayek's at that time.

However, Morgenstern also published a treatise on economic foresight in the same year and explicitly states therein the importance of the economic individuals who stand behind the prices; this focus relates closely to his emphasis on subjectivity:

> Böhm-Bawerk and [von] Wieser have stated clear enough that prices are results from different activities of separate individuals and their wills. But this side of price phenomena became soon out of consideration as "self-evident" and prices got to be operated as independent areas, separate from

judgments and acts of economic subjects standing behind.... But it all matters for the theory of foresight, to come back to the actual behaviors of individuals and to find out the base for the direction of acts of consumers [*Wirtschafter*] and entrepreneurs. Further it is necessary to prove the eventual changeability or stiffness of the points of orientation [*Orientierungspunkte*] which jointly found the subjective rationality of economic behaviors.[5]

(Morgenstern 1928a: 25–6)

According to Morgenstern, subjective value judgments of separate, individual consumers and entrepreneurs are important in the theory of foresight; their subjective "rationality," he states, is founded on several "points of orientation" or landmarks, making it necessary to examine these "points of orientation." He goes on to investigate them, claiming that the economic acts of individuals build a subjectively meaningful cosmos that constitutes a rank or order, and that the variation of points of orientation unknown to an individual leads to a decrease in the rationality of his or her behavior and negatively affects the rationality of others' behavior. The points of orientation can typically be seen in the prices of goods, but these prices are data that result from other individuals' acts; they are not fully given to individuals, but are mere probabilities that correspond to their subjective rationality. Hence, they give rise to the aforementioned repercussive mechanism. We can see that some idea of subjective expectation with regard to probability distribution was imagined here.

Morgenstern then further discusses the subsequent process by which rationality is reduced, wherein a change in unknown directions or "economic fluctuations" could present not only on account of price changes, but also because of many possible changes in areas such as trade, harvest, quantity of money, and volume of production, for which all the people involved are responsible. These can initiate the disequilibrium process.

This portion of the work seems to have been influenced by Pigou, as suggested by a footnote reference to Pigou's book *Industrial Fluctuation*, which he reviewed in yet another article.[6] However, Morgenstern did not forget to add that fluctuations could not necessarily be approached in terms of psychological theory – that there were also cases of fluctuations with "objective" circumstances, like new methods of production, inventions, or catastrophes. Morgenstern's adoption of the antithetical conception of objectivity was a direct criticism of Pigou's monotonous use of the word "psychological." In so doing, Morgenstern posed another question to himself, of whether this objectivity of equilibrium could necessarily be stable.

To this question, Morgenstern answers rather negatively. He explores the circle of mutual dependence among individuals and discusses a case in which the impact of changes in subjective rationality can have an effect on objective rationality, thus implying the instability of objectivity. Here, he briefly mentions the concept of speculation, emphasizing the importance of information vis-à-vis data changes:

But the more reduced subjective rationality of behavior of one consumer means the more reduced objective rationality of the whole system, from which an "error" giving further impact, arises. This error can constitute some "profit" of another one, that is, it can result in an over-proportional transmission of purchasing power into another control power, or it can give rise to pure loss.... The ... final possibility is that I have a monopoly over some knowledge in the change of data and the existence of this monopoly is unknown.... But ... the value of my monopoly continuously decreases. This case is not as hypothetical as it might seem: it plays a considerable role in the stock-exchange speculation.

(Morgenstern 1928a: 29–30)

In discussing the possible instability of the "objectivity" of equilibrium, Morgenstern focuses on stock exchange markets and realizes the importance of one's monopoly or disposal of knowledge of some data and changes therein; in such a situation, there might be some "error" in the market in question, as a result of that person's "profit." The word "profit" is used here as something drawn from speculation, not production. Stock-exchange markets, rather than general markets, were explicitly thought of here, as it is in those general markets that some disequilibrium would be caused by reductions in subjective rationality.

However, as the title of his treatise suggests, Morgenstern did not look into the issue of speculation itself in greater detail. This treatise has usually been interpreted as one that only clarifies the impossibility of prediction methodologically,[7] but we can pinpoint a richer implication for the conception of financial markets and speculation.

Subjectivity in risk and uncertainty

After publishing the aforementioned treatise, Morgenstern continued with a trajectory of research, aided by his acquaintance with F.H. Knight – a colleague who had made the distinction between the concepts of risk and uncertainty, commonly known even today[8] – and published an article in *Zeitschrift für Nationalökonomie* in 1935. There, Morgenstern takes up again the relationship between perfect foresight and equilibrium, and he argues that these two concepts are not inextricable. As is known, this article was translated into English by Knight and was published in a journal for English readers, a happenstance that confirms Knight's high valuation of this article. According to Morgenstern, contradiction rather than equilibrium would be forthcoming if more than two "homo economics" had perfect foresight and sought the maximization of profit for themselves. From the game-theory perspective, in retrospect, one might say that what bothered Morgenstern most was the conflict of interests between those two homo economics: they were not complementary. In this sense, he came to an impasse, not being able to formulate mixed strategies by which he could allocate a probability for each economic player in a situation comprising opposing or cooperative interests. However, as seen in the previous section, Morgenstern went deep into the question of whether subjectivity could possibly penetrate itself in the "social" economy, possibly with more than two individuals.

Hence, the importance of this article lay in the fact that Morgenstern opened a way of looking into the meaning of subjectivity: he discussed the issues relating to subjectivity, including several categories of risk, uncertainty, and expectation, in further relation to the degree of foresight and the degree of that foresight's "effectiveness." In mentioning this effectiveness, Morgenstern briefly examines J.M. Keynes's conceptions and also references Karl Menger's contribution,[9] thus showing that his thought in this direction was influenced by these authors as well as by Knight.

As to the influence of Keynes, Morgenstern, after classifying the economic theorists who had ever questioned the assumption of perfect foresight, wondered critically whether Keynes, in his *Treatise on Money*, thought of imperfect foresight in his mention of "correct forecasting" or "accurate forecasting" (Morgenstern 1935/1976: 170). Morgenstern believed there would be no accuracy or correctness problems, were there not an assumption of perfect forecasting. Here, he introduces the distinction between technical foreseeability and effective foresight, and he argues that the latter could exceed or lag behind the former. Effective foresight could be seen as a variant of subjectivity, but it is arrived at differently, "from the technical data obtainable from time to time ... according to the degree of actual employment of the economic science" (Morgenstern 1935/1976: 178). This statement means that the degrees of diffusion of knowledge or information in economics as a science determines the degree of penetration of correct or accurate forecasting. In this sense, subjectivity would, according to Morgenstern's interpretation of Keynes, be reduced to incorrectness, at least from the vantage of scientific knowledge.

Further, in exploring the meaning of "imperfect foresight," Morgenstern defines the concept of expectation explicitly, as another variant of subjectivity. At the beginning of the article, it is stated that Pigou's concept of "expectations of businessmen" was thought to be assigned a nebulous role in business-cycle theory (Morgenstern 1935/1976: 171):

> With imperfect foresight, with the possibility of other prices, e.g., inability to eliminate factors of disturbance in my expectation, it is always conceivable that I, on the grounds of temperament, of caprice, of daring, etc. form my expectation differently than technical foreseeability would, perhaps, make it necessary for me. For example, I am inclined at one time and at another I am not inclined to undergo a risk. In other words, where really effective final foresight is lacking, the element of expectation appears.... *Expectation depends, thus, only to a limited degree on foresight.*
> (Morgenstern 1935/1976: 189–90; italics in original text)

Here it is shown that "effective" foresight can be determined not only through knowledge of economic theory, but also influenced by the expectations of individuals – each of which is formed by an attitude toward or against some risk, in each case.

The influence of Karl Menger is also clear here, in connection with the concept of risk and uncertainty. Menger delivered in 1934 a presentation on the element of uncertainty in economics – which could instead be called "risk," under the distinction made by Knight – with an example of paradoxical behavior among economic subjects that together constituted the "St. Petersburg's Paradox," something originally noted by Daniel Bernoulli (1738/1956) in the eighteenth century. Menger wrote an article on this issue on the recommendation of Morgenstern, who immediately understood its importance. We can understand why Menger's problem-setting was very persuasive for Morgenstern, as it dealt with subjective expectations.

The St. Petersburg's Paradox was originally considered a risk of insurance;[10] Menger determined that individuals would assume this risk to the corresponding extent of their current assets, the possibility of additional profits, and the probabilities thereof. Menger concludes that people behave in ways different from that predicted by mathematics, rather following the "moral" expectation, as Bernoulli had termed it. Bernoulli defined this "moral" expectation as being identical to the logarithm relating to one's monetary possessions, but the usage of the word "moral" might be replaced by the adjective "subjective," at least as we understand these words here (von Neumann and Morgenstern 1944/1957: 28). Also, from our contemporary perspective of financial markets – including the treatment of insurance markets – this analysis seems quite implicative.

About ten years later, Morgenstern, in collaborative game-theory work with John von Neumann in 1944, still showed this trajectory of research interest, albeit only to a limited degree. At some early part of this book, as the authors point out, they discuss the axiomatic formulation of utility and expectation, and they deal only with the utility corresponding directly to the mathematical expectation. They briefly pose a question, as to whether or not there were some positive or negative utility to the mere act of "taking a chance" in gambling; there, we see a footnote reference to Karl Menger and Bernoulli (von Neumann and Morgenstern 1944/1957: 28). Although they soon answered in the negative, an appendix on the axiomatic treatment of utility was added to the end of the book in the revised 1957 version, where we find a concluding remark on this issue.

In this appendix, after confirming the three necessary characteristics of utilities – namely, completeness, transitivity, and the combination rule – the authors take up the case of Bernoulli, where "the utility of monetary gain should not only be proportional to the gain, but also (assuming the gain to be infinitesimal) inversely proportional to the amount of the owner's total possessions, expressed in money" (von Neumann and Morgenstern 1944/1957: 629). It then follows that "of equal gains and losses the latter are more strongly felt than the former" and that "a 50%–50% gamble with equal risks is definitely disadvantageous." They then explain that a suitable definition of "utility" should eliminate the "specific utility or disutility of gambling, which prima facie appeared to exist" (von Neumann and Morgenstern 1944/1957: 629). They sought to determine whether the combination rule is contradictory at all to the utility or disutility of gambling; although their conclusion was rather negative, the treatment of this issue in itself suggests Morgenstern's consistent interest in the problem of expectation, while using the terminology of gambling.

Subjectivity in line with cognitive psychology

As mentioned, Morgenstern's view was not very popular among economists of the time, but there was at least one exception: his intellectual friendship with Knight was indeed mutual. In 1940, Knight published an article, "What is 'Truth' in Economics?" apparently a critical-review article of a book by T.W. Hutchison, *The Significance and Basic Postulates of Economic Theory*, published in 1938.[11] The critique was sharply directed toward the inconsistency of Hutchison's methodology, but if we take the fact into consideration that Hutchison had investigated Morgenstern's aforementioned article of 1935 considerably and in great detail, we might see Knight's article as a defense of Morgenstern from being misleadingly interpreted by Hutchison. Actually, the chapter in which Hutchison argues the distinction between "subjective" and "objective" rationality was originally published in the same journal, *Zeitschrift für Nationalökonomie*, in 1937, under the title "Expectation and Rational Conduct"; this implies his direct awareness of Morgenstern's contribution two years previous to his. For Knight, although Hutchison had attempted to annihilate or at least ridicule von Wieser's psychological method,[12] the analysis was naïve and ultimately unsuccessful, and so Hutchison rather retreated to von Wieser's position, away from that of Morgenstern.

What is interesting is that Knight, in this article, developed his own view of subjectivity. Without using the precise term "subjectivity," he examines its meaning from the following perspective: "what we perceive, or are able to perceive, is largely a matter of the 'apperceptive mass' – and this involves both expectation and interests" (Knight 1940: 11). That is, for Knight, the function of one's perception of the external world – and therefore one's subsequent judgments – must be explored whenever inner or psychological value theory is discussed. This can be seen as a cognitive psychological version of subjectivity. In so doing – as the title of this article implies – Knight asks the question "What is truth?" in relation to observation and inference in economics. For this purpose, he distinguishes three categories of knowledge that economics is meant to address: the first is knowledge of the external world, the second is the "truths of logic and mathematics," and the third – and the most important one here – is knowledge of human conduct. Knight examines the meaning of "subjectivity" for the second and third categories, and comes to the understanding that the distinction between subjectivity and objectivity is neither self-evident nor absolute.

Knight starts, in connection to the second category, with an examination of the most basic proposition of economics – namely, that individuals maximize their satisfaction or utility – and questions its rigorousness, saying that "in the absence of any technique of measurement, there is no clear differentiation between a subjective state and an objective quality" and that the "reference of an experience to the external world or to the mind is shifting and largely arbitrary." He means here that there is no logically "true" connection between them. He then goes on to the third category and again argues critically, that a really thoroughgoing laissez-faire individualism that accepts individual preferences is theoretically and fundamentally impossible, under any condition:

> it is a fact to be kept in mind and recognized as a condition of talking sense about human interests, that everyone, habitually and inevitably, makes a distinction, which is vital, however vague it may be, between personal preferences and values assumed to be objective.... No discussion of group action can be carried on in propositions which merely state what "I want."
>
> (Knight 1940: 23)

As we can see here, Knight claims that individuals make a distinction between their preferences or the satisfaction of their own wants on one hand, and social values on the other. Though this is rather a critique "from outside," Knight denies the idea that subjectivity in the sense of individual preference would, once confronted with others and collected into a society, "naturally" be absorbed or integrated into objective equilibrium, in a way different from that which Morgenstern suggests.

Further, under these assumptions, Knight discusses the problem of prediction or the limitations of the possibility of prediction; he argues that the basis of prediction would be social psychology, dependent not only on statistical extrapolation but also on individuals' insights and interpretations of what is socially "right," and what they themselves could do with their competence. In this way, Knight also attempts to elaborate upon subjectivity in his own way, and he rather partakes in a fundamental exploration of the morals or ethics around markets.

Subjectivity and the random-walk hypothesis

As was made clear in the previous section, the concept of subjectivity was considerably explored by several economists, from the late 1920s to the early 1940s; they considered it an important issue in the analysis of expectations and forecasting, risk, uncertainty, and disequilibrium. However, this view did not enjoy widespread acceptance: mainstream economics had been formulated around the concept of equilibrium – like that extolled by Hayek – including that pertaining to business cycles and fluctuations.

On the other hand, M.L. Bachelier speaks of a completely different line of history in his 1900 doctoral dissertation, "Théorie de la spéculation," perhaps under the influence of Regnault;[13] he makes clear the random character of the stock market, similar to Brownian motion, without specifically naming it.[14] Bachelier was certainly conscious of the importance of subjective probability in speculation, when he writes of the distinction between two kinds of probability in the transactions within an exchange (Bachelier 1900/2006: 26). The first kind is mathematical probability, which can be determined a priori and leads to the calculation of mathematical expectation. The second is "the probability depending on future events, which is, consequently, impossible to predict in a mathematical fashion," as "it is this last probability that the speculator tries to predict.... His inferences are entirely personal, since his counterpart necessarily has the opposite opinion" (Bachelier 1900/2006: 26). He then proceeds to analyze stochastic probabilities from this assumption.

Since Bachelier's dissertation submission to the Faculty of Mathematics, a further line of development followed in mathematical and technical directions.[15] As a book edited by Paul H. Cootner (1964) shows, several economic theorists – such as Kendall, Osborne, Fama, and Samuelson – wrote much about this issue in the first half of the 1960s, and Morgenstern was among them. Most of them had more interest in the random character of changes, followed by the stochastic probabilities of prices, and so the subjectivity that Bachelier had originally taken into consideration eventually dimmed from their view. From our perspective, this was the phase in which subjectivity had faded from market analysis, and random-walk theory became thus connected to the smooth functioning of the market.

Morgenstern and the random-walk hypothesis

Morgenstern, after publishing collaborative work with von Neumann – who died in the 1950s – needed to play the role of game-theory promoter, to some extent. However, his research interests remained in business-cycle theory and he seemed to seek out a suitable methodology for it: as seen in the previous section, he examined qualitative and quantitative approaches for business-cycle theory in his early career and stated that there were vast research areas yet to be explored. Then, also in the mid-1930s, he expressed his idea in relation to the methodological problem of axiomatizing economics, and he claimed that this formulation did not seem to be suitable for business-cycle theory.[16] Driven perhaps by this motivation, he began to undertake research and to publish articles and books – such as those that deal with stock markets, for example – with a focus on international comparisons and mutual influence.

He then investigated the conception of the random-walk model, in a new collaboration with C. Granger and others. He remembered that he originally planned to write further collaborative papers with von Neumann, and that one of the themes was time-series analysis; this was not realized prior to von Neumann's death.

> we wrote only one of the planned joint papers.... For example, we were both convinced that the then current methods for time-series analysis of economic data were totally inadequate ... and that better methods based on Fourier series could be developed.... It never came to that: in 1955 Johnny was stricken by cancer ... and he died in Washington on 8 February 1957. (I did not give up this plan, but worked towards the development and

application of spectral analysis; the fruit of this is my book with C.W.J. Granger, Predictability of Stock Market Prices, preceded by various papers).
(Morgenstern 1976a: 814)

Although this later collaboration itself did not attract considerable attention – that is, only as Granger's contribution to time-series analysis, which won the Nobel Prize in 2003 – we will follow the subjectivity's fading-out from stock-market analysis research.

In a paper published in 1963, Morgenstern and Granger examine the random-walk hypothesis, believing that the time-sequential changes in the price series of stock markets do not correlate, at least in the limited context of prices in the New York Stock Exchange; as a result, the results were not generalizable and could be "applied only to this sample" (Granger and Morgenstern 1963/1964/1976: 330). Still, the result was a "confirmation of the random-walk hypothesis for weekly and monthly data" (Godfrey et al. 1964/1976: 357). Achieving this result, the authors replied negatively to the question of whether "stock price indices provide useful leading business cycle indicators," emphasizing the huge inaccuracies around the "cycles" (Granger and Morgenstern 1963/1964/1976: 344).

Morgenstern then confessed that he had to modify his earlier statements "made about the alleged existence, duration and interaction of stock market 'cycles,'" referring to one of his own books (Granger and Morgenstern 1963/1964/1976: 345). In this way, Morgenstern seems to have been empirically impeded in his ambition to construct some general theory of business "cycles" while focusing on the stock markets. Even though the random-walk hypothesis originally made some assumption vis-à-vis the subjective expectations of participants, this element was substantially omitted in the process of randomness. The authors (or perhaps Morgenstern) put forth its implications for investment behavior: "To the extent that stock prices perform random walks the short term investor engages in a fair gamble, which is slightly better than playing roulette" and also for the long-term investor, the small margin "will rapidly disappear as it is being made use of" (Granger and Morgenstern 1963/1964/1976: 345). This means that this kind of gamble could be carried only haphazardly, *not* with subjectively rational judgments.

Further collaboration with Granger on random-walk theory generally resulted in a stronger confirmation for Morgenstern that his attention to subjectivity did not leave any room for further theory development. In an article in the following year – again, on the random-walk hypothesis – Morgenstern, as one of the authors, had to accept the adaptive nature of the market:

> If the mechanism were such that the mathematically expected value of the price at future times differed from the current price then an investor could establish a predictive decision rule which would result in a net profit when exercised in the market. However ... the realization ... for profit ... will result in a change of mechanism which will remove this opportunity.
> (Godfrey et al. 1964/1976: 379)

Although there exists some possibility for speculative profit for investors, the market mechanism would win in the long run. The authors briefly mention some possibility of inside information that would influence price changes in a favorable way, but they soon deny its durable validity, in consideration of the self-destroying need to continue to flow in new inside information to maintain profits. In this sense, Morgenstern had to give way to the Hayekian functioning of markets.

From the standpoint of the above conclusions, the assumption of an efficient market model was not far-fetched: as was formulated in an article by E.F. Fama in 1970,[17] the efficient market model assumed "the adjustment of security prices to relevant information subsets" (Fama 1970: 383), which in turn owed to the sound functioning of the market.

> The primary role of the capital market is allocation of ownership of the economy's capital stock. In general terms, the ideal is a market in which prices provide accurate signals for resource allocation: that is, a market in which firms can make production-investment decisions, and investors can choose among securities that represent ownership of firms' activities.... A market in which prices always "fully reflect" available information is called "efficient."
>
> (Fama 1970: 383)

Fama states, albeit with some reservation, that efficiency can be said to have been attained if "sufficient numbers of investors have ready access to available information" (Fama 1970: 388) and the random walk is included in the conditions of the theory, to test this efficiency empirically. Hayek's concept of a market that conveys all available information was formulated for capital markets or markets of securities; since that time, the random walk has come to align explicitly with the efficient functioning of market and is hence at variance with subjectivity, in spite of its apparent affinity with "randomness."

Revival of subjectivity as irrationality

A few years after Fama made his aforementioned basic contribution to the survey of market efficiency theory, B.G. Malkiel published his bestselling book *Random Walk Down Wall Street* (1973/2003), because of which the concept of the "random walk" became very popular in the field of market analysis, not only for professional economists but also for the investing public. Seen from theoretical and empirical perspectives, he approximately follows the contributions of Fama, and this was made clear in his other article of the same period.[18] However, Malkiel also made his own contributions: in his writings, we see the concept of subjectivity being revived within the classification. At the beginning of his book, he describes a random walk as "one in which future steps or directions cannot be predicted on the basis of past actions. When the term is applied to the stock market, it means that short-run changes in stock prices cannot be predicted"

(Malkiel 1973/2003: 24). He then provides a short survey of the history of economic theory, vis-à-vis this concept: he theoretically contrasts "Firm Foundations" and "Castles in the Air" – the former of which argues that an investment instrument has a "firm anchor of something called intrinsic value" (Malkiel 1973/2003: 29), while the latter is closely related to subjectivity and is opposed to the former kind of idea. According to Malkiel, both of these are reactions by academic scholars to the idea of investment and random-walk theory: "taken to its logical extreme, it means that a blindfolded monkey throwing darts at a newspaper's financial pages could select a portfolio that would do just as well as one carefully selected by the experts" (Malkiel 1973/2003: 24).[19]

The purpose of Malkiel's book was to show that one can perform well in investing, in the sense of providing "a method of purchasing assets to gain profit in the form of reasonably predictable income (dividends, interest or rentals) and/or appreciation over the long term" (Malkiel 1973/2003: 26). In his understanding, investment is a rational, logical, and reasonable activity, and it was different from that of "speculating," in his usage of the word, which is psychological and irrational. He almost reproaches speculative bubbles, saying that they were manipulated by savvy institutions and professionals, and he states that too many investors are lazy and careless. According to him, the more cautious investors become, the more predictable – and hence more efficient – stock markets become, which he feels was the "good" functioning of investment. This is, so to speak, an ethical explanation of an efficient market model against, for example, the behavioral finance theory that praises irrationality.

The author's intentions in writing it aside, Malkiel's book provides an interesting grouping of theorists, with regard to subjectivity: our main figure, Morgenstern, who is explicitly mentioned as the early leader of Castle-in-the-Air theory, Keynes, and Robert Shiller, who used mass (crowd) psychology in the "so-called behavioral theories of the stock market" (Malkiel 1973/2003: 32). It was banteringly called the "greater fool" theory to recommend paying, for example, three times what something was worth, so long as later you could find someone innocent to pay five times what it is worth. Keynes was considered representative of this group, with the example of the beauty contest,[20] and Morgenstern was mentioned as believing "that every investor should post the following Latin maxim above his desk, "Res tantum valet quantum vendi potest" [A thing is worth only what someone else will pay for it] (Malkiel 1973/2003: 32–3).

From the viewpoint of the history of economic theory, Malkiel's classification might seem coarse and even misleading. His interpretation of Morgenstern's theory of speculation (which had, in fact, been made in collaboration with Granger), as well as that of Keynes' beauty contest, would immediately provoke some rebuttals. Surprisingly enough, at the very beginning of the 1970 book by Morgenstern and Granger, we find the aforementioned Latin maxim! We need to admit that the episode Malkiel introduced rang true for Morgenstern, at least with respect to his collaboration with Granger.

Revenge of subjectivity?

As Malkiel describes, the Castle-in-the-Air theory and certain psychological theories of stock prices have become more and more popular since the 1990s:

> there have always been both logical and psychological theories of stock prices, and earlier generations of economists, such as John Maynard Keynes, stressed the importance of the fallibility of human decision making. The efficient-market theory was developed on the assumption that market participants are highly rational. But particularly during the 1990s and early 2000s, psychologists such as Daniel Kahneman and financial economists in increasing numbers have argued that the decisions of many investors are strongly influenced by behavioral characteristics such as overconfidence, overreaction, attraction to fashions and fads, and even hubris.
>
> (Malkiel 1973/2003: 243)

It is evident from this quotation that subjectivity in the sense of irrationality – as evidenced in overconfidence, overreaction, hubris, or attraction to superficial things like fashion or fads – is supposed to be important in deciding stock prices, even though those kinds of prices are "fallible" in comparison to those determined through rationality.

Further, this kind of subjectivity corresponds to what Shiller, one of the representatives of behavioral finance theory, calls "irrational exuberance."[21] Shiller ascertained that efficient market theory gave in to behavioral finance theory, based on empirical validity. In a 2003 review article with the title "From Efficient Markets Theory to Behavioral Finance," Shiller notes that the efficient markets theory reached its height of dominance in academic circles in the 1970s and that its adherents – for example, Merton and Lucas – use rational expectations, but that the volatility anomaly ran so deeply that many theoretical attempts arose in the 1980s to revise that theory and demonstrate that some stock-market inefficiency does not damage the theory as a whole. But Shiller concludes that "the level of volatility of the overall stock market cannot be well explained with any variant of the efficient markets model in which stock prices are formed by looking at the present discounted value of future returns" (Shiller 2003: 90). This was a remarkable turning point in the "academic discussion" of economic theorists in the 1990s, as it marks a shifting away from econometric analyses of the time series, toward "developing models of human psychology as it relates to financial markets" (Shiller 2003: 90).

Thinking back to the setback that Morgenstern had experienced in the 1950s – when it was the empirical data of stock markets that prevented him from making further efforts to construct a general theory involving his conception of subjectivity – his intention of that time retrieved its honor here. This "honor" can be seen as the revenge of subjectivity, despite the fact it makes use of that tricky term, "psychology," once again. This kind of economic-theory trend vis-à-vis subjectivity survives to the present, owing to the convincing nature of "psychology," fundamental deficits in finding any other persuasive devices in current economic and financial crisis, as Boyer (2011: 26, Japanese version: 63) laments.

Notes

1 Shortly before these passages, Hayek mentions Morgenstern's 1935 article and points out that the relationship between equilibrium and foresight had been hotly debated. Some researchers point out the influence of Morgenstern on Hayek in shifting his research interest. See Akiyama (2003).
2 See Rellstab (1992) and Leonard (2010). Morgenstern took over this position from Hayek. Please note that we use the term "business-cycle research" rather than "trade-cycle research" as the equivalent of the German *Konjunkturforschung*.
3 Morgenstern analyzed "Business Cycles" by Mitchell, "Industrial Fluctuations" by Pigou, and "Business Cycles and Business Measurements" by Snyder, all of which had been published in 1927. Of course, these authors did not have an Austrian intellectual background, as Morgenstern does emphasize.
4 Tentative English translation, by Nakayama.
5 Regarding the distinction between *Wirtschaftler* and *Unternehmer*, he stated to support that made by Hans Mayer (Morgenstern 1928a, p. 31). In the article referenced, Mayer re-examines the Austrian theory of *Wirtschaften*, which corresponds to theory concerning consumers (Mayer 1922).
6 Morgenstern 1928a: 27 – Pigou also lists such factors as harvest variations, inventions, changes in tastes, etc., to analyze the causes behind varying expectations of profit among businessmen (Pigou 1927/1967, part I, chapter IV). For details, see, for example Collard (1983, 1996); these factors are seen, in part, in Morgenstern's description here.
7 "It was a treatise on the methodology of economic forecasting, in which he determined to prove the futility of all attempts at prediction" (Leonard 2010: 100).
8 For details on this acquaintance and their mutual influence, see Nakayama (2010).
9 Morgenstern mentions Menger's 1934 article, as well as his book of the same year. Nakayama (2010: 239) briefly alludes to this influence.
10 Bernoulli deals with the risk of marine insurance in transporting a commodity between St. Petersburg and Amsterdam. He calculated how many assets the insurance company should hold to commit to this business chance, while assuming risk.
11 Researchers of Hutchison who evaluate this book positively find Knight's article unfairly critical.

> At this distance of time one might say that Knight was perhaps too severe in his attack on such a young and promising academic.... However ... Knight's criticism created a good deal of general interest, among fellow economists, in the book of a little-known economist from England!
> (Ghosh 2007: 164)

See also Hart (2003).
12 Knight quoted a phrase of Hutchison where Hutchison picked up a sentence of von Wieser: "'We can observe natural phenomena only from outside, but ourselves from within.' [This sentence is taken from von Wieser.] The employment of this inner observation is the psychological method [This phrase is provided by Hutchison, following von Wieser's own terminology]" (Knight 1940: 15).
13 See Taqqu (2001: 13–14) and Le Gall (2007: ch. 4).
14 For detailed discussion, see Davis and Etheridge (2006).
15 Exceptionally, Keynes quotes Bachelier in his treatise on probability, as early as 1921 – not from Bachelier's dissertation, but from his other works that deal with probability.

16 "[I]t is not at all certain that the entire economic theory can be formulated axiomatically. Thus this seems to be unlikely for business cycle theory, because in this field there is too much uncertainty about the basic assumptions" (Morgenstern 1936/1976: 397).
17 This was an article surveying theoretical and empirical literature pertaining to the efficient market model; it was also a summary of a presentation at an annual Meeting of the American Finance Association at the end of 1969, in a joint session with the Econometric Society.
18 See Malkiel (2003), an article for which Malkiel extracted and rewrote the content of his book in a more academic style.
19 His use of a humorous tone – like that in this example citing monkeys with darts – seems to be strategic, as this book was directed at experts of finance and general readers who, like him, wished to enter the world of portfolio management and succeed in it, from the world of academic scholarship. This stance has recently been taken by those with careers similar to Malkiel.
20 It is analogous to entering a newspaper beauty-judging contest.... The smart player recognizes that personal criteria of beauty are irrelevant in determining the contest winner. A better strategy is to select those faces the other players are likely to fancy.... The newspaper-contest analogy represents the ultimate form of the castle-in-the-air theory of price determination.

(Malkiel 1973/2003: 31–2)

21 The term "irrational exuberance" was originally used by Alan Greenspan, former chairman of the US Federal Reserve Board, in 1996 during a dinner speech, to describe the behavior of stock market investors – behavior that, soon after the speech, would cause a precipitous drop in the stock markets. This event, says Shiller, inspired him to write the book. See Shiller (2000/2009: 1).

References

Akiyama, M. (2003) "An investigation on Hayek's 'transformation' process: in relation to Morgenstern's 'perfect foresight and economic equilibrium,'" *Mita Gakkai Zasshi*, 95(4): 135–51 (in Japanese).
Bachelier, L. (1900/2006) "Theory of speculation" (originally: "Théorie de la speculation"), in M. Davis and A. Etheridge (trans. and commentary) (2006) *Louis Bachelier's Theory of Speculation: The Origins of Modern Finance*, Princeton, NJ/Oxford: Princeton University Press, pp. 15–79.
Bernoulli, D. (1738/1956) "Exposition of a new theory of the measurement of risk" (originally: "Specimen theoriae nvae de mensura sortis"), *Econometrica*, 22(1): 23–36.
Boyer, R. (2011) *Finance et globalisation: la crise de l'absolutisme du marché* (*Kin-yu Shihonshugi-no Houkai*), translated into Japanese, Tokyo: Fujiwara Shoten.
Collard, D. (1983) "Pigou on expectations and the cycle," *Economic Journal*, 93(370): 411–14.
Collard, D. (1996) "Pigou and modern business cycle theory," *Economic Journal*, 106(437): 912–24.
Cootner, P.H. (ed.) (1964) *The Random Character of Stock Market Prices*, Cambridge, MA: The MIT Press.
Davis, M. and Etheridge, A. (trans. and commentary) (2006) *Louis Bachelier's Theory of Speculation: The Origins of Modern Finance*, Princeton, NJ/Oxford: Princeton University Press.

Fama, E.F. (1970) "Efficient capital markets: a review of theory and empirical work," *Journal of Finance*, 25(2): 383–417, Papers and Proceedings of the Twenty-Eighth Annual Meeting of the American Finance Association.

Ghosh, R.N. (2007) "Obituary of Terence Wilmot Hutchison: my reminiscences, communications and notes from the archives," *History of Economics Review*, 46: 162–9.

Godfrey, M.D., Granger, C.W.J., and Morgenstern, O. (1964/1976) "The random-walk hypothesis of stock market behavior," in A. Schotter and M.I. Nadiri (eds) *Selected Writings of Oskar Morgenstern*, New York: New York University Press, pp. 357–83 (originally in *Kyklos*, 17: 1–30).

Granger, C.W.J. and Morgenstern, O. (1963/1964/1976) "Spectral analysis of New York stock market prices," *Kyklos*, 16: 1–27 (reprinted also in P.H. Cootner (ed.) (1964) *The Random Character of Stock Market Prices*, Cambridge, MA: The MIT Press, pp. 162–88, and in A. Schotter and M.I. Nadiri (eds) *Selected Writings of Oskar Morgenstern*, New York: New York University Press, pp. 329–55).

Hayek, F.A. (1937) "Economics and knowledge," *Economica* (new series), 4: 33–54.

Hayek, F.A. (1945) "The use of knowledge in society," *American Economic Review*, 35(4): 519–30.

Hart, J. (2003) "Terence Hutchison's 1938 essay: towards a reappraisal," *Journal of Economic Methodology*, 10(3): 353–73.

Hutchison, T.W. (1938) *The Significance and Basic Postulates of Economic Theory*, London: Macmillan and Co. Ltd.

Knight, F.H. (1940) "What is 'truth' in economics?" *Journal of Political Economy*, 48(1): 1–32.

Le Gall, P. (2007) *A History of Econometrics in France*, London/New York: Routledge.

Leonard, R. (2010) *Von Neumann, Morgenstern, and the Creation of Game Theory: From Chess to Social Science, 1900–1960*, Cambridge/New York: Cambridge University Press.

Malkiel, B.G. (1973/2003) *Random Walk Down Wall Street*, New York: W.W. Norton & Company, Inc.

Malkiel, B.G. (2003) "The efficient market hypothesis and its crisis," *Journal of Economic Perspectives*, 17(1): 59–82.

Mayer, H. (1922) "Untersuchung zu dem Grundgesetz der wirtschaftlichen Wertrechnung," *Zeitschrift für Volkswirtschaft und Sozialpolitik*, N.F. Bd. II: 1–23.

Morgenstern, O. (1928a) *Wirtschaftsprognose: Eine Untersuchung Ihrer Voraussetzungen und Möglichkeiten*, Vienna: Verlag von Julius Springer.

Morgenstern, O. (1928b) "Qualitative und quantitative Konjunkturforschung," *Zeitschrift für die gesamte Saatswissenschaften*, 85(1): 54–88.

Morgenstern, O. (1935/1976) "Perfect foresight and economic equilibrium'," in Schotter, A. and Nadiri, M.I. (eds), *Selected Writings of Oskar Morgenstern*, pp. 169–83.

Morgenstern, O. (1936/1976) "Logistics and the social sciences," in A. Schotter and M.I. Nadiri (eds) *Selected Writings of Oskar Morgenstern*, New York: New York University Press, pp. 389–404 (originally in German, *Zeitschrift für Nationalökonomie*, 6(2): 196–208).

Morgenstern, O. (1976a) "The collaboration between Oskar Morgenstern and John von Neumann on the theory of games," *Journal of Economic Literature*, 14(3): 805–16.

Morgenstern, O. (1976b) *Selected Writings of Oskar Morgenstern*, edited by A. Schotter and M.I. Nadiri, New York: New York University Press.

Morgenstern, O. and Granger, C.W.T. (1970) *Predictability of Stock Market Prices*, Lexington, MA: Lexington Books (D.C. Heath and Company).

Nakayama, C. (2010) "Involvement of an Austrian émigré economist in America," in H. Hageman, T. Nishizawa, and Y. Ikeda (eds) *Austrian Economics in Transition*, New York: Palgrave Macmillan, pp. 235–53.

Neumann, von, J. and Morgenstern, O. (1944/1957) *Theory of Games and Economic Behavior*, Princeton, NJ: Princeton University Press.

Pigou, A.C. (1927/1967) *Industrial Fluctuations*, 2nd edn., London: Frank Cass & Co. Ltd.

Rellstab, U. (1992) *Ökonomie und Spiele: die Entstehungsgeschicte der Spieltheorie aus dem Blickwinkel des Ökonomen Oskar Morgenstern*, Chur/Zurich: Verlag Ruegger.

Shiller, R. (2000/2009) *Irrational Exuberance*, 2nd edn., revised and updated, New York: Broadway Books.

Shiller, R. (2003) "From efficient markets theory to behavioral finance," *Journal of Economic Perspectives*, 17(1): 83–104.

Taqqu, M.S. (2001) "Bachelier and his times: a conversation with Bernard Bru," *Finance and Stochastics*, 5(1): 3–32.

von Wieser, F. (1889/1893) *Natural Value*, trans. Christian A. Malloch, edited by William Smart, London: Macmillan and Co.

10 Some evolutionary interpretations of the economic systems of Piero Sraffa and John von Neumann in the light of complexity

Yuji Aruka

A new perspective on the economic system derived from J. Holland's genetic algorithm

Alteration of the price concept in the last century

I recall that in the 1970s, the keen interest in the theory of price and production that had dominated the 1920–30s had decreased drastically. J. von Neumann, A. Wald, R. Remak, G. von Cassel, H. F. von Stackelberg, E. Schneider, P. A. Samuelson, and many other great authors developed their own theories of price and production in mathematically rigorous form. These unique contributions motivated many scientists to study economics, which led to the growth of mathematical economics in the mid-1950s. The existence and stability proofs of general equilibrium were thus achieved with remarkable mathematical precision. However, in the 1970s, many books on production and distribution were no longer being sold in bookstores. To my understanding, the state of the shops reflected the metamorphosis of the fundamental business activities in the advanced countries of the last century. The banking business and advanced industries began to computerize their activities.[1]

Here, imperfect or irrational conditions no longer matter. More significantly, equilibrium prices no longer play a primary role in realizing the products in the market. The present mode of production is subject to increasing returns and to the market generating a path-dependent process of trading shares, as Arthur (1994) demonstrates. This process is accompanied by a persistent innovation process, which brings steady change to the economic environment. In this mode of production, the *novelties* of products become more important. This feature is quite similar to biological evolution, as Holland (1992, 1995) noted in his genetic algorithm.[2] In other words, a new mode of production generated at the end of the last century has emerged, and has in turn changed the bidding system. The economic system can operate without resorting to equilibrium prices; producers need not employ the equilibrium price system to survive in it. The agents in an economy should always receive positive feedback from other agents' reactions. In an actual system accompanying persistent innovations, the environment should always be *renormalized*.[3]

Shift of the trading method and the environmental niche

In short, price no longer plays a crucial role in the economy. The equilibrium price system is no longer the sole decisive factor in the fulfillment of trades. While price is still a main source of information for realizing trades, it is not the final determinant to equilibrate supply and demand. The prices actually employed no longer are the so-called equilibrium prices that eliminate excess demand. This alteration suggests that a replacement of the trading method will occur. In fact, the amount traded by the batch auction (*Itayose* in Japanese) has shrunk drastically, while the continuous double auction (*Zaraba* in Japanese) has become much more dominant.[4] The present tendency coincides with the historical path of the market. In the latter method, the settlement is simply attained by a matching of ask and bid according to the time preference principle.[5] This observation is not limited to the stock exchange, but may also be generally applied to the process of selecting a productive plan. Thus, this shift to the double auction is reflected by the metamorphosis of production. In this stage, prices in the sense of general equilibrium are no longer required. The bid/ask mechanism for selecting an adaptive productive plan might be replaced by the bucket brigade algorithm as an internal mechanism, as the evolutionary genetic algorithm shows. The evolutionary process based on this algorithm moves to a new stage via the feedback loop from a consecutively modified environment.[6] The environment in the genetic algorithm is to be interpreted as an "environmental niche," according to Holland (1992: 11; 1995: 22–7). The field might be strategically chosen for the agents. This is called "stage-setting" in a genetic algorithm. Under such an implementation of the environmental niche, the environment for agents in this sense does not settle at a given landscape. Hence, the economic system will not necessarily be bound to an equilibrium state in which equilibrium prices dominate.

Classical steps to attain equilibrium

As Aruka and Koyama (2011: 149) demonstrate, the agent who sets the desired amount of a set of {price, quantity} to trade with an arbitrary agent must have an independent plan, which is never influenced by the environment outside the inner preference. Consequently, the agent must cancel the original offer as things go against the original plan. Suppose that the agent is a buyer who wanted to purchase a desired good at a price lower than the desired price. In this case, a suggested rule will be applied as follows:

1. In the case that there is any market order to sell, any purchase plan could be at least partly fulfilled. Here, let the concerned buyer be the person who obtains a contract.
2. As the quoted price is raised to a price higher than the planned price, the buyer must then give up the contract right to purchase.

3. The buyer must then become a seller of the obtained amount, adding to the market supply. However, this transition from buyer to seller must be not realized in the Walrasian *tâtonnement*, because all the contracts obtained before equilibrium are cancelled.

Application of a genetic algorithm to the economic system

In the Holland system, evolution will be achieved by the following mechanisms.

1. the learning process to find a rule;
2. the credit assignment on rules;
3. rule discovery.

These mechanisms have been carefully incorporated into the classifier system of Holland (1992, ch. 10; 1995, ch. 2) to guarantee genetic evolution. In particular, the learning process has an interactive mechanism involving the defector (on input), effector (on output), and environment. The key issues for motivating an evolutionary system are the stage setting and adaptation of the rule to the environment, which are taken into consideration by the bucket brigade algorithm. These considerations are also set out in the classifier system. Decisions (or intentions) in an economic system might be regarded as "stage-setting moves" (Holland 1992: 177).

In such a feedback system, agents cannot necessarily identify equilibrium prices immediately. The environment where the agents operate will be changed before equilibrium has been detected; practically, then, equilibrium prices might be replaced by quasi-mean values in a dynamic process of production and trading. In parallel with this replacement, the bidding process for production costs might also be changed. Thus, a feedback system will change the world of equilibrium into a true evolutionary economic process.[7]

In a genetic algorithm, a gene can *evolve* by bidding or asking its own rule at the cost of posting, if its asking price should match a receiver's (consumer's) offer.[8] In this trade, a kind of double auction is at work.[9] However, there is no auctioneer or neutral mediator in the bidding field. Therefore, the participants refer only to expected mean advantages or the quasi-mean *fitness* of a concerned ensemble of genes. Suppliers might use such a mean value as the basis for asking their rules.

In the following, we discuss the von Neumann economic system in light of Holland (1992, 1995). Holland ingeniously envisaged that the von Neumann economic system could be reformulated in the framework of a genetic algorithm, although von Neumann's original bid/ask mechanism differs from new bid/ask systems such as a bucket brigade algorithm. Here, an emphasis is placed on the *adaptive* capability of a process on the basis of its environment. This chapter will focus on the internal selection mechanism of the original von Neumann balanced economic system, in light of a genetic algorithm. Finally, this argument may also provide a new insight into the Sraffa standard commodity, which is also found in the original von Neumann model.

The von Neumann balanced growth model

General production process

Von Neumann (1937) considered an economic system as a non-decaying system at any point of time t. The economic system can then be iterated.

At the initial set for an economic system, there are given regenerative factors such as water or solar power. In the original von Neumann system, primitive factors such as labor also are regarded as unlimited. Other factors of production must be mutually produced by means of a set of appropriate operators to transform them. Taking into account the differences in the primary factors of production $\kappa_i(t)$,[10] that is, land and labor, the intermediate product $\iota_i(t)$, and the final product $\zeta_i(t)$, the productive process can be described as follows:[11]

The original von Neumann system includes the storage and disposal of goods. If there are no disposal costs without loss of generality, the inequality formulation can be transformed into an equality formulation. This transformation may be attained according to the rules of free goods and profitability.[12]

The von Neumann theorem in the original model

In describing the process of production, we distinguish inputs from outputs. We usually assume $m \neq n$. Therefore, we define as follows:

Process $i = 1, \ldots, m$
Good $j = 1, \ldots, n$.

It then generally follows the process of production:

$$a_i = (a_{i1}, \ldots, a_{in}) \to b_i = (b_{i1}, \ldots, b_{in})(i = 1, \ldots, m).$$

Let the number of productive processes i be m. a_{ij} represents the requirement of good j per unit of activity x_i to produce good j. b_{ij} is the output produced by a unit of activity x_i.

$$a_i x_i = a_{i1} x_i + \ldots + a_{in} x_i.$$

The configuration of the whole system's activities $\{x\}$ is

$$x = (x_1, \ldots, x_m).$$

Table 10.1 The vertically integrated process and horizontally cross-operated process

Time	The primary factor	The intermediate product	The final product
The initial period	$\kappa_1(0)\ \kappa_2(0)$	–	–
The first period	$\kappa_1(1)\ \kappa_2(1)$	$\iota_1(1)$	$\zeta_1(1)$
The second period	$\kappa_1(2)\ \kappa_2(2)$	$\iota_1(2)$	$\zeta_1(2)$

The system of production is as follows:

$$(a,b) = \sum_{i=1}^{m} x_i(a_i, b_i) = (xA, xB),$$

where A is the matrix of m by n, called "input matrix"; B is also m by n, called "output matrix." For each output j, we can define the expansion rate of technology in terms of activity vector x:

$$\alpha_j(x) = \frac{xb^j}{xa^j}, \alpha(x) = \min_j \alpha_j(x).$$

On the other hand, we can define the expansion rate of the economy in terms of price vector y as a column vector.

$$y = (y_1, \ldots, y_n)',$$

$$\beta_i(y) = \frac{b_i y}{a_i y}, \beta(y) = \max_i \beta_i(y).$$

Von Neumann's theorem

1. $\alpha xA \leq xB$
2. $\alpha x a^j < xb^j \rightarrow y_j = 0$
3. $\beta Ay \geq By$
4. $\beta a_i y > b_i \rightarrow x_i = 0$

Condition 1 defines the feasibility of the activities. Condition 4 defines cost–price feasibility. Condition 2 is called "the rule of free goods," while condition 4 is called "the rule of profitability." Von Neumann proved that there were guaranteed nonnegative vectors $x \geq 0$, $y \geq 0$ and the positive values α, β, fulfilling conditions 1–4. Optimally, conditions 1 and 3 can be held in equality.

From Holland's perspective, the feasible activities are reformulated in discrete time:

$$Bx_{t-1} \geq Ax_t.$$

Given the initial supply of goods, under the production system,

$$(a,b) = \sum_{i=1}^{m} x_i(a_i, b_i) = (xA, xB),$$

An example of von Neumann technology can be depicted as the following production sequence $\{x_t\}$.

$$x_0, x_1, \ldots, x_{t-1}, x_t, \ldots.$$

The original interpretation

Following von Neumann's (1937) original article, we set the expansion rates of technology and economy as follows:

$$\alpha(x) = \min_j \alpha_j(x) = 1+g, \beta(x) = \min_i \beta_i(x) = 1+r.$$

We call g the uniform rate of growth, and r the uniform rate of interest. The von Neumann theorem can then be written as:[13]

1. $(1+g)xA \leq xB$
2. $(1+g)xa^j < xb^j \rightarrow y_j = 0$
3. $(1+r)Ay \geq By$
4. $(1+r)a_iy > b_i \rightarrow x_i = 0$

It then follows

1. There could be uniquely established nonnegative solutions x, y.
2. The golden rule of growth (the maximum rate of growth) is attained at $r = g$.

The payoff function

Von Neumann imposed the normalization or probability conditions on vectors x and y:

$$x_1 + \ldots + x_m = 1, y_1 + \ldots + y_n = 1.$$

Following Thompson (1956: 281) and Nikaido (1960: 238–45), we define the payoff matrix of the von Neumann game as follows:

$$\Pi(\rho) = B = \rho A.$$

Here ρ is a parameter satisfying $r = g$.[14] The payoff function of the game is

$$\upsilon(\rho) = x\Pi(\rho)y.$$

It immediately follows that

$$\min_i \sum_{j=1}^{n} \pi_{ij}(\rho)y_j \leq \upsilon(\rho), \upsilon(\rho) \leq \max_j \sum_{i=1}^{m} \pi_{ij}(\rho)x_i$$

Thus, the player employing the activities is the maximizing player, while the player setting the prices is the minimizing player.[15]

The optimization of the payoff function is achieved by the two-player game between the price and activity players. The price vector y can then be interpreted with a mixed strategy of the price player, and the activity vector x can be interpreted with a mixed strategy of the activity player. This kind of game proof suppresses the internal process of selecting a profitable process.

Adaptive plans in the von Neumann economy

We define the admissible set of activities X in the von Neumann model of production as follows.

1. $x_t \in X$
2. $x_t A = x_{t+1} B$
3. $x_0 B = X(0)$ [initial supplies]

An activity mix is the so-called mixed strategy satisfying the above admissible set X. We denote the time series of feasible programs by X_θ, and the time series of chosen programs by C_θ:

Feasible programs: $X_\theta = \{x_{\theta,t}(t = 0,1,\ldots)\}$

Chosen programs: $C_\theta = \{c_{\theta,t}(t = 0,1,\ldots)\}$.

The feasible programs are technologically bounded from the upper limit. So the maximal welfare level will be guaranteed.

The society that chose $c_{\theta,t}$ can uniquely specify the welfare level $u(c)$. For convenience, the level may be regarded as the expected net output or profit. In this case, we utilize the von Neumann payoff function as the welfare level. Thus, the welfare level that the program θ accumulates during the period $(0, T)$ is

$$U_\theta(T) = \sum_{t=0}^{T} u(c_{\theta,t}).$$

Program θ is preferred to any other program θ' if

$$U_\theta(T) > U_{\theta'}(T).$$

The optimal program is θ, satisfying the condition

$$\underset{c_\theta \in C}{\mathrm{glb}} \underset{T \to \infty}{\liminf} [U_{\theta^*}(T) - U_\theta(T)] \geq 0.$$

An adaptive plan τ is such that a production program C_θ is chosen on the basis of information received from the economy (E, the environment). Our problem is to choose a certain adaptive plan approaching an optimal program in a broader domain of the environment.

Our illustration above is Holland's original interpretation. Referring to Holland (1992: 39), we can summarize the set of variables required to define our problem:

X, the set of admissible activity vectors x;
Ω, transformations of X into itself, so as to bring about a beneficial process by applying an appropriate operator: $\omega_i \in \Omega$;
$\mathcal{J}$, plans for selecting a program $\langle c_t \rangle \in C$, where c_t is an activity vector in X, on the basis of observed utilities $\{\mu_E(c_{t'}), t'<t\}$, that is, the payoff-only plans;
$\mathcal{E}$, an indexing set of possible utility functions $\{\mu_E \colon X \to \Re\}$. Here, the von Neumann payoff function μ_E may be used;
χ, a requirement for adaptation: the limiting rate of accrual of an adaptive plan τ becomes the rate of the best possible program $C_{\beta^*}(E)$ in each $E \in \mathcal{E}$, for all utility functions (the net expected output or profit):

$$\lim_{T \to \infty} \frac{U_\tau(T)}{U_{\beta^*(E)}(T)} = 1.$$

Thus, the von Neumann production system underlies a framework that is similar to the framework of genetic adaptation ($\mathcal{J}, \mathcal{E}, \chi$) on which the adaptive plans as a whole evolve.

A genetic adaptive plan[16]

"The fantastic variety of possible genotypes, the effects of epitasis, changing environments, and the difficulty of retaining adaptations while maintaining variability, all constitute difficulties which genetic processes must surmount" (Holland 1992: 35).

Framework for a genetic adaptive plan

According to Holland (1992: ch. 2), the world of evolving genes consists of two base building blocks:

$\mathcal{G}$: populations of chromosomes, that is, genotypes and species (in economics, production process or activities X); each $g \in G = \{G_1, \ldots, G_n\}$. Under plan 1, let the set of genotypes be G_1. Here the probability assigned to g is the fraction of the total population consisting of that genotype.[17]
Ω: genetic operations, that is, mutation and crossover (in economics, market selection for a beneficial process); each genetic operator $\omega_i \in \Omega$ is accompanied by a fixed probability $p_i > 0$ (in economics, each intensity or price of activity).

The evolutionary mechanism then works. In this setting, we can define the framework ($\mathcal{J}, \mathcal{E}, \chi$), whose elements are as follows:

$\mathcal{J}$: the reproductive plans τ (in economics, the productive activities) as applied by the genetic operator;
$\mathcal{E}$: $\{\mu_E \colon G \to \Re\}$, the set of possible functions, usually as a function of combinations of co-adapted sets; and

χ: comparison of plans according to average fitness of the population produced.

In this framework, the genetic adaptive plan develops in terms of an ever-changing population of chromosomes, which on interacting with the environment, provides a concurrent sequence of phenotype populations (Holland 1992: 33). Holland (1992: 11) interpreted "niche" in a broader sense and did not limit it to the environmental features particularly exploited by a given species. "Environmental niche" thus is defined as a set of features of the environment, which can be exploited by an appropriate organization of the phenotype. We denote the environmental niche by E. Hence, the von Neumann system of production has a framework common to the genetic adaptive plan.

Fitness and the selection mechanism

The fitness of an allele critically depends on the influence of other alleles (epistasis). The fitness of each allele may be based on E. We also suppose that E belongs to the domain $\mathcal{E}$. Let an allele be σ_i. The fitness of the allele is denoted as $\mu_E(\sigma_i)$. The fitness of the set of the alleles $\{\sigma_1, \ldots, \sigma_n\}$ is denoted by

$$\sum_{i=1}^{m} E(\sigma_i).$$

The ranking of genetic adaptive plans

The ranking of genetic adaptive plans is derived by comparing the fitness of the plans. Let the set of the possible plans be $\mathcal{J}: \tau \in \mathcal{J}$. We rank the plans τ according to robustness over $E \in \mathcal{E}$.

We introduce the idea of *evolutionary game*. An adaptive plan τ is chosen in terms of the average fitness of the populations it produces. A plan will be chosen if its fitness is greater than the average fitness. The extinction of plan τ will occur when the population produced by τ becomes negligible, relative to the population produced by τ'. The average fitness in E of a finite population of genotypes $G_\tau(t)$ produced by τ is given by

$$\bar{\mu}_E(\tau,t) = \frac{\sum_{g \in G_\tau(t)} \mu_E(A)}{M(\tau,t)}.$$

Here, $M(\tau, t)$ is the number of individuals in $G_\tau(t)$.

$$\operatorname*{glb}_{E \in \mathcal{E}} \operatorname*{glb}_{t} \operatorname*{glb}_{\tau' \in \mathcal{J}} \frac{\bar{\mu}_E(\tau,t)}{\bar{\mu}_E(\tau',t)}.$$

Here, glb is the greatest lower bound. This value indicates the possibility of extinction for plan τ relative to the plan τ'. The criterion ranks plans according to

The classifier system as an internal selection mechanism

Holland's design of a *classifier* as a genetic algorithm run by a computer is a great academic contribution. Holland also provided economists with good insight on the von Neumann economic system by applying the same idea to it. We briefly illustrate the *classifier* system according to Holland (1992: ch. 10). The system is capable of rewriting itself using a genetic algorithm.

All messages in the classifier system are bit-strings $(0,1)^k$ of the same length k, similar to how the register size is set for a computer. For simplicity, all interaction between rules is mediated by messages. Usually, the rule is divided into two parts: conditions and actions. The condition clause is described by appropriating the symbol #. # implies "don't care," that is, it permits either 0 or 1. The action part of the rule indicates a particular behavior to the classifier.

In the classifier, the set of all conditions is represented by the set $\{1, 0, \#\}^k$. In details, for instance, the set may be a particular form:

$$\{1,0,\#\}^k = \overbrace{\{\#,\#,0,1,0,\ldots,\#\}}^{k}.$$

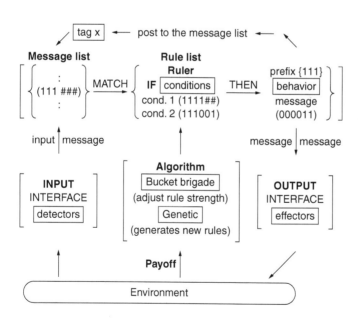

Figure 10.1 Classifier system.

Note
This figure originally appeared in Aruka (2004: 71) in Japanese.

The rule is constituted by the conditions part and a single action part. If the conditions part were fulfilled at time t, the action part would post the message to the message list incorporated at time $t+1$. The rules are applied to an address that can be used by other rules when useful. If a rule ψ is given by (111# ... #), the particular prefix "111" is reserved for rule ψ alone. This prefix serves as a *tag* to make any message associated with the prefix direct to rule ψ. We show an example of such a rule selection.[18]

An example of rule selection[19]

> Let the following message be put into the detector
>
> *long* and *thin*: either true or false
> *hairy*: true
> *big*: either true or false
>
> In the message list, thus, (#1#1) will be entered. If the predator rule is (0001), the classifier will then be:
>
> IF (#1#1), THEN (0001).
>
> Hence, the output must be "prey on the object." However, it is difficult to identify "cat" with "worm." If a bird should be the agent to use the classifier, the classifier could not be regarded as particularly reliable.

The bucket brigade algorithm

We define the strength of a rule ψ by $s(\psi)$. The strength $s(\psi)$ represents the average past usefulness. The larger the strength of the rule, the higher the survival probability is in the competition. The rule participates in a competition to post its message any time its conditions are satisfied. The actual competition is based on a bidding process. Each satisfied rule makes a bid on the basis of its strength and specificity. Following Holland (1992: 176), for simplicity, we take the bid for a rule r of strength $s(\psi)$ in the form:

$$Bid(\psi) = c \cdot s(\psi) \cdot \log_2[specificity(\psi)].$$

Here c is a constant set $c<1$. "A rule that both has been useful to the system in the past (high strength) and uses more information about the current situation (high specificity) thus makes a higher bid" (Holland 1992: 176).

Rules making higher bids are favored in the competition. The adaptation (coordination) of the strength of the rule is based on the bucket brigade algorithm. This algorithm consists of two main parts.

1. the credit assignment
2. the rule discovery.

Credit assignment

The system in which the rules are competing is made up of suppliers and consumers:

[Supplier] The group of rules satisfying the conditions of an outgoing message.
[Consumer] The group of rules satisfying the conditions of an incoming message.

A $Bid(\psi)$ by the consumer thus implies payment for the "right" to post a message. The amount of $Bid(\psi)$ is considered the payment to the supplier. The winning rule is the rule that received payment $Bid(\psi)$. The supplier as the winning rule reinforces its own strength, that is, *capital*. On the other hand, the receiver of the winning rule decreases its strength by $s(\psi) - Bid(\psi)$. The way to reimburse this payment is to find a consumer who pays for the next winning rule. The rule is then activated at the time when the system receives the payoff from the environment. The payoffs are allocated among the rules activated at the moment when the payoffs are generated. The strengths of these rules are thus increased. A numerical example of the exchanges in the above process is shown in Figure 10.2.

Stage setting

During the continuation of activation in similar situations, the system must determine a distribution of strength reinforcement on the rules for *stage setting*, by resorting to the bucket brigade algorithm. The bucket brigade algorithm works because rules become strong only when they belong to sequences leading to payoff (Holland 1992: 177).

In Figure 10.2, C' is first a consumer (of C) and then a supplier (of C''). The classifier C' receives a message from C and pays $Bid=6$ to C in exchange for the message. The strength of C' at time t decreases by 6 (to 114 from 120), while C at t increases its strength by 6 (to 106 from 100). C'' at time $t+1$ receives a message from C', and then pays $Bid=12$ to C'. The strength of C'' decreases by 12 (to 148 from 160), while C' increases its strength by the payment from C''

Bucket brigade algorithm

Time of activation	Classifier(C)				Strength		
		tag x			C	C'	C''
[t−1] C	cond. 1	cond. 2	≡	message	100	120	160
					+6	−6	
[t] C'	tag x ≡|		tag y ||| message	106	114	160
						+12	−12
[t+1] C'' ||||			message	106	126	148

Figure 10.2 Bucket brigade algorithm.

(to 126 from 114). This process can generate "a backward rewarded process" in which a reimbursed supplier benefits the suppliers of the supplier, finally reducing to the initial suppliers, that is, the original rules for *stage setting*.

Remarks on bucket brigade bidding

At the beginning of this chapter, we referred to the shift of trading method from the batch auction to the double auction. We remarked on the difference between the game theory of auction and the bucket brigade algorithm exposited above. In the game theory of auction, however, the trade object is usually limited to a smaller number of targets. If there should be a greater number of trade targets, an institutionally grand design like the stock exchange could be required for a continuation of the auction. On the other hand, the bucket brigade algorithm is irrelevant to the explicitly institutional designs, although its environment is implicitly connected with various institutional settings. It is crucial that the positive feedback mechanism be implemented in the algorithm. The supplier, by simulating (asking) profitability in exchange with the consumer (bidder), can reinforce the adaptive plan. In these evolving simulations, the reference point will be an ensemble mean of the adaptive plans.

Significance of standard commodity discovered in the context of genetic algorithm

The classical meaning of prices

The publication of Sraffa (1960) has spawned many arguments on various topics. Nevertheless, the significance of the standard commodity has not necessarily been elucidated in a fully satisfactory manner.[20] One of major reasons for the ambiguity associated with the standard commodity may arise from the impossibility of it occurring in a general case such as a joint-production system, such as the von Neumann economic system. This view can easily lead to the devaluation of the contribution of Sraffa's standard commodity. However, the devaluation of the standard commodity was apparently driven in view of the idea of equilibrium, as there does not exist a proper equilibrium in a more general case. Sraffa's original concern, however, was irrelevant to the price equilibrium. The classical principle of political economy refers to the natural price, or prices other than the equilibrium prices, as the center of gravity in the economic system. It is apparent that the classical meaning of prices is not the same as that of prices in general equilibrium.

Property of the original von Neumann solution based on the constancy of the environment

The solution of the von Neumann economic system contains the optimal prices and quantities as its components. As described in a preceding section, the solution is derived by referring to the payoff function (the value of the game). Von Neumann employed the two-person strategy game of the growth-maximizing player and cost-minimizing player to prove the solution and to establish equilibrium. However, it is difficult to interpret his original proof with an actual counterpart because, as previously pointed out, both players are aggregate players, a kind of hypothetical agent. In this construction, equilibrium in terms of a quasi-stationary state only attains optimality over time. The balanced growth or sustainability thus simply requires constancy in its environment. Once the equilibrium has been attained, the state should be constant forever. There then is *missing* the internal selection mechanism: the exchange of information with the environment in the original von Neumann system. As the environment changes before the end of the time horizon on a productive plan, equilibrium cannot help but be changed or revised. The constancy of the environment must be relaxed, which will be accompanied by *the feedback system* as in the bucket brigade algorithm.

Introduction of a genetic algorithm into the original Sraffa system

The same limitation in the von Neumann system seems to be found in the Sraffa system. However, Sraffa's original intention was to measure the fluctuating price movements in terms of the invariant measure of value of the standard commodity.[21] Any idea of scale of production was not presupposed by Sraffa's essential image of the "production of commodities by means of commodities." Hence, his system did not need constancy of environment. The standard commodity in the original sense is rather to be interpreted as a picture taken at one point of production. In other words, the standard commodity simply gives a momentary profile (characteristics) of the system. As time goes by, the standard commodity must be changed. That is to say, the continuously updated standard commodity must be indispensable.[22] If we extend our vision to the future evolution of the economic system, there must not only be the sole invariant standard commodity; it must evolve.

The standard commodity represents a reference point for the sustainability of the system. The process of selection among productive plans requires an anchoring point by which reference the process should be evaluated.[23] Hence, we must look for a basis for calculating the mean value of the profitability of the economic system. However, it is natural that the actual systems do not always provide a square matrix and unique maximal vector. Therefore, some approximation is needed[24] to find a *surrogate* system nearly equivalent to the actual system.

Derivation of the standard commodity

As stated above, the linearity of the production process is not a requirement to derive the standard commodity. However, the assumption of linearity is convenient for proving the standard commodity, as the special commodity is the same idea as the nonnegative eigenvector of the input matrix in the linear form of the production system. In the following, we assume the linearity of the production system similarly to the von Neumann production system. However, labor l, as the sole primary factor of production, may be explicitly treated as a limitational factor in the Sraffa production system, which can take into account the distributive effects on the price system. In the following, we denote such an extended production system by $[A, B, l]$.

We have already given an exact description of the existence proof of the standard commodity in Aruka (1991, 2011) and elsewhere. Here, we only show the significance of the standard commodity in the simplest production system. The preparation for this proof is given as follows.

Suppose a linear production system without joint production, where each process produces a single product. Labor is the sole primary factor of production and is indispensable in operating each process. A is an $n \times n$ square matrix of input coefficients a_{ij}; a^0, a labor input vector; p, a price vector; and r, the rate of profit. I is a unit matrix, which has all 0 elements except for 1 on the diagonal. The simplest price system will then be an in-homogeneous equation system:

$$[I-(1+r)A]p = a^0. \tag{10.1}$$

Here, the price of labor – the wage rate – is fixed at unity, and prices of produced goods are therefore expressed in terms of labor. As argued by many authors, we could obtain, as a solution, a nonnegative vector by virtue of the following assumptions:

i   An input matrix A is *productive*: $q[I-A] \geq 0$ for any $q \geq 0$.
ii An input matrix A as a whole is nonnegative and *irreducible*, and its eigenvalue is smaller than $1/(1+r)$.

Either guarantees a non-negative solution:

$$p(r) = [I-(1+r)A]^{-1} a^0. \tag{10.2}$$

In particular, (ii) confirms a unique nonnegative solution.

We can then prove the transformation of the Sraffa price system in view of the commutable matrices, that is, $[I-(1+r)A]^{-1}A$ and A are commutable:

$$[I-(1+r)A]^{-1} A \cdot A = A \cdot [I-(1+r)A]^{-1} A \text{ for } r \leq R. \tag{10.3}$$

Sraffa theorem (Aruka 1990, 2011: ch. 2)[25]

i   Suppose $sa^0 \neq 0$ for $s \neq 0$, any left-hand eigenvector of matrix A (or $a^0 \neq (1+R)Aa^0$). If and only if $a^0, Aa^0, A^2a^0, \ldots, A^{n-1}a^0$ are linearly independent, does there then exist a p such that

$$Ap = \frac{m}{1+m(1+r)} p \text{ for some non-zero number } m.$$

There also then exists a left-hand side eigenvector s such that

$$sA = s\frac{m}{1+m(1+r)}p \text{ for some non-zero number } m.$$

Here, s is the standard commodity.

ii Normal modes of the Sraffa price system are equivalent to the necessary and sufficient condition (i) of this theorem.

The balancing proportion

Sraffa originally demonstrated "the balancing proportion" for the prices against the changes of a distributive variable. In the present framework of the production system, the balancing proportion may be represented in the following expression:

Let m be the ratio satisfying the condition

$$m = \frac{a_i p}{a_i^0} = \frac{a_i A p}{a_i a^0} = \frac{a_i A^2 p}{a_i A a^0} = \ldots \text{ for } r \in (0, R]. \tag{10.4}$$

The ratio m is just "the balancing proportion" for the prices against the changes of the rate of profit. The activity vector s preserving this critical proportion must satisfy the following condition:

$$m = \frac{sA^n p}{a_i A^{n-1} a^0} \text{ for } r \in (0, R]. \tag{10.5}$$

It is easy to ascertain that there exists a unique nonnegative eigenvector to support "the balancing proportion m" (Aruka 1991, 2011).

The standard commodity in the Sraffa joint production system

It is easy to insert the von Neumann system into the Sraffa production system as a special case. According to Gale (1956: 286), this kind of model is obtained by adding the next two conditions to the von Neumann model:

1. The number of basic production processes is the same number of the basic goods.
2. The number of outputs is only one good for each process.

On the other hand, we also define the Sraffa joint-production system $[A, B, a^0]$. Here, input and output matrices are of *square* forms. The price system of the joint-production system will be:

$$Bp = (1+r)Ap + wa^0.$$

The solution will be given in the form, if $[B-(1+r)A]^{-1}$ exists:

$$p=[B-(1+r)A]^{-1}a^0.$$

Here, $w=1$. Moreover, we introduce the assumption that $[B-A]$ can be *invertible*. The solution could then be transformed into

$$p=[I-r[B-A]^{-1}A]^{-1}[B-A]^{-1}a^0.$$

The latter form of the solution reflects the idea of a vertically integrated system by which a joint-production system can be reduced into a virtual single production system. We call the latter form the price system of a vertically integrated system:[26]

$$[[B-A]^{-1}A, I, [B-A]^{-1}a^0].$$

In this bracket, $[B-A]^{-1}A$ may be regarded as input, I as output, and $[B-A]^{-1}a^0$ as labor l in terms of an integrated system.[27] For convenience, we denote as follows:

$$Z=[B-A]^{-1}A; \ l=[B-A]^{-1}a^0$$

It is easy to find the nonnegative eigenvector $h \geq 0$ if $Z=[B-A]^{-1}A \ 0$:

$$hZ = h\frac{\mu}{1+\mu r} \quad \text{for some non-zero number } \mu. \tag{10.6}$$

Here, μ is the balancing proportion of the joint production system in terms of a virtual single production system, that is, a renormalization of m.

$$\mu = \frac{hZ^n p}{z_i Z^{n-1} l} \tag{10.7}$$

The nonnegative eigenvector $h \geq 0$ may then be regarded as the standard commodity equivalent to the modified joint production system. Thus, we have applied the same reasoning to the vertically integrated system to deduce the standard commodity equivalent corresponding to the joint production case. In this case, we have restricted the domain of the von Neumann system of $[A, B]$ to a square system by adding fictitious commodities,[28] and in addition implemented a limitational primary factor l into the modified system.

Significance of the standard commodity

Finally, we compare the results of the Sraffa theorem with the payoff function of the original von Neumann system. It holds from the Sraffa theorem for the eigenvectors s and p that

$$sAp = \frac{m}{1+m(1+r)} sp \text{ for some non-zero number } m. \tag{10.8}$$

On the other hand, we assume $B=I$ in the original von Neumann system. We then apply the eigenvectors s and p to the payoff function of the von Neumann system:

$$x(I-\rho A)y = 0 \Rightarrow sAp = \frac{1}{\rho} sp \tag{10.9}$$

If we interpreted $m/(1+m(1+r))$ with $1/\rho$, expressions (10.8) and (10.9) could be regarded as equivalent. Thus, it has been verified that the payoff function of the appropriately restricted von Neumann system by the condition $B=I$ could be represented in terms of Sraffa's standard commodity by employing the balancing proportion m.

A standard commodity in an extended system

The invertibility of $[B-A]$ was indispensable to setting up the Sraffa joint-production system. In fact, Sraffa (1960) skillfully implemented a new set of fictitious processes and commodities to complement the system to make the matrix $[B-A]$ *square*. This is a necessary condition for the invertibility of $[B-A]$. A fictitious process could realize a potential set of commodities.[29] This realization may induce the preparation of the new environment for either a newly emerged commodity or a new efficient process.

Suppose the actual production system to be a general joint-production system. The system does not necessarily confirm its solution in general. The nonexistence of a solution (equilibrium prices) does not necessarily imply the impossibility of trading/production. Even without knowing the equilibrium prices, producers can trade with other producers under the double auction process underlying the changing environment, as mentioned in the first section of this chapter.

A standard commodity as the weight to measure the profitability of the fictitious processes/commodities in an extended system

Each producer is assumed to have the right to *post* a new fictitious process or commodity. Here, we imagine the market as a field such as *the bucket brigade algorithm* in which agents can post their rules.

For example, if the number of commodities is greater than the number of processes in the existing production system, the system is under-determinant. If the under-determinant production system successfully selected some of the *posted* fictitious processes to implement into itself, a standard commodity at the point of time could be then assured. In other words, a standard commodity can be fabricated in a proposed system. However, a chosen standard commodity may vary according to the method of selection of a set of new fictitious ones. In order to generate a standard commodity in an extended system, there may exist a kind of combinatorial number corresponding to the difference between the number of commodities n and the number of processes m. Hence, the standard commodity of an extended system is not always unique.

A derived standard commodity in the above procedure will be a useful measure for producers who posted their fictitious processes to decide whether those processes are more profitable.[30] That is to say, the payoff function of this virtual system will be evaluated by employing a derived standard commodity s as its weight. In this sense, a standard commodity is regarded as the weight to measure the profitability of the fictitious processes and commodities in a virtually implemented system. The implication of the standard commodity given here must coincide with what Sraffa originally defined as the invariant measure of value.

The measure, even if hypothetical, could work as a reference point for a new system. This kind of measure could be regarded as the quasi-mean average of the concerned ensemble generated by the base production set. In this context, the mean average can be calculated by employing a standard commodity generated by the fictitious processes and commodities. Thus, we have given new insight into the Sraffa standard commodity in an extended system.

Updating a standard commodity

Competition among the multiple standard commodities will orientate the future direction of the production system, which must provide feedback to its environment.

---

1. In order to guarantee the solution, some fictitious processes of commodities should be added to the original system. However, the solution depends on the method of taking a certain fictitious set. It may be multiple.
2. The profitability of the additional processes and commodities can be judged by the use of the standard commodity s expected as a result of their addition.
3. A standard commodity will give a virtual expected mean of the average profitability of the system.
4. Another standard commodity will give another virtual expected mean.
5. The competing standard commodities will prepare for a new environment in which a new standard commodity can be updated.

Finally, we provide an intuitive scheme of our procedure given above. We can still use many detailed empirical analyses to compute the actual different standard commodities among the actual national economies. These attempts will allow the shedding of new light on the application of our new principle to some empirical studies.[31]

$t = 0 \quad (x_0 A, x_1 B) \xrightarrow{\text{posting a new process}} s_1^* \in \{s_1^1, s_1^2, \ldots\}$

$t = 1 \quad (x_1' A', x_2' B') \xrightarrow{\text{posting a new process}} s_2^* \in \{s_2^1, s_2^2, \ldots\}$

$t = 2 \quad (x_2'' A'', x_3'' B'') \xrightarrow{\text{posting a new process}} s_3^* \in \{s_3^1, s_3^2, \ldots\}$

$\vdots$

$(A, B) \xrightarrow[s_1^*]{\text{judging profitability}} (A', B') \xrightarrow[s_2^*]{\text{judging profitability}} (A'', B'')$

Time series generated

$\overbrace{x_0, x_1}^{s} \xrightarrow[s_1]{\text{updating}} x_1'$

Figure 10.3 Updating a standard commodity.

Notes

1 Businesses obtained the ability to develop complex plans. An example was the prevalence of derivative option operation in the futures market. See Arthur (2009: 151–6).
2 John Holland is an eminent scientist who successfully connected evolution with adaptation by defining a "complex adaptive system" (CAS). Holland is considered the father of a genetic algorithm. Similarly, Brian Arthur, who shared a house with Holland at the Santa Fe Institute, formulated a complex adaptive system (see Arthur 1994: Preface).
3 Arthur (2009) used the term "redomaining" rather than "renormalization." His "domain" is interpreted according to the environment of Holland (1992). See Arthur (2009: chs. 4 and 8).
4 Japan was the first nation in the world to construct a complete futures stock market. The Tokyo Stock Exchange (TSE) thus inherited from our historical custom the traditional terms for trading such as *Itayose* and *Zaraba* (Taniguchi *et al.* 2008). Each market method must similarly retain its own historical difference. A further examination of these differences will show that the market method is institutionally sensitive. Theoretically speaking, *Zaraba* in the TSE is a kind of continuous auction. However, this auction method is uniquely bounded by the TSE's own rules and customs. Therefore, the TSE even now employs the term "*Zaraba* auction" instead of "continuous auction" (www.tse.or.jp/english/faq/list/stockprice/p_c.html).
5 The price will be settled within the range of {ask, bid}. In the TSE, the price movement limit is institutionally imposed to promote settlement. Here, the theory of auction often discussed in game theory does not necessarily hold. Rather, the bucket brigade algorithm fits our bid/ask discussion for a productive plan.
6 In this process, the environment undergoes some destruction or creation.
7 The artificial market experiment in the U-Mart system precisely depicts the details of an ongoing trading process, which differs from the classical equilibrium formation. In the U-Mart system, the futures market is always influenced by the spot market. Agents must revise their reactions by adapting to the changes of internal and external environments. Trading in the *Zaraba* market runs without any shape to supply and demand curves.

As for the U-mart system, see Shiozawa *et al.* (2008). The U-Mart Project began in 1998 as V-Mart (Virtual Mart). Now, it is the Unreal Market as an Artificial Research Test-bed. The development of the U-Mart system over these ten years was mainly engineer driven (www.u-mart.org/html/index.html). The U-Mart system is now internationally recognized as a good platform for AI markets.

8 In the futures market, agents, whether asking or bidding (selling or buying), must pay their "margin money" to the stock exchange. Therefore, trading on margin is like paying a "posting cost."
9 In the U-Mart system, trading agents are of a hybrid type. One is a "human agent," while the automatic trading agents are called "machine agents." The U-Mart can be compatible with the machine agents whose moves are designed by a genetic algorithm. We have already observed that such a machine agent could be a powerful agent in the market.
10 Here land is denoted by $\kappa_1(t)$ and labor by $\kappa_2(t)$.
11 If you track the diagonal elements, you can read the vertically integrated process in this scheme of production. While the row elements of the table are the horizontally cross-operated process.
12 See Morishima (1969).
13 In the following, a_i represents a row vector and a^j represents a column vector. a_{ij} then represents an element of matrix A.
14 Morishima (1969: 120) used the fair wage rate as a parameter, because he reformulated the von Neumann model to introduce explicitly a limitational labor factor. The payoff matrix of the model must be revised.
15 The above game was interpreted as a game with the price player as the minimizing player and the activity player as the maximizing player. Here, the minimizing player strives for cost minimization, while the maximizing player strives for growth-rate maximization. The problem is that the two players are aggregate players. The maximizing player, as a single player, manipulates all the activities. Similarly, the minimizing player, as a single player, sets all the prices. These players do not actually exist in the market. Thus, these are only fictitious players existing exclusively for the proof.
16 This section relies heavily on Holland (1992, 1995). The figures and examples employed have been appropriately modified by the author. These are partly useed in Aruka (2004) in Japanese.
17 Here $G(t)$ is considered a reservoir of co-adapted sets.
18 The basic execution cycle of the classifier system consists of an iteration of the following steps (Holland 1992: 175):

  1 Messages from the environment are placed on the message list.
  2 Each condition of each classifier is checked against the message list to see if it is satisfied by (at least one) message.
  3 All classifiers that have both conditions satisfied participate in a competition, and those that win, post their messages to the message list.
  4 All messages directed to effectors are executed (causing actions in the environment).
  5 All messages on the message list from the previous cycle are erased (i.e., messages persist for only a single cycle, unless they are repeatedly posted).

19 This example originally appeared in Aruka (2004: 72) in Japanese.
20 To date, the interpretation by Schefold in Nachwort on the German edition of Sraffa (1960) is referred to. Readers will discover a set of meaningful understandings on the standard commodity. See Schefold (1976b).
21 The original analysis by Sraffa on the price change primarily focused on price changes caused by the change of the distributive relationship between the wage rate and the rate of profit.
22 The bucket brigade algorithm suggests the updating process.
23 This may be employed as the basis to calculate the expected mean value.
24 In a joint production, the introduction of some fictitious process of production aids in proving the existence of a standard commodity. Such a hypothetical operation may be justified to "approximate" the actual system of production.

25 Similar statements of this theorem (i) were originally discussed in Schefold (1976a).
26 We then suppose $[B-A]^{-1}A > 0$. We also set

$$Z = [B-A]^{-1}A;\ l = [B-A]^{-1}a^0.$$

It then holds for an appropriate rate of profit

$$p(r) = 1 + rZ\,l + r^2 Z^2 l + \ldots + r^n Z^n l + \ldots > 0.$$

Or, equivalently,

$$p = [I - rZ]^{-1}l.$$

Replacing Z with A, the latter form is a solution for a single-production price system with the exhaustive distribution principle. In view of a vertically integrated system, the Sraffa joint-production system can be considered a single production system with the exhaustive distribution principle being imposed. See Aruka (2011: ch. 3) for details.

27 In this context, our production of goods is considered the reduced relation of input–output given by a series of reduced inputs tracing back to the primary factor (labor) as a whole.
28 If the number of processes m is greater than the number of commodities n, the additional commodities are to be added by the difference $m-n$. Otherwise, additional processes must be added. The former case is the over-determinant system; the latter, the under-determinant for the solutions.
29 This case corresponds to the over-determinant system for prices.
30 Such producers may be involved in forming a new innovative coalition with their neighbors. Sometimes, this coalition can cause an *environmental niche*.
31 See, for example, Mariolis and Tsoulfidis (2011).

References

Arthur, W.B. (1994) *Increasing Returns and Path Dependence in the Economy*, Ann Arbor, MI: University of Michigan Press.
Arthur, W.B. (2009) *The Nature of Technology*, New York: Free Press.
Aruka, Y. (1991) "Generalized Goodwin Theorems on General Coordinates," *Structural Change and Economic Dynamics*, 2(1): 69–91; reprinted in J.C. Wood (ed.) (1996), *Piero Sraffa: Critical Assessments, IV*, London: Routledge; and also incorporated in Y. Aruka (2011) *Complexities of Production and Interacting Human Behaviour*, Heidelberg: Physica Verlag (Springer).
Aruka, Y. (2004) *Mathematical Method to Evolutionary Economics* (in Japanese), Tokyo: Kyoritsu Shuppan.
Aruka, Y. (2011) *Complexities of Production and Interacting Human Behaviour*, Heidelberg: Physica Verlag (Springer).
Aruka, Y. and Koyama, Y. (2011) "The Matching of Interactive Agents in the Future Stock Market and the U-Mart Experiment," in V. Caspari (ed.), *The Evolution of Economic Theory: Essays in Honour of Bertram Schefold*, London: Routledge, pp. 145–67.
Gale, D. (1956) "The Closed Linear Model of Production," in H.W. Kuhn and A.W. Tucker (eds.), *Linear Inequalities and Related Systems*, Princeton, NJ: Princeton University Press, pp. 285–330.
Holland, J.H. (1992) *Adaptation in Natural and Artificial Systems*, Cambridge, MA: MIT Press.
Holland, J.H. (1995) *Hidden Order: How Adaptation Builds Complexity*, New York: Basic Books.

Mariolis, T. and Tsoulfidis, L. (2011) "Eigenvalue Distribution and the Production Price-profit Rate Relationship in Linear Single-product Systems: Theory and Empirical Evidence," *Evolutionary and Institutional Economic Review*, 8(1): 87–122.

Morishima, M. (1969) *Theory of Economic Growth*, Oxford: Clarendon Press.

Nikaido, H. (1960) *Mathematical Methods in Modern Economics* (in Japanese), Tokyo: Iwanami Shoten.

Schefold, B. (1976a) "Relative Prices as a Function of the Rate of Profit," *Zeitschriftfür Nationalökonomie*, 36(1–2): 21–48.

Schefold, B. (1976b) "Nachwort," in P. Sraffa, *Warenproduktion mittels Waren*, Frankfurt am Main: Suhrkamp Verlag, pp. 129–226.

Shiozawa, Y., Nakajima, Y., Matsui, H., Koyama, Y., Taniguchi, K., and Hashimoto, F. (2008) *Artificial Market Experiments with the U-Mart System*, Tokyo: Springer.

Sraffa, P. (1960) *Production of Commodities by Means of Commodities*, Cambridge: Cambridge University Press.

Taniguchi, K., Ono, I., and Mori, N. (2008) "Where and Why Does the Zaraba Method have Advantages over the Itayose Method? Comparison of the Zaraba Method and the Itayose Method by Using the U-Mart System," *Evolutionary and Institutional Economic Review*, 5(1): 5–20.

Thompson, G.L. (1956) "On the Solution of Game Theoretic Problem," in H.W. Kuhn and A.W. Tucker (eds.), *Linear Inequalities and Related Systems*, Princeton, NJ: Princeton University Press, pp. 274–82.

Von Neumann, J. (1937) "Über ein ökonomisches Gleichungssztem und eine Verallgemeinung des Brouerschen Fixpunktsatzes," *Ergebnisseeines Mathematischen Kolloquiums*, 8: 73–83, Leipniz and Vienna: Franz-Deuticke. (English translation: (1945–46) "A Model of General Economic Equilibrium," *Review of Economic Studies*, 13: 1–9).

Index

acatallactic theories 118
act psychology 79
aggregates 55
Allen, R.L. 122n35
Alter, M. 91
altruism, reciprocal 13, 14
Anderson, J. 23
applied economics 64, 68
approbation 17
à priori reasoning 51, 56n9
Aristotle 76, 79, 92
Armentano, D. 140n9
Arrow, K.J. 40, 45n9
Arthur, W.B. 162, 181n1, 181n2, 181n3
artificial market experiment 181n7
Aruka, Y. 8–9, 162–84
asymmetric information 45n11
atomistic method 102
Austrian School of Economics 3, 7, 8, 108, 146; economics and philosophy 78–80; later development 95, 120; Menger as founder 91; subjectivism 73–90; values 78
average, concept of 7, 52–3, 54
axiomatic approaches 30, 31, 34, 40, 44n3

Bachelier, M.L. 152, 153, 158n15
Bain, A. 55
balanced growth model (von Neumann) 9, 165–9; adaptive plans 168–9; details of theorem 166–8; general production process 165; original interpretation of theorem 167; payoff function 167–8; von Neumann theorem in original model 165–6
Barro, R.J. 104
barter 54, 128; in labour theory of value 12, 13, 14, 18, 22
Batson, H. E. 122n45

behavioural economics 4, 73
behavioural finance theory 145
Being 79–80, 81; as prestructure of knowledge 86; social-science implications 87–8
Being and Time (Heidegger) 81
Benassy, J.P. 104
Bentham, J. 39, 50, 55
Bernoulli, D. 150, 158n10
bidding 162; bucket brigade algorithm 174
Black, R. 49, 54–5
Boehm, S. 105n2
Böhm-Bawerk, E. von 9n2, 79, 108–25, 126, 146; on economic and noneconomic motives 131; habilitation paper (1879) 118; Innsbruck lectures 121n7; intertemporality 112, 115–16, 119; and Menger 108, 109–11, 120; and Mises 113, 116–19, 128, 129; objectivism of 8, 108–25; past-present-future point of view of price objectiveness 117–18; and Schumpeter 114–15, 117; time preference theory 141n25; transformation of objectivism 113–19, 120; and Wieser 113–14, 120
Böhm-Bawerk–Fisher intertemporal discount theory of interest 109
Boyer, R. 144, 145
Brentano, F. 74, 75, 78–9, 80, 89
bubbles, economic 38
bucket brigade algorithm 163, 164, 172–4
business-cycle theory 146, 149, 153, 154

Cannan, E. 16
capital and land, prices of 67
capitalist economy 38, 44
Carr, E.H. 30
Cassel, G. von 162
Castles-in-the-Air theory 156, 157

catallactics (science of exchange) 118, 136
causal theory/cause and effect 49–50, 51, 76
central planning board 41–2
circular flow theory (Schumpeter) 83
Cirillo, R. 70n7
class exploitation concept 2
classifier system, genetic adaptive plan 171–2
coefficients of production 66
cognition 7
cognitive psychology, and subjectivity 151–2
collective economy 8
collective subjective judgment/valuation 5–6
commercial society 15–16
commodities: definition of value of commodity 31; real value 16–21; resources 31; scarcity 31, 32; standard *see* standard commodity (Sraffa); two-agent, many-commodity model/ two-commodity, many-agent model 37
competitive equilibrium 29, 39–40, 111
competitive price theory 37–8
complex adaptive system (CAS) 181n2
Condillac, É.B. de 31, 32, 34
content psychology 79
cooperative game theory 40, 42, 45n8
Cootner, P.H. 153
corn: nutritional value 24; representation of value of labour 11; setting of prices 53
Corn Laws 48
cosmopolitanism 101
cost–benefit analysis 40
Cournot, Antoine Augustin 63
credit assignment, bucket brigade algorithm 173
critical realism 92
Čuhel, F. 131–2, 140n14

Dalrymple, J. 53
Darwin, C. 13, 26n3
Dasein (human being) 80, 85, 88; as agent of thrown projection 81, 82, 83, 84, 86, 88; as Being-in-the world 82; characteristics 81–2
Davenant, C. 53
Davies, D. 27n10
Debreu, G. 40
demand and supply theory 116
De Morgan, A. 48–9
descriptive psychology (Brentano) 78
desires 7, 13, 74; and goods 76; Menger on 75–6; true 76, 77

de Wall, Frans 13, 14, 26n3
Dilthey, W. 79, 80
division of labour 6, 11–12
dominant strategy mechanisms 42, 43
Douglas, P.H. 17

Ebeling, R. 73
economic efficiency 77–8
economic foresight, place of subjectivity in 146–8
economic liberalism 99
economic progress 66
economics: Austrian 78–80; microfoundation of 3, 8, 103–4; pure 63–9; as a science 5, 6, 7; welfare economics, fundamental theorems 29, 30, 38–41
Eden, F.M. 27n10
Edgeworth, F.Y. 45n8, 55
efficiency 69, 77–8; *see also* Pareto efficiency
efficient markets theory 145, 157
Elements of Pure Economics (Walras) 62, 63, 68, 69, 70; *rareté* concept in 64–5
empiricism 3, 49
English Classical School 97; and German Historical School 92, 99–103
enjoyment, laws of 39
Enlightenment 89
Epistemological Problems of Economics (Mises) 130, 131
epistemology/ontology distinction, application to economics 4, 6
equilibrium: classical steps to attain 163–4; competitive 29, 39–40, 111; in history of economic analysis 2, 3, 5; and microeconomic theory 29; objectivity of 148; *see also* general equilibrium theory
equilibrium price 111, 115, 117, 162, 163
essentialism: of Aristotle 79; methodological 76
esteem value 37
evolutionary game 170
evolutionary theory 5, 6
exactness 50, 51, 52
exchange power 111, 115–16, 119
exchange rate 14
exchange-relations 119
exchange value 11, 118, 119; defined 111; and individual value 37; propensity to exchange 13; real measure of 16–21; theory of 34–8; two-agent, many-commodity model/two-commodity, many-agent model 37

Index 187

experimental economics 4
experimental psychology 78
externalities 29, 40

factor substitution 66
fair wage rate 181n14
Fama, E.F. 155
Farr, W. 49
financialization phenomenon 144
Fitzgibbons, A. 26n1
foresight: economic foresight, place of subjectivity in 146–8; effective 149–50; imperfect 149; Morgenstern on 145–52; in ontological hermeneutics 84
free competition system 61, 69
free-rider problem 40–1
free will 7, 49
Frege–Popper criterion 120
French tradition of utility theory of value 59
Friedländer, E. 110, 121n15
From Mises to Shackle (Lachmann) 137

Gale, D. 177
Galiani, F. 31, 32, 38
gambling 150
game theory 29–30, 40, 42
general equilibrium theory 29, 30, 31, 38, 45n9, 45n11, 63, 65, 69, 70n2, 76; founding of 40, 59; as interdependent theory 76; and Morgenstern 146; and Wieser 122n32; *see also* Walras, Léon
genes 164, 169
genetic adaptive plan 169–74: bit-strings 171; bucket brigade algorithm 172–4; classifier system as internal selection mechanism 171–2; fitness and selection mechanism 170–1; framework for 169–70; ranking 170–1; rule selection example 172
genetic algorithm (Holland): application to economic system 164; classical meaning of prices 174–5; introduction of genetic algorithm into original Sraffa system 175; new perspective on economic system derived from 162–4; property of original Von Neumann solution based on constancy of environment 174–5; significance of standard commodity discovered in context of 174–80
German Historical School: and English Classical School 92, 99–103; German Historical School of Jurists and German Historical School of Economics 102

Gibbard, A.F. 42
Gibbard–Satterthwaite theorem 43
gold 116
goods: concept of 109–10; and desires 76; equilibrium-theoretic indifferent classification of 117; exchange power 111, 115–16, 119; imaginary 92, 93–4; Menger on 75, 76; proportionality of values 65; public goods problem 29
Gossen, H.H. 39, 68
Granger, C. 153, 154
Greenspan, A. 159n21
Grossman, H.I. 104
Grundsätze (Menger) 8, 74, 76, 77, 91; aggregation of preference ordering 96; and Böhm-Bawerk 108, 109, 110, 120; concept of economy 95; economic models in 95–6, 104; exchange model 96; imaginary goods 93–4; methodological foundations 92–9; non-market economy 77, 78; Preface 92, 93, 95, 96; "simplest elements" in 92–3, 98–9; "strict types" 98; "types" 93, 97, 99; "typical relationships" 97; *see also* Menger, Carl

Haberler, G. 122n35
Hahn, F.H. 45n9
happiness maximization *see* utilitarianism
Haraya, N. 105n1
Hayek, Friedrich A. 2–3, 4, 41, 42, 126, 139n5, 144, 145, 146, 158n1; and Mises 139n5, 140n8; *Pure Theory of Capital* 103, 106n11
Heidegger, M. 7, 70–81; *Being and Time* 81; on "jumping or leaping" 83–4, 87
Heidegger=Schumpeter theses 85–8, 89; Being as prestructure of knowledge 86; *Dasein* as agent of thrown projection 81, 82, 83, 84, 86, 88; isomorphic duality 86; nature of projection and thrownness 74, 87; rationality and time, relationship between 88
hermeneutical circles 80, 83, 86, 87
hermeneutics 7, 73–90; in Austrian economics 73; background/description 80–1; dialogue on innovation and routine 81–4; dialogue on prestructure of science 84–5; epistemological content 85; hermeneutical economics 73, 74; hermeneutical situation 84; as meta-economic theory/economic philosophy 74; as philosophy of interpretation 73; time horizon in 74, 86; *see also* Being; *Dasein* (human being)

Historical Setting of the Austrian School of Economics (Mises) 141n27
History of Economic Analysis (Schumpeter) 59
history of economic analysis, subjectivism and objectivism in 1–9
Hobbes, T. 19, 44
Holland, J. 9, 166, 168, 169, 171, 181n2, 181n16; genetic algorithm of *see* genetic algorithm (Holland)
Hollander, S. 23, 26n8
Holt, A. 26n9
homo economicus, in standard economics 84
Horwitz, S. 139
Hülsmann, J.G. 138, 139n6, 140n10, 141n26
human nature 13, 50, 56n3
Hume, D. 44, 56n9
Hurwicz, L. 42, 45n10, 45n12
Husserl, E. 74, 78, 79–80
Hutchison, T.W. 76, 151, 158n11

ideal type: true desires as 76; Weberian concept 3, *4*
Ikeda, Y. 8, 91–107
imaginary goods 92, 93–4
impossibility theorem (Arrow) 40
incentive compatibility 29–30, 42, 43
incentives, and mechanism design 41–3
indirect exchange, subjectivist theory of Mises 127, 132–5
individualism: laissez-faire 152; methodological 91, 92, 103
individual rationality and mechanism, microeconomic theory *see* microeconomic theory
individual value: and exchange value 37; structure of theory 31–4
Industrial Fluctuation (Pigou) 147
innovative entrepreneur 83
Inoue T. 7, 48–58
instinct 13
intentionality (Brentano) 74, 78–9
interest 112, 118, 138
interpretation 7; hermeneutics as philosophy of 73
intertemporality 112, 115–16, 119
invisible hand 38
irrational exuberance 157, 159n21
irrationality, subjectivity as 155–6
isomorphic duality 86
Ito, M. 105n1

Jaffé, W. 64, 69, 70n7, 70n15

Japan Society for the Promotions of Science (JSPS) 70n1
Japan Society of the History of Economic Thought 6
Jevons, William Stanley 7, 35, 39, 44n7, 45n8, 65; average, concept of 7, 52–3, 54; background 48; exchange value theory 37; fictitious mean 54; formation of view of science 48–51; intellect, evolutions 48–51; *Principles of Science, The* 53–4; Quételet's influence on 48–58; in Sydney 49; trading body concept 53–4, 55, 56n12; at University College London/School 48, 49; and Walras 70n2
John Law's system 38

Kahneman, D. 157
Kalai–Smorodinsky solution 40
Kant, I. 80, 92
Katzner, D.W. 31
Kauder, E. 76
Kawamata, M. 6–7, 29–47, 105n1
Keynes, J.M. 70, 156, 157; *Treatise on Money* 149
Keynesian economics 104
King, G. 53
Knies, K. 9n2, 99, 112
Knight, F. 8, 148, 150, 151, 152, 158n11, 158n12
Koyama, Y. 163
Kuhn–Tucker conditions of utility maximization problem 33, 44n4, 44n6

labour theory of value: biological foundation 23–5; commercial society 15–16; common stock 11, 12, 13; division of labour 11–12; institutionalist interpretation 15–16, 20; labour as real measure of exchange value 16–21; and marginal utility theory of value 59; of Marxists 1; Menger on 110; pin manufactory example 12, 26n1; productivity increase, reasons for 12; propensity to exchange 13; purchasable labour 19; real and nominal price of labour 21–3; reciprocal altruism 13, 14; of Smith (Adam) 6, 11–27; sympathy 11, 13, 14, 17, 26n3; truck, barter and exchange, general disposition to 12, 13, 14
Lachmann, Ludwig M. 73, 127, 141n23; *From Mises to Shackle* 137
land nationalization, Auguste and Léon Walras on 59, 61, 63, 67–8

Lange, O. 41
Lange–Lerner scheme of market socialism 41–2
Latzer, M. 122n37
Lavoie, D. 73
Law, J. 38
law of indifference 35, 37
Lawson, C. 92
Lectures on Jurisprudence (Smith) 17, 26n7
Leonard, R. 158n2
Lerner, A.P. 41
Lindahl, E. 41, 43
Linnés, C. 13
Liverpool, England 48
loan, legal concept 118
Locke, J. 44, 56n9
Locke, J. 48

Machlup, F. 126
macroeconomics 112; disputes in 3
Mäki, U. 105n7
Malkiel, B.G. 155, 156, 157
Manchester, England 48
marginal productivity theory 66
Marginal Revolution 30, 73, 74, 104
marginal utility theory of value 3, 55, 59, 114; microeconomic theory, history 30, 31, 34, 36, 37, 44n7
market efficiency theory 155
market failures 7, 29, 40
market interest 138
market mechanism 29, 38, 40; *see also* mechanism design
market price 109, 110, 114, 119, 120
market socialism, Lange–Lerner scheme 41–2
Marshall, A. 40, 55, 57n14
Marx, K. 83
Marxists, objectivism of 1
Mas-Colell, A. 29
Maskin, E. 43, 45n10
mathematical science 7, 50–1, 52, 61, 153
mechanism design 29, 30, 41–3
Menger, C. 3, 7, 8, 9n2, 33, 39, 44n7, 73, 91–107, 126, 139n6, 145; and Böhm-Bawerk 108, 112, 120; on direct and indirect manners 110; economic theory 75, 76, 77; as founder of Austrian School 91; *Grundsätze see Grundsätze* (Menger); horse-trading model 110; methodology 91–2; and Mises 105n4, 128, 129, 131; and non-mainstream economics 77; ontology, interpretation of 74–8; second subjectivism of 109–11; subjectivism of 108, 109–11; on technical direction and efficient or economizing direction 76, 77; *Untersuchungen* 93, 97, 105n7; and Walras 70n2; "Wesen" 105n3
Menger, K. 8, 149, 150
meta-economic theory, hermeneutics as 74
metals, precious 116, 118
meteorology 49, 53
methodological essentialism 76
methodological individualism 91, 92, 103
microeconomic theory 6–7, 91, 99, 109; exchange value theory 34–8; general equilibrium theory 29, 30, 31, 38, 40, 45n9, 45n11; history, individual rationality and mechanism in 29–47; incentives and mechanism design 41–3; individual value, structure of theory 31–4; UTILITY and scarcity theory 29, 30–8; welfare economics, fundamental theorems 29, 30, 38–41
Microeconomic Theory (Mas-Colell) 29
microfoundation of economics 3, 8, 103–4
Milford, K. 91, 105n3
Mill, J.S. 39
Misaki, K. 7, 59–72
Mischler, P. 94
Mises, L. von 8, 41; and Böhm-Bawerk 113, 116–19, 128, 129; *Epistemological Problems of Economics* 130, 131; and Hayek 139n5, 140n8; *Historical Setting of the Austrian School of Economics* 141n27; and Menger 105n4, 128, 129, 131; on monetary calculation 127, 130, 131, 134–5; *Nationalökonomie* 132, 133, 139; *Notes and Recollections* 132; as a pure subjectivist 127, 136–9; and Schumpeter 141n20; *Theory of Money and Credit, The* 127, 129, 130, 132; time preference theory 138; and Wieser 129, 139n5; *see also* subjectivism of Mises
money 115, 133; classifications of 117, 118; indirect exchange, subjectivist theory of 127, 128, 132–5; monetary calculation 118, 119, 120, 127, 128, 130, 131, 134–5; origin 128; as price index 128
monotonicity 43
Morgenstern, O. 8, 139n5; and random-walk hypothesis 153–5; speculation theory 156; on subjectivity and foresight 145–52; and von Neumann 153; von Neumann–Morgenstern utility function 40

Morishima, M. 69–70, 181n14
Muldrew, C. 27n10

Nakayama, C. 8, 76, 144–61
Nash solution 40, 43
natural price 6
natural science 7, 51, 80
natural value 8, 114
Negishi, T. 45n8
neoclassical economics 2, 3, 59; on static reality 82–3
Neumann, J. von 8–9, 150, 162, 164, 177; balanced growth model *see* balanced growth model (Von Neumann); and Morgenstern 153; property of original solution based on constancy of environment 174–5; von Neumann–Morgenstern utility function 40
Neurath, O. 140n8
neuroeconomics 104
Newton, I. 51
new welfare economics 40
Nikaido, H. 167
non-convexity problems 29, 40
Notes and Recollections (Mises) 132

objectiveness, static or atemporal 111, 120
objectivism: of Böhm-Bawerk 8, 108–25; in history of economic analysis 1–9; integration with subjectivism 2, 3; *see also* subjectivism
objectivity: of equilibrium 148; terminology 3; and theory of property 7
Okon, H. 8, 126–43
O'Neill, John 141n24
ontology: and hermeneutics 73, 80–1; of Menger 74–8; ontology/epistemology distinction, application to economics 4, 6
optimality concept 39
ordinal utility 40
original interest 138

Pareto efficiency 29, 34, 39, 40
past theory 30
perfect knowledge, assumption of 2–3
period-of-production model 112
perpetualism 101
phenomenology 79
philosophical realism 76
philosophy, Austrian 78–80
Picard, P. 63, 70n13, 70n15
Pigou, A.C. 40, 147, 158n3
plural subjectivities 4–6

points of orientation 147
Polanyi, K. 73, 77, 140n8
political economy 59, 68, 69
Popper, K. 76, 91
potatoes, cultivation 27n10
power of exchange 111, 115–16, 119, 122n37
precious-metal-value principle 116, 118
present theory 30
price: classical meaning 174–5; composite 23; concept *see* price concept, alteration of in last century; equilibrium 111, 115, 117, 162, 163; market 109, 110, 114, 119, 120; market process of formation 111; objective 8, 14; objectivism of Böhm-Bawerk 108, 111; pricing process theory, based on subjectivism (Mises) 135–6; quantitative theory of determination 17; and *rareté* concept 62; real and nominal price of labour 21–3; UTILITY and scarcity theory 36; and value 37; Walras on 63, 66–7
price concept, alteration of in last century 162–4; equilibrium, classical steps to attain 163–4; shift of trading method and environmental niche 163, 174
Principles of Science, The (Jevons) 53–4
probability, 8, 153
products: novelties of 162; prices of 66
profit 148
progressive society 61, 62, 65–8
projection: *Dasein* as thrown projector 81, 82, 83, 84, 86, 88; nature 87
propensity concept 13
property theory 60
Proudhon, Pierre-Joseph 61
psychology 73; act 79; cognitive 151–2; content 79; descriptive 78; experimental 78
public goods problem 29
pure economics: definition 64; object of 68–9; Walras (Léon) on 63–9; *see also Elements of Pure Economics* (Walras)
Pure Theory of Capital (Hayek) 103, 106n11

Quételet, A. 7; on *à priori* reasoning 51, 56n9; influence on Jevons 48–58; "social body" 53, 54, 57n12; "social man" 52, 54; on speculative sciences 51, 56n9; *Treatise on Man* 49, 51–2; as "true founder of exact social science" 51

radical subjectivism 105n4, 138

random-walk hypothesis, and subjectivity 152–8
rareté concept 59–72; definitions 7, 62; at early stage (Léon Walras on) 61–3; in *Eléments* 64–5; objectivity of 59; as ratio 60, 62; and utility 60; *see also* UTILITY and scarcity theory
rational behaviour 3, 4, 6, 34
rationality and time, relationship between 88
Rau, H. 94
reciprocal altruism 13, 14
Rellstab, U. 158n2
Remak, R. 162
renormalization 162, 181n3
rent, surplus value in a progressive society 61
"representative consumer/firm," assumption of 5
revealed preference concept 9n1
Ricardo, D. 62, 70
rigorousness 50
risk, subjectivity in 148–51
Rorty, R. 85
Roscher, W. 94, 109
Roscoe, W. 48
Rousseau, J.-J. 56n9
Royston, P. 26n4

Salerno, J. 139
Samuelson, P.A. 9n1, 162
Satterthwaite, M.A. 43
Savigny, Fr. 101–2
Say, J.B. 59, 60, 61, 68, 69
scarcity, scientific meaning 64; *see also rareté*; UTILITY and scarcity theory
Schmitz, S.W. 122n37
Schneider, E. 162
Schumpeter, J.A. 7, 9n2, 74, 80, 81, 84, 85, 91; and Böhm-Bawerk 109, 114–15, 117, 122n37; circular flow theory of 83; *History of Economic Analysis* 59; and Mises 141n20; *see also* Heidegger=Schumpeter theses
science: dialogue on prestructure 84–5; economics as 5, 6, 7; Jevons' view of 48–51; natural 7, 51, 80; of observation 51; relevance of history 88; speculative 51, 56n9; subjectivism and objectivism as alternative positions in 1
self-interest 99, 100
services, prices of 66–7
Shackle, G. 137
shares, trading of 162

Shiller, R. 156, 157
Shionoya, Y. 7, 73–90
silver 116
Sjöström, T. 45n10
Smith, A. 56n9, 62; as founder of economics 44; on invisible hand 38; labour theory of value *see under* labour theory of value; *Lectures on Jurisprudence* 17, 26n7; *Theory of Moral Sentiment* 11, 13, 14, 17, 18, 21; *Wealth of Nations* 6, 11, 13, 14, 16, 17, 22–3, 25
Smith, B. 91
social body (Quételet) 53, 54, 57n12
social choice rules 43
social economics 64, 68–9
social goals 42
socialist concept of planned economy 8
social man (Quételet) 52, 54
social values, vs. wants 152
speculation theory 152, 156
Sraffa, P. 8–9, 174; genetic algorithm introduced into original system of 175; joint production system 9, 177–8, 182n26; objectivism of Sraffian economists 1; standard commodity of *see* standard commodity (Sraffa); theorem 176–7
Stackelberg, H.F. von 162
stage setting, bucket brigade algorithm 163, 173–4
standard commodity (Sraffa) 164, balancing proportion 177; derivation 175–8; in extended system 179–80; feedback system 175; significance, discovered in context of genetic algorithm 174–80; in Sraffa joint production system 9, 177–8, 182n26; updating 180; as weight to measure profitability of fictitious processes/commodities in extended system 179–80
static economy 83
statistics methodologies 7, 49, 51, 53
Stephenson, G. 48
stock-exchange markets 148, 157, 163
St. Petersburg's Paradox 150
strategic interdependence, and uncertainty 144–61
subjectivism: Austrian 73–90; in history of economic analysis 1–9; integration with objectivism 2, 3; second, of Menger 109–11; terminology 1, 3, 91; turn toward, in late nineteenth century 2; *see also* objectivism

Index

subjectivism of Mises 126–43; elimination of inconsistencies 127–32; indirect exchange, subjectivist theory of 127, 128, 132–5; persistence of 130–2; pricing process theory based on 135–6; *see also* Mises, Ludwig Edler von
subjectivity: and cognitive psychology 151–2; elimination, in Jevons' theory 55–6; epistemological/ontological 4, 6; and foresight *see* foresight, and subjectivity; and random-walk hypothesis 152–8; revival of as irrationality 155–6; in risk and uncertainty 148–51; terminology 1
Suzumura, K. 45n10
symmetric information 45n11
sympathy, and labour theory of value 11, 13, 14, 17, 26n3
synthesis of subjectivism and objectivism, neoclassical 2, 3
Systema Naturae (Linnés) 13

Taka, T. 6, 11–27
tâtonnement process, Walrasian 41, 42, 164
teleological causality 76
Theory of Money and Credit, The (Mises) 127, 129, 130, 132
Theory of Moral Sentiment (Smith) 11, 13, 14, 17, 18, 21
Theory of Political Economy, The (Jevons) 52–3, 54, 55, 56
Thirsk, J. 27n10
Thompson, G.L. 167
thrownness: *Dasein* as thrown projector 81, 82, 83, 86; nature 87
time preference theory 138, 141n25, 163
Tokyo Stock Exchange (TSE) 181n4
Tomo, S. 8, 108–25
trading body, concept 53–4, 55, 56n12
tranquility, ideal of 21
transaction value 114
Treatise on Man (Quételet) 49, 51–2
Treatise on Money (Keynes) 149
true desires 75–6, 77
Turgot, A.R.J. 31, 32, 33, 34, 35–6, 37, 38–9

U-mart system 181n7, 181n9
uncertainty 8; and strategic interdependence 144–61; subjectivity in 148–51
United States (US), modern Austrians in 95
universal rational action, assumption of 2–3
utilitarianism 7, 50
UTILITY and scarcity theory 29, 30–8, 44n1; exchange value 34–8; individual value, structure of theory 31–4; reconstructed and original theory 31
utility maximization 2

value: in bilateral relationships 139n6; concept 37; exchange *see* exchange value; individual 31–4, 37; labour theory of *see* labour theory of value; marginal utility theory of 3, 30, 31, 34, 36, 37, 44n7, 55, 59; Menger's theory of 33; natural 114; and price 37; proportionality of values of goods and services 65; real, of commodities 16–21; in trilateral relationships 129, 133; utility theory of, French tradition 7, 69; Walras (August) on theory of 7, 60–1
values, hermeneutical economics 75, 78, 87, 88
verification 49, 56n2
Vienna stock market 110

Wald, A. 162
Walras, A. 59, 62–3, 68, 69; on theory of value 7, 60–1
Walras, L. 40, 60; definition of progress 65, 66; *Elements of Pure Economics* 62, 63, 64–5, 68, 69, 70; general equilibrium theory of *see* general equilibrium theory; on nationalization of land 59, 63, 67–8; price theory 63, 66–7; as progenitor of neoclassical economics 59; on progressive society 61, 62, 65–8; pure economics 63–9; on *rareté* at early stage 7, 61–3; three divisions of economics 64, 68–9; at University of Lausanne 63
wants 31, 55; imaginary 105n4, 131; vs. social values 152
wealth 19, 118
Wealth of Nations (Smith) 6, 11, 13, 14, 16, 17, 22–3, 25
Weber, M. 3, 9n2
Weber–Fechner's law 3
welfare economics, fundamental theorems 29, 30, 38–41
Wicksell, K. 40–1
Wieser, F. von 8, 9n2, 126, 145, 146; and Böhm-Bawerk 113–14, 119, 120; and Mises 129, 139n5; on "simple economy" 103

will, liberty of 49, 50, 51
Williamson, A.W. 48, 49
Wiseman, J. 141n21
Wundt, W. 78, 79

Yagi, K. 1–9, 122n35
Yeats, J. 48
Yeats, J. Y. 48